Damned If You Do

Damned If You Do

Dilemmas of Action in Literature and Popular Culture

Edited by Margaret S. Hrezo and John M. Parrish

LEXINGTON BOOKS
A DIVISION OF
ROWMAN & LITTLEFIELD PUBLISHERS, INC.
Lanham • Boulder • New York • Toronto • Plymouth, UK

Published by Lexington Books
A division of Rowman & Littlefield Publishers, Inc.
A wholly owned subsidiary of The Rowman & Littlefield Publishing Group, Inc.
4501 Forbes Boulevard, Suite 200, Lanham, Maryland 20706
http://www.lexingtonbooks.com

Estover Road, Plymouth PL6 7PY, United Kingdom

British Library Cataloguing in Publication Information Available

Library of Congress Cataloging-in-Publication Data
Damned if you do : dilemmas of action in literature and popular culture / edited by
Margaret S. Hrezo and John M. Parrish
   p.   cm.
  Includes bibliographical reference and index.
  ISBN 978-0-7391-3813-7 (cloth : alk. paper)
 1. Literature and morals. 2. Ethics in literature. 3. Politics in literature. 4. Popular
culture—Moral and ethical aspects. I. Hrezo, Margaret S. II. Parrish, John M.
  PN49.D2555 2010
  809'.93353—dc22
                                                                    2010004075

∞ ™ The paper used in this publication meets the minimum requirements of
American National Standard for Information Sciences—Permanence of Paper
for Printed Library Materials, ANSI/NISO Z39.48-1992.

Printed in the United States of America

~

Contents

~

Preface

This volume began as a panel on moral dilemmas in literature and popular culture at the Annual Meeting of the American Political Science Association in 2008. The idea for the panel was conceived in a conversation between Charles Turner and John Parrish at the previous year's meeting. Paul Cantor and Joel Johnson offered to present papers on the panel, while Susan McWilliams and Travis Smith agreed to serve as the panel discussants, and Margaret Hrezo stepped in as the panel chair. When the opportunity to develop a volume of essays arose, Craig Waggaman also agreed to provide an essay to round out the collection. Margaret and John undertook to jointly edit the volume, but all the contributors participated in discussions about the volume's aims and form, and in that sense it is truly an ensemble production. The essays themselves, of course, represent a wide range of methodological approaches and of political and philosophical views—indeed, an unusually eclectic range among collections in the field of politics and literature—and so each author's claims, including ours in the introduction, should be understood as ultimately belonging to them alone.

At Lexington Books, Margaret and John would like to thank Joseph Parry for commissioning and helping to develop the volume and Jana Wilson and Tawnya Zengierski for their extensive helpful advice in guiding us through the production process. Loyola Marymount University and Radford University each provided resources and support that assisted in bringing the volume to completion.

The following artists and publishers permitted the use of their work for the volume:

Material from the works of Stephen King in chapter 3 is reprinted with permission of Scribner, a Division of Simon & Schuster, Inc., from *Everything's Eventual* by Stephen King. Copyright © 2002 by Stephen King.

Excerpts from *The Lord of the Rings* by J. R. R. Tolkien, edited by Christopher Tolkien. Copyright ©1954, 1955, 1965, 1966 by J. R. R. Tolkien. Copyright © Renewed 1982, 1983 by Christopher Tolkien, Michael H. R. Tolkien, John F. R. Tolkien, and Priscilla M. A. R. Tolkien. Copyright © Renewed 1993, 1994 by Christopher R. Tolkien, John F. R. Tolkien, and Priscilla M. A. R. Tolkien. Reprinted by permission of Houghton Mifflin Harcourt Publishing Company. All rights reserved.

Chapter 5 is reprinted from *Essays in Philosophy* Vol. 10, No. 1 (January 2009), with permission of the author and the general editor, Michael Goodman. *Essays in Philosophy* can be accessed at www.humboldt.edu/~essays/.

The quotations in chapter 7 from the *Harry Potter* series are reproduced with the permission of the author, J. K. Rowling, as follows: *Harry Potter and the Sorcerer's Stone* copyright © J. K. Rowling 1997; *Harry Potter and the Chamber of Secrets* copyright © J. K. Rowling 1998; *Harry Potter and the Goblet of Fire* copyright © J. K. Rowling 2000; *Harry Potter and the Order of the Phoenix* copyright © J. K. Rowling 2003; *Harry Potter and the Half-Blood Prince* copyright © J. K. Rowling 2005; *Harry Potter and the Deathly Hallows* copyright © J. K. Rowling 2007.

Quotations in chapter 8 from *Paradise* by Toni Morrison, copyright © 1997 by Toni Morrison. Used by permission of Alfred A. Knopf, a division of Random House, Inc.

Quotations in chapter 9 from *A Simple Plan* by Scott Smith, copyright © 1993 by Scott B. Smith, Inc. Used by permission of Alfred A. Knopf, a division of Random House, Inc.

We owe special debts of gratitude to our families for their support. John's contribution benefited as always from the patience of his wife, Lynn, and the happiness he finds in the company of his family: Lynn, Sophie, and George. Margaret expresses her gratitude to her husband, Bill, her daughter and son-in-law Kate and Donnie, and her grandson Kai for their support during the past year.

The volume is dedicated by Margaret to Bill, Kate, Donnie, and Kai, who understand the power of stories; and by John to Bob McGill, Kevin Stenzel, Charley Turner, Scott Wasson, and the other residents of Doniphan House, in whose fine company he read a lot of books and watched a lot of TV.

~

CHAPTER ONE

Moral Dilemmas
and the Narrative Arts

Margaret S. Hrezo and John M. Parrish

At the heart of drama lies conflict: conflict between individuals, conflict within societies, conflict with the external world, conflict within the heart. All these forms of conflict, in one way or another, are driven by conflicts of moral values, and thus ethical conflict is at the very center of the driving impulse behind all the narrative art forms. When value conflicts become so serious as to be not just challenging but seemingly irresolvable, we call them *moral dilemmas*. Much of our greatest literature—and a fair bit of our not-so-great literature as well—focuses on depicting moral dilemmas, because it is these situations which often bring into sharpest relief the conflicts between competing values which motivate so much of the narrative arts—and so much of political life.

That, at least, is the premise of this book, and of the eight case studies in literature and popular culture which comprise it. *Damned If You Do* examines the problem of moral dilemmas as a persistent concern in literature and popular culture. These essays showcase the value of the narrative arts in examining the complex conflicts of value in moral and political life and explore the philosophical problem of moral dilemmas as that problem finds expression in ancient drama, classic and contemporary novels, television, film, and popular fiction. From Aeschylus to *Deadwood*, from Harriet Beecher Stowe to Harry Potter, our authors show how the narrative arts constitute some of the most valuable instruments for complex and sensitive moral inquiry.

Problems of individual moral choice have always been closely bound up with the larger normative concerns of political theory. There are several reasons for this continuing connection. First, the value conflicts involved in private moral choice often find themselves reproduced on the public stage: for example, states may find it difficult to do right by both justice and mercy in much the same way individuals do. Second, we frequently find conflicts among the values at stake in private and public life, such that the moral choice we must make is *between* private and public goods. Loosely speaking, choices which express either of these sorts of conflicts are what philosophers call moral dilemmas: choices in which no matter what one does one will be forfeiting some important moral good, in which wrongdoing is to some degree inescapable, in which one is (perhaps literally) damned if one does and damned if one doesn't.[1]

The narrative arts—whether in the classical forms of poetry, drama, and the novel, or in the more widely consumed forms of film, television, and popular fiction—afford a unique forum in which to explore both politically pregnant cases of individual moral choice and the conflicts between private and public moral values. One reason for this is that the narrative arts, which by their nature focus on and indeed seek out conflict—are unusually sensitive instruments for discovering and then exploring cases of conflicting values. Additionally, the narrative arts permit us to investigate cases of moral conflict with a concreteness and vividness that do not readily emerge from abstract philosophical analysis. At the same time, however, the narrative arts permit us to retain and, through artistic selection, focus on the precise philosophical and ethical features that specify the value conflict in question.

Novels, dramas, films, even television shows, can be among our most potent tools of philosophical exploration and among our most powerful teachers. And in truth, we have little choice but to take these art forms seriously as philosophical forums, since their influence on our society's moral education is pervasive and only seems to grow with time. Ordinary people have much more extensive contact with the narrative arts than with philosophy, and more so today than at perhaps any point in history. So the narrative arts will by necessity be among the principal teachers most people have for what moral dilemmas are, and therefore, implicitly, for a good chunk of how ethics works (the chunk that has to do with value conflicts). Our aim in this volume is to contribute to showing how this process of moral education works in the narrative arts as they stand today—in the hopes that someday it will work better.

Conflicting Values and Moral Dilemmas

The idea of a moral dilemma, as we will be using the term, refers to choice situations in which wrongdoing is inescapable. These are not just difficult moral choices, but (in some sense) impossible ones: not choices that cannot be made, but rather choices that cannot be made well—not without wrongdoing. This involves two elements: value conflicts across competing and incommensurable spheres of value, and the inability to resolve these conflicts satisfactorily without a morally unacceptable loss within (at least) one of the spheres.

Consider for example one of the oldest stories in Western literature: the myth of the sacrifice of Iphigenia.[2] In the myth, King Agamemnon, the supreme commander of the Greek forces bound for the Trojan War, is presented with an ultimatum by the goddess Artemis. The winds have faltered, and the Greeks will only be able to continue sailing for Troy if Agamemnon consents to sacrifice his daughter Iphigenia.[3] Here Agamemnon is faced with a choice of conflicting values, grounded in his competing roles (to borrow a term from the narrative arts) as a political leader on the one hand and as a loving father on the other.

This is the stuff of which dilemmas are made. To us it may seem obvious that there is a right way to resolve this conflict—it seems grotesque to modern readers that one should sacrifice an innocent child for any reason (though it may have seemed less so to the audiences of the ancient tragedies). But there is nonetheless here at least one of the key elements of a moral dilemma which we moderns can still recognize: namely, that there is a conflict between different *spheres* of value. If Agamemnon fails to protect his daughter, he fails as a father; if he fails to sacrifice his daughter, he fails as a political leader, since his fleet will never get to Troy. Perhaps the loss of these political goals is well worth accepting to save an innocent child—though again, this might not be so obvious to an ancient spectator. But it is in any event a *sacrifice* of a good in one moral sphere that is not entirely made up for by the good gained in the other sphere: when the tearful family reunion is done, the fleet will still be stranded, the political loss still remains.

A moral dilemma properly speaking is just a version of such value conflict that is essentially *irresolvable*: in which, while it may be possible to make a choice between actions serving competing values, it is not possible to make a *right* choice, because any action one takes will still, in some sense, be morally wrong (from the perspective of the sacrificed sphere of value).

Modern moral and political theory has been dominated by two competing broad normative approaches—the *consequentialist* and the *deontological* models of systematic ethics—which both happen to be peculiarly unreceptive to the idea of moral dilemmas.[4] For both the consequentialist and the deontologist, it is possible to have moral conflicts, but not moral dilemmas. Consequentialism, also known in its most familiar form as utilitarianism,[5] continues to be the starting point for much contemporary normative evaluation, particularly in the political and social spheres.[6] Its core premise is that the defining feature of right action is its tendency to maximize good outcomes and minimize bad ones, as is seen for example in the utilitarian maxim of "the greatest good for the greatest number."[7] According to consequentialism, then, good consequences are the only aspect of action that matter directly when evaluating its morality. All other moral values are commensurable, with good consequences as the common measure. There may be ostensible moral conflicts, say between parental duty and public duty, but they are resolvable by comparing the overall good consequences for everyone concerned of each course of action.

So to return to our example, the consequentialist ultimately sees no genuine dilemma in the choice confronting Agamemnon. What matters is the public benefit. If the Greeks' need to go to Troy outweighs the significance of a single human child (as in the Greeks' minds it plausibly would have), then Agamemnon acts rightly in consenting to sacrifice his daughter. Indeed more: not only does he act rightly, but he does nothing wrong in so acting. It is of course possible to argue against the sacrifice of Iphigenia on consequentialist grounds. We might say, for example, that the overall negative consequences to society of exhibiting such an outrageous example of parental failure might outweigh even the great good of launching the fleet; or we might argue that the Trojan War itself is a bad thing and that anything that facilitates it is wrong for that reason. The point is that on the consequentialist account this is a contingent matter: the rightness or wrongness of what we do depends on the (contingent) results of our calculations about the outcomes of our actions, and not at all on any intrinsic properties of goodness or badness which the action itself might hold.[8]

If consequentialism is the most intuitive approach to moral questions in contemporary thought, then deontological ethics is perhaps the most influential approach among professional moral and political theorists. Deontological approaches, exemplified in classical ethics by Immanuel Kant and in contemporary political theory by John Rawls, identify right action (or at the political level, right policy) as defined by the qualities of the rational principle which inspires it.[9] Kant frames these defining qualities of right action in terms of universal applicability and respect for persons: right action proceeds from the principle that the actor does not subjectively privilege herself above others, but instead acts on reasons which others should be able to accept and which treat others as equally valuable with herself.[10] Rawls's political theory adapts this ethical view to a larger social context; for Rawls, public policies are just when they could in principle be accepted by any rational agent abstracted from her particular perspectives, interests, and aims.

On the deontological view, these qualities of the rational principles (or in Kant's terminology, "maxims") underlying our actions are what define them as right or wrong. Questions of consequences may enter into our choices as prudential considerations, but they are not strictly speaking "moral" questions at all—and moral questions have a strict priority over all non-moral considerations. This feature of deontological theories is why Michael Walzer, in his famous treatment of moral dilemmas, characterizes such views as "absolutist": they are unwilling to admit of any compromise between the abstract rational principles of morality and consequentialist considerations about the outcomes that result. The old saying "let justice be done though the heavens fall" is one the deontological thinker would approve. So to return again to our example, the deontological theorist like the utilitarian sees no dilemma in the case of Agamemnon's sacrifice—though he is likely to come to a diametrically opposed conclusion about its solution. From his perspective, the only moral question which arises is whether the principle of the action—always sacrifice the innocent when great consequences will befall the polity—is one that can be universally justified to all, and which shows genuine respect for all persons as of equal human worth. Supposing that it cannot (and it seems like it would be a hard sell to at least a few rational agents, such as Iphigenia herself and all similarly situated potential sacrificial victims), consequential considerations about the welfare of the polity cannot rightly enter into the equation at all. Wrong is wrong; no dilemma about that.

Moral conflict need not of course be restricted to consequences on the one hand and rational moral imperatives on the other. Other kinds of moral good may also come into play. Until the last few centuries, one form that would have been an obvious factor to most observers is the question of virtue. Right actions, according to both the ancient and Christian traditions, were actions that proceeded from virtuous character. This virtue ethics model of moral thinking (which has experienced a revival of contemporary interest in the past few decades) is more open to the possibility of dilemmatic moral conflict, since the plurality of the virtues necessarily implies that they may conflict internally with one another.[11] And there are other competing sources of value as well. Beauty, for example, is something we may count as

a moral good, but not because of its good consequences or its rational principle or its contribution to virtue. And contemporary individualism sees an
intrinsic moral worth to be found in self-actualization and self-expression,
not independent of but at least distinguishable from the various other spheres
of value outlined above.[12]

To get the idea of a moral dilemma off the ground, we need the possibility
that values may conflict *irresolvably*: which is to say, we need the possibility
of the *plurality* and *incommensurability* of moral values.[13] What consequentialism and deontology share is the view that value is essentially monistic, and
that conflicts among values, while real, are nevertheless commensurable or
otherwise rationally resolvable. This view was shared by most ancient philosophers as well, almost all of whom thought there was one and only one true
good. They just didn't agree what that one good was: the Epicureans thought
it was pleasure; the Stoics, virtue; Plato, the Form of "The Good" knowable
only by reason. Aristotle alone among the ancients believed that goods were
plural, and that while comparable, they were not commensurable.[14] Genuine
conflicts could exist between them.[15]

In contemporary thought, those who hold some version of this view are
commonly known as *value pluralists*: and they range all over the political
and philosophical spectrum.[16] What they share in common is a belief in the
plurality and incommensurability of the different spheres of value, a conviction that there is no single good in terms of which all other values may be
cashed out and all other value conflicts resolved. We may be able to make
comparisons, but sometimes they will be between apples and oranges; we
may be able to make choices, but sometimes they will be Hobson's choices.
Sometimes a gain in one sphere of value, however important, will never be
able to make up for the loss it costs us in another; sometimes the rightness
of one course of action according to one sphere of value, however clear, will
never be able to make up for its wrongness from the perspective of another
sphere. Sometimes it will not even be clear to us what spheres of value are
truly at stake in making a choice.

The narrative arts show us, in ways that are too direct, immediate, and
powerful to deny, that conflicts between rival spheres of value are real and
often difficult if not impossible to resolve. The fact that the dominant
ethical theories of our modern age have a difficult time conceptualizing
the problem of moral dilemmas is symptomatic of a broader problem those
theories have in engaging directly with much of the content of our moral
world that is most important to us. The tendency of consequentialism and
deontology to reduce conflicts among values to misapprehensions or failures
of calculation not only denies something real in human moral experience; it

also points out a systematic shortcoming in the modes of inquiry and analysis we presently use to make such sense as we can out of the moral world around us. Our aim in this book is to offer examples of how at least one alternative mode of moral inquiry and analysis—the narrative arts—can get at philosophical truths that our more familiar systems tend systematically to discount or overlook.

Politics and Literature

The narrative arts are thus an indispensable mode of moral inquiry. But they are equally indispensable to political inquiry. To see this, we must understand that politics itself is always, at least in part, a narrative act. Every political community seeks to fashion for itself a pattern of order within which citizens can develop meaningful and flourishing lives. Politics is therefore at its heart an act of evocation, as a society calls into being the reality of a political order through the power of language. We are shaped, deeply, by the stories we tell each other about who we are and who we are not.[17]

For the consequentialist, the ends will almost always justify the means. However, for the deontologist an evaluation of the means of achieving an end are just as important as the ends themselves. Thus, most modes of moral inquiry about the political world that go beyond the consequentialist model must include analysis of many different values in terms of both the acceptability of the means and the importance of the end sought. Simone Weil wrote that politics is a "composition on a multiple plane."[18] This phrase captures the insight that politics must balance multiple human needs and concerns, with conflicting moral values perhaps the most important among them. It is this attempt to evoke some harmony among the various levels and aspects of human life that provides a foundation for the construction, deformation, reconstruction—or redemption—of social space.[19]

Much of political science, even political theory, has remained resistant to the idea that public order is essentially a creative act, dependent on a community's social and moral consciousness. Thus, the narrative arts have often been compelled to take the lead in exploring certain moral conflicts and dilemmas and in examining their implications for communal as well as individual life. Through the evocative power of their language, and through their ability to explore simultaneously so many of Weil's "multiple planes," the narrative arts are able to contribute to the description, evaluation, and improvement of public order. These arts mirror the social consciousness that both influences and is influenced by the political sphere. The essays in this book attempt to shed light on the role of moral choices in framing, illuminating, and shaping that pattern of order, as well as how moral dilemmas reflect the underlying value conflicts which exist within the political order.

The narrative arts begin with a localized event. In exploring that event, however, they often offer a tiny pinprick of insight into the whole of human life, as the timeless briefly flashes into the concrete world of time and necessity. These insights inform politics, Martha Nussbaum argues, by providing a framework for "a valuable form of public reasoning, both within a single culture and across cultures."[20] Any narrative originating in the moral questions and dilemmas that drive individual and communal action may offer a point of entry into understanding the intersection of consciousness, moral reasoning, and the evocation of public order. The more attuned a narrative is to the way real human beings experience the world, the more the narrative can contribute to the evocation of that order. The philosopher Iris Murdoch wrote that "literature, morals, and politics must all concern themselves with reality."[21] All three rely on *le monde vécu* (the world as lived or experienced) for their raw materials and it is this reliance on reality that allows at least a partial overcoming of crude dichotomizations of facts and values, idealism and materialism, and theory and praxis.[22] Although the multiplicity of value systems in today's world makes difficult the discussion of the moral aspects of politics (in particular analysis of the ends of governance), it does not render the attempt either impossible or irrelevant.

Over the past 30 years political philosophy increasingly has come to follow the lead of the narrative arts and to understand that literature and popular culture also offer important insights into the moral element of political life. This acknowledgment of the connection between the *philosophos* (lover of wisdom/knowledge of the good) and the *philokalon* (lover of beauty) has led to the development of the politics and literature movement in political theory. There is neither need nor space to trace the history of this movement; many students of literature and political philosophy have contributed to its development and their work pursues myriad themes. Thus, we limit our description to setting forth some of the major themes of this rich and varied literature.

Some scholars root their discussions in the techniques of literary criticism, such as Charles Embry in his examination of Eric Voegelin's approach to twentieth-century literature, Irving Howe in his classic study of revolution in literature, and George A. Panichas in his analysis of more than twenty British, continental, and American authors' responses to the "brokenness" of the modern world.[23] A second category of studies focuses on defense of the American regime and on elucidating the effects of the American regime on character.[24] Covering such ideas as the effects of liberalism on the soul, the conflict between the natural passions and the requirements of civilization, civic education, and the American self, this second set of scholars offers rich insights into the political values that underlie the American political system.[25]

Third, there exists a diverse body of scholarship that undertakes regime criticisms from the perspective of family, gender, or colonial power.[26] Most of these, however, do not discuss the American regime, with some important exceptions (such as the interaction between women and the law in Heidi Setterdahl Macpherson's *Courting Failure*).

Finally, a fourth group of studies, focusing on the connection between virtuous citizens and a flourishing society, attempts to illuminate the link between moral choice and the formation of ethical citizens.[27] These scholars tend to follow the approach of Martha Nussbaum, who casts her work within an Aristotelian ethical perspective by connecting ethics to a conception of a flourishing human life that emphasizes: (1) the non-commensurability of valuable things; (2) the priority of the particular; (3) the ethical value of the emotions; and (4) the ethical relevance of uncontrolled happenings. The overall emphasis is on the ability of good literature to provide examples of moral choice that foster ethical citizens and hence more flourishing political societies.[28]

What binds together these different approaches is a commitment to studying intentionally and carefully aspects of political life that are not fully accessible through traditional empirical or philosophical methods. These scholars reflect on and respond to their social, political, and cultural environment. Thus, they make it possible for us to uncover the moral dimensions of politics and acknowledge that it is sometimes difficult to measure two valued things according to the same standard. The study of popular culture and literature are invaluable assets to political theorists engaged in asking what Glenn Tinder described as the perennial questions—those involving what it means to be human, the nature of justice and injustice, estrangement and community, freedom and obligation, equality and hierarchy, power and authority.[29] The narrative arts offer us insight both into our current answers to these questions and into the ways in which the values that ground those assumptions may change dramatically from culture to culture and from generation to generation, often without explicit philosophical acknowledgment.

The study of popular culture and literature can show us a great deal about the nature of order and disorder, both individual and communal. In the end, political philosophy is itself a story—a narrative about and a commentary on the human search for order, based on societal beliefs concerning what it means to be a human being, the existence and nature of God or the gods, how human beings should relate to one another in society, the nature of reality, and the place of human beings in the universe. Regimes both reflect and form the character of their citizens, and at bottom these aspects of consciousness have a moral basis. Culture and politics are connected integrally in the search for societies that can allow human beings to establish happy, flourishing, and meaningful lives.

We hope to contribute to this field by dealing with questions that have not yet become a focus of the politics and literature movement—the moral implications and moral obligations of political action in a variety of difficult circumstances. As the narrative arts demonstrate, systematic consequentialist and deontological theories may not do full justice to the richness and complexity of either the moral or the political world—or in some cases, to certain simple truths that often get obscured by heavy philosophical systems and by the human tendency to try to justify even one's worst behavior. Moral inquiry in the political sphere will remain difficult and any solutions to moral dilemmas will be tentative no matter how sincere and conscientious our efforts. However, through their ability portray individuals' and communities' experience of life and the political, the narrative arts can assist us in reflecting on the conflicts among competing values that pervade both the political and moral world.

The Essays

The essays collected in this volume consider political dilemmas associated with: (1) political stability; (2) public leadership; (3) institutional evil; and (4) the effects of community on moral choice. In the first section, Paul Cantor and Charles C. Turner examine dilemmas associated with political stability and regime change as developed in the HBO television series *Deadwood* and in Stephen King's novels and short stories. Cantor's chapter on the HBO series *Deadwood* questions the human tendency to consider law and order as an inseparable pair. In particular, he focuses our attention on the loss of individual freedom that law requires and asks whether order is possible where law is minimal or non-existent, as it was in the town of Deadwood. To analyze this issue he turns to Thomas Hobbes, John Locke, and Jean-Jacques Rousseau who used the state of nature as a device for exploring the dilemma of freedom versus law. Cantor argues that Hobbes forsakes too much liberty in order to achieve order and that Rousseau, although correct in his assessment of the loss of freedom brought about by government, is insufficiently attuned to human pride and self-interest. For the creators of *Deadwood*, Cantor maintains, economic rationality can orchestrate a rough order even without a formal government to enforce that order. Ultimately, "government is at best a necessary evil, but we must be skeptical about its claims to serve the public interest, and always remain vigilant to resist its perennial tendency to increase its power and encroach upon personal freedom." The most stable regime, in this view, is the smallest and most limited one in which responsibility for political decisions rests at the local level whenever possible.

Turner explores why popular fiction, and in particular the widely read works of Stephen King, seems open to the notion of morally justified political assassination in a way that contemporary political theory generally is not. To investigate this impulse, Turner directs his attention to two of the political theorists who have engaged most explicitly and sympathetically with the idea of justified political assassination: Leon Trotsky (in "Their Morals and Ours"), whose concern is primarily with the extent of an assassination's transformational effects, and Hannah Arendt (in *On Violence* and other works), whose concern is primarily with the unpredictability of its consequences. Turner then compares the application of these theories in the scenarios depicted in King's short story "Everything's Eventual" and in his novel *The Dead Zone*.

The second section confronts dilemmas associated with public leadership, as Craig Waggaman and John M. Parrish consider the ethical conflicts presented in Aeschylus's classical dramas *The Suppliants* and *The Persians*, J. R. R. Tolkien's *Lord of the Rings*, and in the contemporary FOX television series *24*. Both essays deal with dilemmas of moral leadership in extreme situations. For Waggaman, *The Suppliants* and *The Lord of the Rings* provide examples of mature moral decision making by political leaders and citizens. In both these works moral inquiry begins but does not end with custom and law. In his reading of Aeschylus and Tolkien, the focus of decision making is discourse among participants rather than the application of abstract principles. In these works, he argues, mature moral decision making requires (1) that leaders and followers understand rational decision making as the connection of pragmatic ends to some vision of the Good itself and (2) procedures that both are transparent and include participation by citizens in moral discourse concerning the choice to be made.

Parrish's goal in his essay on *24*, on the other hand, is to call attention to a political falsehood that results in the deadening of moral sensibility and to trivializing and sensationalizing the political problems engendered by moral dilemmas. By refusing to see hard ethical choices as "*being* hard cases" the show may make it harder for us both to recognize difficult cases and to make the sorts of judgments that those difficult cases require. Thus, the show may make it more difficult to understand the nature and characteristics of virtuous citizenship. Focusing specifically on *24*'s Season Five (the year the show won the Emmy for Best Dramatic Series), the chapter concludes that 24's creators have substituted in the public mind almost a parody of the standard philosophical account of a moral dilemma in place of the traditional notion. In so doing they subtly de-value the moral stakes in the more pedestrian variety of moral conflicts Jack Bauer and company must overcome in their quest to keep America safe whatever the cost.

In the volume's third section on institutional evil, Joel A. Johnson and Susan McWilliams examine dilemmas of slavery, as they emerge in Harriet Beecher Stowe's classic novel *Uncle Tom's Cabin* and in J.K. Rowling's *Harry Potter* series. As Johnson writes with regard to *Uncle Tom's Cabin*, both these works address "what is now to most people a dead issue." Why include works with slavery as a central theme in a book that examines the place of moral dilemmas and the role of moral reasoning about such dilemmas in politics? The chapter on *Uncle Tom's Cabin* provides the reader with one possible answer—as an aid to understanding "how arguments, passions, violence, and suffering interact at points of grave moral crisis." Most importantly, he argues that Stowe's classic work provides a continuum of responses to and a useful typology of human reactions to serious moral dilemmas and, in fact, addresses the factors that might change one's attitude toward some classes of injustice.

McWilliams reinforces this theme in her study of J.K. Rowling's *Harry Potter* series. As in *Uncle Tom's Cabin*, the main characters respond to the slavery of the house elves in a variety of ways. In addition, just as slavery in the United States raised questions about America's commitment to its most deeply held values, the problem of slavery in the world of wizards raises questions about Hogwarts as a bastion of moral magic. McWilliams goes further, however, arguing that these books illustrate that "freedom is inseparable from virtue." Just like the creatures in Rowling's stories, we demonstrate virtue, good citizenship, and freedom when we are willing to make sacrifices to achieve the common good. Thus, freedom to act is essential to both individual and civic virtue.

Margaret S. Hrezo and Travis D. Smith consider dilemmas of community and choice in Toni Morrison's novel *Paradise* and in the contemporary film *A Simple Plan* in our final section. Hrezo's essay explores two complementary visions of the religious moral view—those of Nobel Prize winner Morrison in *Paradise* and of German theologian Dietrich Bonhoeffer. Hrezo's analysis reveals interesting similarities in Morrison's and Bonhoeffer's vision of a moral life and its implications for politics and community. Both display a complex moral and ethical sensibility rooted in living a "responsible life"—one committed to both freedom and to the obligation to act with concern for real people and sacrifice for a common good. Both warn of the dangers inherent in individual and communal lives that stress absolute adherence to set moral codes and exclusion of those who are different, and both highlight the importance of *opsis* (clear-sightedness) in reaching individual and communal moral decisions. They offer a glimpse of spiritualities that transcend conventional understandings of religion in seeking a moral ground for individual and political action.

Finally, Smith examines the similarities between the film *A Simple Plan*—a story about what to do with "found" money—and ideas treated by Plato, Aristotle, Machiavelli, and Hobbes. The film, he argues, pits modernity's goals of controlling the vagaries of fortune and achieving material success at any cost against classical ethical concerns based in character. To Smith, the film demonstrates "the fragility of conventional justice premised on material self-interest, the inadequacy of treating the power to satisfy appetites as the measure of happiness, and the vanity of man's attempt to conquer fortune." Implicit in the film is a warning concerning the dangers to political community of an ethical framework that encourages the individual to become a law unto himself focused primarily on satisfying personal appetites and securing individual prosperity.

Although these chapters cover a wide variety of thinkers and narrative arts, taken together, the essays in this book pursue several common themes that recur again and again when the political world is faced, as it always will be, with moral dilemmas. They ask us to reflect upon: (1) the differences among law, convention, and order; (2) the connections among virtue, freedom, and citizenship; (3) obligation to self versus other; (4) the relevance of character and justice to moral decision making; and (5) the possibilities and limits of politics. The common themes treated in this work echo Willa Cather's words in *O Pioneers!*: "there are only two or three human stories, and they go on repeating themselves as fiercely as if they had never happened before."[30] Philosophy, literature, and culture help us find provisional answers to the moral issues that haunt political life. The never-ending stories told by philosophy and the narrative arts are a testament not only to how provisional our answers as human beings must be, but also to how important it is to continue the search for such answers as we can attain in daily life and in politics.

Notes

Thanks to Joel Johnson and Susan McWilliams for their helpful comments on this chapter.

1. On the philosophical concept of a moral dilemma, many of the best sources are collected in Christopher Gowans, ed., *Moral Dilemmas* (Oxford, 1987). On the specifically political application of the problem, see Michael Walzer, "Political Action: The Problem of Dirty Hands," *Philosophy and Public Affairs* 2 (1973): 160-80. On the historical development of the conceptual problem, see John M. Parrish, *Paradoxes of Political Ethics: From Dirty Hands to the Invisible Hand* (Cambridge, 2007).

2. Two of the most famous representations of the story are to be found in Aeschylus's *Agamemnon* and in Euripides's *Iphigenia at Aulis*. On this story as representative of a moral dilemma, see Martha Nussbaum, *The Fragility of Goodness* (Cambridge, 1986), ch. 2.

3. The grounds for Artemis's requirement differ from story to story in the ancient versions of the myth. In some Agamemnon offended Artemis by poaching one of her sacred animals; in others his fault is that he boasted he was a better hunter than Artemis was. Neither one seems a particularly rational reason for requiring the death of a child, but as Plato points out, the gods do some strange things in Greek myths.

4. On the conceptual development of these rival normative traditions, see among many excellent studies J.B. Schneewind's classic *The Invention of Autonomy* (Cambridge, 1998).

5. Properly speaking, utilitarianism is a form of consequentialism that specifies a theory about what the good to be maximized is: namely, pleasure, and the absence of pain. See Philip Pettit, "Consequentialism," in *A Companion to Ethics* ed. Peter Singer (Blackwell, 1991).

6. Though consequentialism is no longer the force it once was, its influence is still extensive: the most influential textbook on contemporary political theory asserts that "in our society consequentialism operates as a kind of tacit background against which other theories have to assert and defend themselves." Will Kymlicka, *Contemporary Political Philosophy*, 2nd ed. (Oxford, 2002), 10. Moreover, many of the key intuitions of modern political science, from the cost-benefit analyses prevalent in public policy studies to the preference-maximization models found in political economy, formal theory, and much democratic theory, find their roots in consequentialist premises.

7. For the classical articulations of the theory, see Jeremy Bentham, *An Introduction to the Principles of Morals and Legislation* (Dover, 2007) and John Stuart Mill, *Utilitarianism* (Hackett, 2002). For an influential adaptation of consequentialist ethics to normative problems in contemporary politics, see Robert Goodin, *Utilitarianism as a Public Philosophy* (Cambridge, 1995).

8. Consequentialists also rely on the assumption that moral agents can know the outcome of a specific decision in advance—a hubristic assumption that the narrative arts often undermine. Oedipus in *Oedipus the King* and Creon in *Antigone* each act on the belief that they can predict the future consequences of their actions with certainty—and each winds up shattering the world they inhabit as a result.

9. Kant's classic formulation may be found in *Groundwork of the Metaphysics of Morals*, Mary Gregor, ed. (Cambridge, 1998); Rawls's in *A Theory of Justice* (Harvard, 1971) and *Political Liberalism*, expanded edition (Columbia, 2005).

10. Kant has a third formulation, that regarding the idea of a "kingdom of ends," which has been less directly influential on contemporary moral and political theory. Many of the best interpretive insights on this subject are collected in Christine Korsgaard, *Creating the Kingdom of Ends* (Cambridge, 1996).

11. The work most responsible for this contemporary revival of interest in the virtues is Alasdair MacIntyre, *After Virtue*, 3rd ed. (Notre Dame, 2007). For a collection of many of the most important essays on the subject, see Roger Crisp and Michael Slote, ed., *Virtue Ethics* (Oxford, 1997).

12. For a further elaboration of these spheres of value and possible conflicts between them, see Thomas Nagel, "The Fragmentation of Value," in Gowans, *Moral Dilemmas*.

13. On these concepts see especially Michael Stocker, *Plural and Conflicting Values* (Oxford, 1990) and Ruth Chang, *Incommensurability, Incomparability, and Practical Reason* (Harvard, 1998).

14. Aristotle, *Nicomachean Ethics*, ed. David Ross (Oxford, 1991).

15. On the possibility of conflicting goods in Aristotle, see Michael Stocker, *Plural and Conflicting Values*, ch. 3.

16. Some important contributors to the development of the theory of value pluralism include Max Weber, "Politics as a Vocation," in *From Max Weber: Essays in Sociology*, H.H, Gerth and C. Wright Mills, eds. (Oxford, 1946); Thomas Nagel, "War and Massacre," *Philosophy and Public Affairs* 1(1972): 123-44, and "The Fragmentation of Value," cited above; Bernard Williams, "Ethical Consistency," in Gowans, *Moral Dilemmas*, and "Conflicts of Value," in his *Moral Luck* (Cambridge, 1982); Isaiah Berlin, "Two Concepts of Liberty," in his *The Proper Study of Mankind* (Farrar, Straus, and Giroux, 1997); John Gray, *Isaiah Berlin* (Princeton, 1996); Michael Walzer, "Political Action: The Problem of Dirty Hands"; Michael Stocker, *Plural and Conflicting Values*; Charles Taylor, *Sources of the Self* (Harvard, 1989); Ruth Chang, *Incommensurability, Incomparability, and Practical Reason*; and Joseph Raz, *The Practice of Value* (Oxford 2003).

17. See, for example, K. Anthony Appiah, *The Ethics of Identity* (Princeton University Press, 2005), ch. 3; William Connolly, *Identity/Difference: Democratic Negotiations of Political Paradox* (University of Minnesota Press, 2002), ch. 3; Patchen Markell, *Bound by Recognition* (Princeton University Press, 2003); and Charles Taylor, *The Ethics of Authenticity* (Harvard University Press, 1992) and "The Politics of Recognition" in *Philosophical Arguments* (Harvard University Press, 1997).

18. Simone Weil, *The Need for Roots* (Putnam, 1952), 216-19.

19. Gaston Bachelard, *The Poetics of Space* (Boston: Beacon Press, 1964).

20. Martha Nussbaum, *Poetic Justice* (Oxford, 1995), 8.

21. Iris Murdoch, "The Existentialist Political Myth" in *Existentialists and Mystics* (New York: Penguin Books, 1997), 284.

22. Ibid., 132.

23. Charles Embry, *The Philosopher and the Storyteller* (University of Missouri Press, 2008); George A. Panichas, *The Politics of Twentieth Century Novelists* (Hawthorn

Books, 1971); Irving Howe, *Politics and the Novel* (Columbia, 1992); and Robert Coles, *Politics and Leadership: Stories of Power and Politics from Literature and Life* (Modern Library, 2005). Leonidas Donskis' *Power and Imagination: Studies in Politics and Literature* (Peter Lang, 2008) also belongs with this group of scholars. Using works by Thomas Mann, Thomas More, Shakespeare, Cervantes, Melville, Milosz, Orwell and others, Donskis' work persuasively argues that novels often anticipate future political movements.

24. See, for example, Joel Johnson's *Beyond Practical Virtue: A Defense of Liberal Democracy Through Literature* (University of Missouri Press. 2007); Catherine Zuckert, "The Political Thought of Nathaniel Hawthorne," *Polity* 13 (Winter 1980): 163-83 and "On Reading Classic American Novelists as Political Thinkers," *Journal of Politics* 43 (August 1981): 683-706; Patrick Deneen and Joseph Romance, eds., *Democracy's Literature* (Rowman & Littlefield, 2005); Peter Augustine Lawler, *Democracy and Its Friendly Critics* (Lexington, 2004); John Whalen-Bridge, *Politics and the American Self* (University of Illinois Press, 1998); James Boyd White, *Acts of Hope: Creating Authority in Literature, Law, and Politics* (University of Chicago Press, 1994); and Cyrus R.K. Patel, *Negative Liberties* (Duke University Press, 2001).

25. Mary P. Nichols' wide-ranging work, for example, often emphasizes the effects of liberal individualism on the soul and the conflict between natural passions and the requirements of civilization. Patrick Deneen and Joseph Romance's *Democracy's Literature* examines works of literature that the individual essayists believe foster American civic education. In their works Cyrus Patel and John Whalen-Bridge discuss the American idea of the self. Patel, for example, uses the works of Thomas Pynchon and Toni Morrison to highlight the differences between a situated self and what Michael Sandel categorized as the "unencumbered self" in Michael Sandel's "The Procedural Republic and the Unencumbered Self," *Political Theory* 12 (1984): 81-96.

26. See Amy Kaminsky, *Reading the Body Politic: Feminist Criticism and Latin American Writers* (University of Minnesota Press, 1992); Ngugi Wa Thiongo, *Decolonising the Mind: The Politics of Language in African Literature* (Heineman, 1986); Ketu H. Katrak, *Politics of the Female Body: Postcolonial Women Writers of the Third World* (Rutgers University Press, 2006); and Rajeshwari S. Vallury, '*Surfacing*' *the Politics of Desire: Literature, Feminism and Myth* (University of Toronto Press, 2008). For readings that develop new understandings of particular groups within the United States see Claudia Johnson, *Jane Austen: Women, Politics, and the Novel* (University of Chicago Press, 1990) and Viet Thanh Nguyen, *Race and Resistance: Literature and Politics in Asian America* (Oxford, 2002).

27. See Catherine Zuckert, "The Political Thought of Nathaniel Hawthorne," and "On Reading Classic American Novelists as Political Thinkers"; Patrick Deneen and Joseph Romance, *Democracy's Literature*; John Whalen-Bridge, *Politics and the American Self* (University of Illinois Press, 1998); James Boyd White, *Acts of Hope*; and Cyrus R.K. Patel, *Negative Liberties*.

28. Martha Nussbaum epitomizes the work of this group. See *The Fragility of Goodness* (Oxford, 1986); *Love's Knowledge* (Oxford, 1990); and *Poetic Justice* (Ox-

ford, 1995). Anne Crippen Ruderman also has written on the connection between political ideas and the *Pleasures of Virtue* (Rowman & Littlefield, 1995) in Jane Austen's books. Marion Montgomery pursues a similar examination of Flannery O'Connor in *Why Flannery O'Connor Stayed Home* (Sherwood Sugden and Company, 1981). Wayne Booth's *The Company We Keep* (University of California Press, 1988) is an excellent argument for the importance of ethical criticism in literature as a foundation for moral choice.

29. Glenn Tinder, *Political Thinking: The Perennial Questions*, 6th ed. (Longman, 2003).

30. Willa Cather, *Early Novels and Stories: O Pioneers!* (New York: Library of America, 1987), 196.

PART I

DILEMMAS OF STABILITY
AND REGIME CHANGE

CHAPTER TWO

~

The *Deadwood* Dilemma
Freedom Versus Law
Paul A. Cantor

The State of Nature and the American Frontier

The American Western, with its setting on the frontier between civilization and barbarism, has throughout its history provided an excellent opportunity for exploring a fundamental human dilemma—the perplexing choice between freedom and law. Do we wish to live free of the shackles of the law, even at the risk of seeing society descend into anarchy and violence—everything we fear when we speak of "lawlessness"? Or, are we willing to give up our freedom so that law and order will prevail in society, under the aegis of a strong government? The abstract dilemma of freedom versus law is concretely embodied in the standard Western plot, which typically pits a lone individual against the forces of society in one form or another. Some Westerns celebrate the rugged individualism of the gunfighter; others show how problematic the life of the outlaw can be and champion the imposition of law and order on the frontier community. One reason the Western has played a central role in American popular culture is the fact that it takes us straight to the heart of the great American experiment—the dilemma of a nation that attempted to found a communal order based on the principle of the freedom of the individual. American democracy is premised on the hope that there is a way out of the freedom/law dilemma, that order and freedom might be made compatible under the rule of law.

The American Western thus in effect investigates an important issue in political philosophy, the question of the state of nature. As developed by a series of European thinkers, chiefly Thomas Hobbes, John Locke, and Jean-Jacques Rousseau, the enquiry into the state of nature became a way to analyze the dilemma of freedom versus law. The idea of the state of nature was an attempt to conceptualize the pre-political existence of humanity, life without codified laws, public officials, or other manifestations of government power. Imagining human life without political institutions offers a way of analyzing the need for and value of such contrivances. In *Leviathan*, Hobbes presents such a horrific portrait of the state of nature as a war of all against all that he ends up endorsing any form of government, no matter how absolute, as better than none; Hobbes prefers law over freedom. By contrast, in creating an attractive portrait of the state of nature as idyllic, peaceful, and noncompetitive, Rousseau in his *Second Discourse* raises serious doubts about the legitimacy of civil society as an alternative, especially given its economic, social, and political inequalities; Rousseau prefers freedom over law. In the *Second Treatise of Government*, Locke crafts an image of the state of nature roughly midway between the extremes of Hobbes and Rousseau—less warlike than in Hobbes but more competitive and conflicted than in Rousseau. As a result, Locke's version of the state of nature allows him to legitimate political authority, while still reserving the right to criticize the specific forms it takes; Locke attempts to combine freedom with law, offering a law-abiding state as the guarantor of freedom.

Given the importance of these thinkers to the question of freedom versus law, it is not surprising that American popular culture has sometimes been influenced, directly or indirectly, by Hobbes, Locke, and Rousseau, especially in the Western. This influence is particularly evident in the HBO television series *Deadwood* (2004-2006), created by writer-producer David Milch. Widely recognized as one of the most sophisticated and artistic shows in the history of television, *Deadwood* is thoughtful, intelligent, and as close to philosophical as popular culture ever gets. Milch has been unusually forthright and forthcoming in discussing the show, in interviews, DVD commentaries, and his book about the series, *Deadwood: Stories of the Black Hills*. As a result, we have a rare opportunity—to study the philosophical underpinnings and implications of a television show as explicitly formulated by its creator.[1] At the same time, analyzing *Deadwood* helps clarify the issues at stake in the debate among Hobbes, Locke, and Rousseau about the state of nature and the dilemma of freedom versus law.

Milch was attracted to the story of Deadwood, a mining camp in the late 1870s in what is now South Dakota, by a unique set of circumstances. In 1875, rumors began to spread of gold finds on Indian land in the Black Hills. Because of the US government's treaty with the Sioux, this land belonged to them and was outside federal jurisdiction (as for the state of South Dakota, it did not even exist at the time). Thus the people who poured into the Deadwood camp in search of gold and other ways to make their fortune were there illegally to begin with, and were not subject to any government authority, municipal, state, or federal. Almost the first words we hear in the first episode of the series come from a jailed criminal in Montana saying wistfully: "No law at all in Deadwood?"[2]

The situation in Deadwood thus allowed Milch to explore a subject he had become fascinated by during years of working on television police dramas such as *Hill Street Blues* and *NYPD Blue*—the potential disjunction between law and order:

> A misapprehension that can distort one's understanding of Deadwood—and the world in which we live today—arises from the way that law and order are commonly conjoined. The phrase "law and order" can easily create the impression that these two very different social phenomena arise from a common human impulse, or that they are somehow one and the same. Law and order are not the same. It is common for us to try to retrospectively apply the sanction of law to the things we do to maintain order. Our desire for order comes first, and law comes afterward.[3]

In short, what intrigued Milch about Deadwood is how a motley group of human beings, pursuing—sometimes viciously—their own self-interest could in the absence of any legal institutions or established government nevertheless manage to organize themselves into a community and pursue some form of common good. Or to formulate the issue another way: Can human beings spontaneously arrive at rules that make possible and facilitate their productive social interaction, or are they dependent on the central authority of the state to create and enforce law and only thereby to make life in society feasible?

Thus in looking in *Deadwood* at "an environment where," in Milch's words, "there was order and no law whatsoever," he is raising the same question that is at the heart of state of nature thinking: how does the pre-political existence of humanity define the parameters of political life?[4] If there can be order without law, if human beings can find ways of organizing their social life safely and productively in the absence of the state, then the state cannot claim to be the sole source of human order and must respect the independently evolved order of society. In short, the idea of order without law sets limits on state authority and makes room for human freedom. On the other hand, if there can be no order without law, then the state, as the sole source of social order, can lay claim to unlimited authority, to absolute power, and freedom will suffer as a result.

The Hobbesian War of All Against All

The latter alternative is the core of Hobbes's state of nature teaching and his doctrine of absolute sovereignty. Hobbes espouses the position Milch rejects. He identifies law and order, arguing that all social order, all lawfulness in society, is ultimately the result of positive law, law made and maintained by the state. To be sure, Hobbes talks about "natural law" and the "laws of nature," devoting chapters XIV and XV of *Leviathan* to the subject, and thus seems to allow for some kind of pre-political social order. But "natural law" quickly turns out to be a fiction in Hobbes's account:

> For the Laws of Nature (as *Justice, Equity, Modesty, Mercy*. . .) of themselves, without the terrour of some Power, to cause them to be observed, are contrary to our naturall Passions, that carry us to Partiality, Pride, Revenge, and the like. And Covenants, without the Sword, are but Words, and of no strength to secure a man at all. Therefore notwithstanding the Laws of Nature, . . . if there be no Power erected, or not great enough for our security; every man will and may lawfully rely on his own strength and art, for caution against all other men.[5]

In short, for Hobbes, natural law turns out to be unnatural ("contrary to our naturall Passions") and wholly ineffectual on its own. In his view, only by creating the Leviathan State are human beings able to achieve any kind of reliable social order, and for Hobbes an unreliable order is no order at all. Hobbes's blanket endorsement of a centralized political authority, and his basic indifference to the distinctions among the different forms authority might take, are exactly the results Milch is trying to avoid when he insists that order is separable from law and pre-exists it.[6]

Thus we need to resist the strong temptation to describe the vision of *Deadwood* as simply Hobbesian. To be sure, *Deadwood* is filled with violence, and one aspect that sets it apart from most television series is the fact that from its very first episode, it conditions us to believe that any character might be suddenly killed at any moment. Under these circumstances, it seems at first apt to apply to the show the words with which Hobbes famously describes the state of nature—as a state of "continuall feare, and danger of violent death; And the life of man, solitary, poore, nasty, brutish, and short."[7] People who frequent Al Swearingen's Gem Saloon may indeed find that life in Deadwood is "nasty, brutish, and short," but, aside from the obvious fact that the camp is far from poor, Milch's most basic point in the series is that human life is *not* solitary, but takes communal forms even in the absence of the state and in the midst of bitterly divisive economic and social forces. Milch rejects Hobbes's vision of the state of nature as solitary because he realizes that if community is not in some sense natural to human beings, then they will be hopelessly subject to the dictates of the Leviathan State, the artificial construct created to correct the defects of the state of nature.[8]

Nevertheless, despite Milch's fundamental difference from Hobbes, life in Deadwood shares many characteristics with the state of nature portrayed in *Leviathan*. Milch may want to show that community is natural to human beings, but he does not wish to portray it as coming easily to them. In his view, human beings must struggle to achieve community, and must overcome many potential sources of conflict to do so. On the sources of that conflict, Milch and Hobbes are in remarkable agreement. Hobbes identifies three forces that lead to the war of all against all in the state of nature: "So that in the nature of men, we find three principall causes of quarrell. First, Competition; Secondly, Diffidence; Thirdly, Glory. The first, maketh men invade for Gain; the second, for Safety; and the third, for Reputation."[9] The same array of forces is at work in Milch's Deadwood. Hobbes writes: "if any two men desire the same thing, which neverthelesse they cannot both enjoy, they become enemies."[10] That is exactly what we see happening in Deadwood, as the characters fight, often to the death, over women, as well as gold, land, and other forms of wealth and property. In addition, both Hobbes and Milch see murderous violence arising from the radical insecurity of living without a clear government authority in place. Because any man may be attacked by any other at any time, he must forestall his potential enemies and attack them first.

Life in Deadwood continually follows this model of the pre-emptive strike. In Season 1, Episode 2, contrary to the traditional image of the honorable gunfighter, Wild Bill Hickok draws first and shoots a man who has not yet reached for his gun, merely because he senses—correctly as it happens—that the man meant to kill him. Many of the episodes turn on the issue of whether to neutralize an enemy by killing him before he can kill you. This issue reaches its apex on the communal level in the third season, when the "native" citizens of Deadwood, under Al Swearingen's leadership, must decide how to respond to the appearance in town of the mining magnate George Hearst, who draws upon his great wealth to build up a private army of Pinkerton agents, which he increasingly employs to impose his will on the camp. All of Al's instincts tell him to strike first against Hearst and his army.

Swearingen begs a meeting of Deadwood's elders to tell him why he should not undertake a pre-emptive strike while he still has a chance of defeating Hearst's continually strengthening forces.

We can readily understand why men fight over the same desired object or to defend themselves or to protect their family and property. But the violence in Deadwood is so widespread because it often seems irrational and unmotivated—men fighting, it seems, merely for the sake of fighting. But here, like Hobbes, Milch uncovers the deepest source of instability in any community: masculine pride and aggressiveness. Milch portrays Deadwood as a community of alpha males, who are constantly fighting to establish their individual dominance, to maintain a pecking order in the town. Hobbes explains this situation with his typical clear-sightedness: "For every man looketh that his companion should value him, at the same rate he sets upon himselfe: And upon all signes of contempt, or undervaluing, naturally endeavours, as far as he dares (which amongst them that have no common power, to keep them in quiet, is far enough to make them destroy each other,) to extort a greater value from his contemners."[11]

Hobbes here explains for us the fight between Swearingen and the ex-lawman and businessman Seth Bullock that begins the second season of *Deadwood*, as well as the violent struggles between Hearst and a host of other characters in the series. This violence always seems disproportionate to its ostensible and proximate cause in some minor incident. As Hobbes puts it, men "use Violence. . . for trifles, as a word, a smile, a different opinion, and any other signe of undervalue, either direct in their Person, or by reflexion in their Kindred, their Friends, their Nation, their Profession, or their Name."[12] Because of all these sources of sensitivity, Deadwood is a powder keg of violence. Given the underlying struggle for domination in the town, the slightest incident may trigger an outbreak of murderous violence.

The Right to Property

The extent of the agreement between Milch and Hobbes on the sources of violence among human beings only highlights their more fundamental difference. For Hobbes, only the institution of the Leviathan State can end the cycle of violence in the state of nature. By contrast, *Deadwood* shows that even in the absence of government, human beings have motives for and means of limiting their violence on their own, which is another way of stating Milch's principle that order is possible without law. Here is where Milch displays his greater affinity with Locke, who, unlike Hobbes, conceives of forms of order in the state of nature. The crux of the difference between Hobbes and Locke can be seen in the issue of property.[13] For Hobbes, there is no property in the state of nature: "Where there is no common Power, there is no Law: where no Law, no Injustice. . . It is consequent also to the same condition, there be no Propriety, no Dominion, no *Mine* or *Thine* distinct; but onely that to be every mans [sic] that he can get; and for so long, as he can keep it."[14] It is entirely characteristic of Hobbes that he views the right to property as created only by the state. If the state creates the right to property, then it can take that right away at will—a key example of what Hobbes means by the state's absolute sovereignty.[15]

By contrast, Locke argues that the right to property exists in the state of nature and thus pre-exists the state, indeed any communal action: "I shall endeavour to show how men might come to have a property in several parts of that which God gave to mankind in common, and that without any express compact of all the commoners."[16] For Locke, rather than the state being the origin of property, property becomes in effect the origin of the state: "The great and chief end, therefore, of men's uniting into commonwealths and putting themselves under government is the preservation of their property."[17] Since the right to property exists prior to the state in Locke's account, he sets limits on the state's treatment of private property. If the express end of government is to protect the right to property, it cannot legitimately seize property at will. Locke's vision of limited government as opposed to Hobbes's absolute sovereignty follows from his argument that the right to private property exists prior to the nation-state:

> But though men when they enter into society give up the equality, liberty, and executive power they had in the state of nature into the hands of the society, . . . yet it being only with an intention in every one the better to preserve himself, his liberty and property—for no rational creature can be supposed to change his condition with an intention to be worse—the power of society. . . can never be supposed to extend farther than the common good, but is obliged to secure every one's property by providing against those . . . defects ... that made the state of nature so unsafe and uneasy. And so whoever has the legislative or supreme power of any commonwealth is bound to govern by established standing laws, promulgated and known to the people, and not by extemporary decrees; by indifferent and upright judges who are to decide controversies by those laws.[18]

In contrast to Hobbes, then, Locke offers an example of what Milch means by order without law. Although Locke eventually concedes that the state is necessary to *secure* property rights, he insists that they can develop in society without the intervention of the state. This may seem like a trivial

distinction—both Hobbes and Locke view the state as ultimately necessary—but if one looks at the conclusions they draw from their contrasting
understanding of property, the difference is of the utmost importance. Locke's
conception of the state of nature as allowing for property rights gives him a
basis for evaluating different forms of government and championing those that
secure property rights as opposed to those that violate them with impunity.

Locke's argument for a right to private property prior to the state grows
out of his theory of self-ownership:

> Though the earth and all inferior creatures be common to all men, yet every
> man has a property in his own person. . . . The labour of his body and the work
> of his hands, we may say, are properly his. Whatsoever then he removes out
> of the state that nature hath provided and left it in, he hath mixed his labour
> with, and joined to it something that is his own, and thereby makes it his
> property. It being by him removed from the common state nature hath placed
> it in, it hath by this labour something annexed to it that excludes the common
> right of other men.[19]

Locke's argument applies particularly to land as property. He maintains that
the value of land does not reside solely in the land itself, but more importantly in what is done with it. If a man fences in and cultivates a piece of
land, he thereby increases its productivity and adds to its value, and that in
turn entitles him to its use and makes it his own. As Locke puts it: "As much
land as a man tills, plants, improves, cultivates, and can use the product of,
so much is his property."[20]

The key to Locke's defense of property rights is that he does not view the
dividing up of the world into private property as a zero-sum game. It may
seem that by making a piece of land his own, a man is depriving his fellow
men of something. But Locke stresses the way an owner improves a piece of
land by laboring on it and thereby increases the general stock of humanity.
He even offers a mathematical demonstration of his point:

> He who appropriates land to himself by his labour does not lessen but increase
> the common stock of mankind; for the provisions serving to the support of hu-
> man life produced by one acre of enclosed and cultivated land are—to speak
> much within compass—ten times more than those which are yielded by an
> acre of land of an equal richness lying waste in common. And therefore he
> that encloses land, and has a greater plenty of the conveniences of life from
> ten acres than he could have from a hundred left to nature, may truly be said to
> give ninety acres to mankind; for his labour now supplies him with provisions
> out of ten acres which were by the product of a hundred lying in common.[21]

Here is the magic of private property for Locke: if ten acres of cultivated land are more productive than one hundred acres of uncultivated, then a farmer who appropriates ten acres of land to himself will nevertheless effectively provide his fellow human beings with the benefit of at least an additional ninety acres of land. Hobbes conceives of the state of nature as a zero-sum game, a realm of scarcity in which men struggle over severely limited goods. Locke, by contrast, offers the increased productivity of private property as a way of generating a new abundance in the state of nature that works to everybody's benefit and creates a common interest in having land owned privately.

Locke and the Old Homestead

We can now see the root of the difference between Locke and Hobbes. Locke can imagine an economic order independent of the political order. Economic logic can dictate as complicated a social development as the dividing up of the world into private property, even in the absence of a government to enforce the results. Locke's argument for the priority of economic order over political is the most important example of what Milch means by order without law, and perhaps a clearer way of formulating the idea. In Hobbes's view, human beings left to themselves will simply start killing each other, and only the Leviathan State can stop them. In Locke's more optimistic view, human beings left to themselves will set to work cultivating their gardens (the killing starts much later). Locke makes his difference from Hobbes explicit: "And here we have the plain difference between the state of nature and the state of war which, however some men have confounded, are as far distinct as a state of peace, good-will, mutual assistance, and preservation, and a state of enmity, malice, violence, and mutual destruction are one from another."[22]

Milch displays his affinity with Locke on the priority of economic over political order in a pointed exchange between his two heroes in Season 1, Episode 4. Wild Bill Hickok has a vision of the future of Deadwood: "Camp looks like a good bet. . . . They'll get the Sioux making peace. Pretty quick you'll have laws here and every other thing." In Milch's terms, Hickok makes the mistake of viewing law as the pre-requisite of all social order. Seth Bullock replies to Hickok's political vision with a more basic economic consideration: "I'll settle for property rights." In the process of laboring on a house for his family, Bullock realizes the importance of the economic foundations of society. He is not interested in grand political visions; he wants his economic circumstances clarified and determined before he will worry about political issues, and he believes that Deadwood can find ways to settle property disputes on its own.

The emphasis on property rights is the most Lockean aspect of *Deadwood* and comes naturally to a show dealing with a gold rush, where the fundamental issue for most people is staking out claims to mining territory. Milch shows that even in the absence of conventional legal institutions, Deadwood is able to evolve ways of establishing and arbitrating property rights. We learn in the first episode that a land deal in Deadwood is ratified by spitting in one's palm and shaking hands with the other party. Precisely because legal methods of enforcing contracts are unavailable in Deadwood, its citizens take the customs they have evolved for making deals very seriously. For all the force and fraud we see interfering with honest commerce in Deadwood, we still observe a basically functioning economic community, in which people can roughly rely on each other's word—or handshake—in a business deal. Since no business can take place in an environment of complete hostility and distrust, it is to everyone's advantage to observe at least a minimum of civility and probity in their dealings with each other.

Deadwood even operates with a Lockean definition of property. The premise of the series is that a mining claim is yours as long as you actively work it. When Claggett, a representative of the territorial government, arrives in the camp, he makes this policy official: "The territory respects the statutes of the Northwest Ordinance, which state that a citizen can have title to any land unclaimed or unincorporated by simple usage. Essentially if you're on it and improve it, you own it" (1,9). This passage is so close to Locke's analysis of property that, for a moment, it sounds as if he deserves a writing credit for *Deadwood*. Actually, this scene is evidence of Locke's profound influence on the development of American political institutions. The Northwest Ordinance did in fact establish this principle of land ownership precisely because the governing powers in Washington, DC, were thoroughly familiar with Locke and his arguments for private property.[23] The great American principle of homesteading, which successfully transformed millions of acres of unproductive land into productive private property, was deeply Lockean in spirit. Even if Milch was not familiar with Locke's writings on the subject, his thorough knowledge of American history led him in a Lockean direction in his treatment of the issue of property in *Deadwood*.

Commerce Tames the Alpha Male

The Lockean understanding of property in *Deadwood* points to a larger Lockean spirit in its economic and political understanding of the American

West. The show reflects Locke's hope that economics might trump politics, that the peaceful and cooperative spirit of commerce might triumph over the warlike and divisive impulses of political life. As we will see, David Milch is no friend of capitalism in the form of Big Business, and cannot be described as a champion of the free market. Nevertheless, for someone who is deeply suspicious of businessmen, he is surprisingly open to arguments for the positive effects of commerce on human relations. In *Deadwood* commerce is the chief force that works to produce order without law. Above all, it seems to be the only force that can get the alpha males to set aside their differences, give up their fighting to the death, and work together for their mutual benefit.

The way in which economic logic can dictate social peace is most clearly evident in the career of Al Swearingen. As the owner of the Gem Saloon, he hardly seems to be a model citizen. He is involved in crooked gambling and prostitution, and we quickly learn that he is also guilty of shady land deals and runs a gang of highway robbers. He is responsible for a whole string of murders in the opening episodes. He has a hot temper and is brutal in his treatment of women and his subordinates. A perfect example of an alpha male, he seeks to dominate all around him and regards himself as the unofficial ruler of Deadwood. In short, in the early episodes he shows every sign of being the chief villain in the series and the most destructive force in the community.

Yet in the course of the series, Swearingen emerges as the chief architect of order without law in Deadwood. Of all the many alpha males in town, he is the most rational and the most able to control his emotions, especially his anger. He realizes when and where economic necessities demand that he restrain his violent impulses and work for peace. When the threat develops of Deadwood being annexed to the Dakota territory, thus becoming subject to the rule of outside forces, it is Al who organizes the influential citizens of the camp to respond to developments. One day he announces to the elders of the camp: "Be in my joint in two hours—we're forming a fuckin' government" (1,9). He is constantly working to get the other powerful males in town to recognize their mutual self-interest and unite against their common enemies from outside the camp.

In the first season of *Deadwood*, one might well think that Milch was setting up a simple contrast between Al Swearingen as villain and Seth Bullock as hero. But the intellectual complexity of the series is evident in the way that Swearingen, the criminal, turns out to be a force for order in the community, while Bullock, the lawman, turns out to be a force for disorder. Although Bullock is genuinely good-hearted and well-intentioned, he cannot control his emotions, especially his anger and his pride. Bullock is as much of an alpha male as Swearingen, and, as we have seen, their rivalry comes to a head at the beginning of the second season in a brutal fight. But it is Swearingen who realizes that they need to work together against the outside forces threatening the camp, and he swallows his pride in order to make the conciliatory gesture of returning Bullock's guns to him and thereby to solidify an alliance with a man he initially distrusted and despised. Swearingen continually struggles to calm Bullock's hot temper and to get him to act rationally in the complicated circumstances in which they find themselves. In the third season, Swearingen is willing to take calmly a terrible insult from Hearst (he chops off one of Al's fingers), whereas Bullock, provoked by mere words, hauls Hearst off to jail by the ear, thereby threatening to upset all of Swearingen's delicate negotiations with Hearst.

In line with Locke, then, and in contrast to Hobbes, Milch portrays how human beings, following their economic interests, can find ways to control their anger and their pride—and thus their violent impulses—and achieve forms of social order even in the absence of the state. They quickly reach the point where they themselves realize that killing each other is simply bad for business. Without presenting Milch as the Milton Friedman of the Western, one may note many instances in *Deadwood* of the market being portrayed as a positive force in the community. When a rival bordello opens in town, and Swearingen raises the prospect of colluding to set rates, the new madam, Joanie Stubbs, tells him: "As far as pussy, Al, we'll want to let the market sort itself out" (2,3). In the second season, Hearst's geologist and advance-man, Francis Wolcott, proclaims: "it's always preferable to allow the market to operate unimpeded" (2,4).

To be sure, Wolcott turns out to be the creepiest villain in the series, and Milch presents the business policies he pursues on Hearst's behalf in an extremely negative light. But these policies could justifiably be described as the very opposite of the way a free market operates. Hearst is trying to buy up mining claims in an effort to create a monopoly, and doing so, not by straightforward market means, but instead by using force, fraud, and political influence. Hearst represents the intrusion of outside forces, on a national scale, into the local marketplace of Deadwood. Here we see Milch's distrust of large-scale business allied with the state, as opposed to the small-scale independent entrepreneurship he generally admires. And when Hearst learns of the way Wolcott has murdered several prostitutes, he fires him and drives him to suicide—not because of any moral outrage, but simply because Wolcott's behavior is bad for business. Many of the best outcomes in *Deadwood* happen for the "wrong" reasons—that is, not out of moral idealism but out of the apparently crudest material motives. Milch views that as characteristic of

America, and a cause for celebration, not condemnation. He wants us to be clear-eyed about America and to recognize how its vices are bound up with its virtues:

> None of us want to realize that we live in Deadwood, but all of us do. . . .
> After first recoiling in horror, we come to love the place where we live, in all of its contradictions. . . . American materialism, in all of its crassness and extravagance, is simply an expression of the fact that we have organized our-selves according to a more energizing principle than any civilization that came before us.[24]

From what we see in *Deadwood*, that "energizing principle" is the market economy.

"What Some People Think of as Progress"

As much as Hobbes and Locke differ about the state of nature, they agree that human beings must move beyond it to the state of civil society. Thus Rousseau is relevant to *Deadwood* because he challenges this view and calls into question the triumphalism of the state of nature narratives in both Hobbes and Locke. They view the movement from the state of nature to the state of civil society as progress, a distinct improvement in the human condi-tion. By contrast, Rousseau does not believe in the inevitability of the move-ment from the state of nature to civil society, and he is not at all convinced that this transition should be called "progress." He insists that the movement out of the state of nature, far from being a necessary development as Hobbes and Locke present it, resulted from a "chance combination of several foreign causes which might never have arisen and without which [man] would have remained eternally in his primitive condition."[25] Moreover, Rousseau argues that even after humanity left the state of nature, its development might have stopped at a stage well short of the full-blown nation-state, and humanity would have been happier as a result.[26] Human beings in Rousseau's state of nature live in peaceful harmony, largely because they are scattered in the forests and hardly have anything to do with each other. There are no alpha males in Rousseau's state of nature, and therefore no violence and in fact no competition whatsoever. His natural men and women enjoy the peacefulness and happiness of grazing animals. In contrast to Hobbes, Rousseau views the state of nature as a realm of abundance, and in contrast to Locke, he views the development of property as generating artificial scarcities among human beings.[27]

Because Rousseau's state of nature is so much more attractive than that of Hobbes or even Locke, his writings serve as a powerful indictment of existing governments, and helped to fuel modern revolutionary movements. Rousseau's state of nature offers a model of human freedom and autonomy. To be sure, Rousseau explicitly denies that the message of his work is "Back to Nature!"[28] But his political writings are devoted to the difficult task of re-capturing as much of the positive aspects of the state of nature as is possible in modern civil society. He was highly critical of the way civic institutions have in his view distorted human nature, especially through the inequalities a modern economy creates, with its property rights and division of labor. The most famous sentence Rousseau ever wrote is the beginning of *The Social Contract*: "Man is born free, and everywhere he is in chains."[29]

Deadwood embodies a similar skepticism about the value of government and modern civilization. It may present the town's movement toward devel-oping municipal institutions and being incorporated into the United States as inevitable, but it questions whether this truly constitutes progress, an improvement in the lives of Deadwood's citizens. In the spirit of Rousseau, Milch raises doubts about the triumphalism of the traditional Western. The standard pattern of the Western is the myth of the closing of the frontier, the bringing of civilization to the Wild West. Typically, a lawless community, overrun by rampaging gunfighters, must be tamed by a brave lawman or two in concert with civic-minded businessmen, a crusading newspaper editor, and a beautiful schoolmarm waiting in the wings to educate a new generation of law-abiding city dwellers.

One can hear this standard narrative of progress in the historical fea-turette "Deadwood Matures" included in the DVDs of the third season. The historians tell a familiar tale of the town's march toward civilization, sparked by technological developments such as the telegraph and the railroad, as well as the growth of civilizing influences such as the schoolhouse and the theater. A kind of Hegelian optimism informs these narratives—events in the West happened in the way they had to happen and no other outcome could have been better. Civilization must be good because it is what history led to. Elements of the Western myth of progress are present in *Deadwood*, especially in Season 3, when outside forces truly begin to transform the town. But Milch evaluates this transformation quite differently, and refuses to view it simply as progress. More than any other Western I know, *Deadwood* dwells upon what is lost when a town makes the transition to civilization and be-comes part of the nation-state. What is lost is freedom.

The second season of *Deadwood* begins with Al Swearingen observing the new telegraph poles going up in the town and ruefully commenting: "Messages from invisible sources, or what some people think of as progress." Al is right to be skeptical about the benefit to Deadwood of becoming connected to the outside world. Its citizens will be kept better informed of gold prices in the East, but the telegraph will also allow the East to exert greater control over the West, and proves in fact to be the harbinger of a federal takeover of Deadwood. The upside of Deadwood's initial isolation is its local autonomy. The bureaucratic and corporate forces that invade the town in the second and third seasons take away the camp's control of its own destiny, and have little concern for the welfare of its citizens. Politicians and businessmen eye Deadwood as a place to plunder. The government officials who come to Deadwood are mostly looking to be bribed. With no intention of settling in the town themselves, they plan on governing it from afar, with little or no knowledge of what is actually going on there.

During the first season of *Deadwood*, one might well think that no one could be more evil or worse for the town than Al Swearingen. It is a measure of Milch's doubts about the so-called civilizing process that by the third season, Al has become a sort of hero in *Deadwood* for leading the resistance to the outside forces trying to "modernize" the town. We certainly start rooting for him in his struggles against Hearst, and the mining magnate becomes the new villain in the series, indeed chilling us with a degree of cold-bloodedness that Al could not muster on his worst days. What are the differences between Swearingen and Hearst that make the latter the greater villain in Milch's eyes and ours? Swearingen is a tyrant, but he is Deadwood's own tyrant. As a homegrown boss, he is by nature limited in his evil. When Al kills someone, he usually has to look him—or her—straight in the eyes. In general, he has to live with the consequences of his evil deeds. Indeed, he lives among the very people he preys upon. This fact does not stop him from preying upon them, but it does moderate the way he treats them. He never kills indiscriminately. More generally, Al is a better man than his carefully cultivated public image as a cutthroat would suggest. Despite giving the impression that he is purely self-interested, he actually takes a certain civic pride in Deadwood, and from the balcony of the Gem Saloon, he secretly watches the public life of the town with a sort of seignorial satisfaction.

By contrast, in his portrait of Hearst, Milch shows all the dangers of a man who seeks to rule people as a complete stranger to them. The quality Milch associates with Hearst is abstraction. He has one goal in life—to find and extract gold from the land—and Milch acknowledges that this ability to abstract from all other considerations gives remarkable energy to Hearst's economic endeavors. But it also means that he is blind to all ordinary human concerns and tramples over anyone standing in his way. Unlike Swearingen,

Hearst does not know the men he has killed and he always acts through intermediaries. He tries to keep as much distance as possible between him and the dirty deeds that make his business empire possible. For Milch, Hearst stands for the tyranny of abstraction, and symbolizes everything that is questionable about life in the modern nation-state, which places the seat of power remote from the communities it rules.

Deadwood begins as a small town, and the locus of small business, with impoverished men trying to make their fortunes in mining, accompanied by entrepreneurs like Bullock, who hope to make their living by providing necessary goods and services to the miners. Milch shows much that is questionable about the economic behavior that goes on in the isolation of this small town. Yet he seems to find it preferable to what happens when Big Government and Big Business invade Deadwood. As we have seen, there is something self-regulating about economic life in Deadwood, where everybody knows everybody else and people deal with each other face-to-face. It is the facelessness—the abstraction—of Big Government that Milch seems most to question. Big Business presents the same problem. Hearst represents corporate interests, and therefore Swearingen and others see no point in killing him when other shareholders in his corporation would simply take his place. Hearst's almost magical invulnerability in the third season symbolizes the implacable power of corporate—or what might be better called state—capitalism. What troubles Milch is the alliance between Big Government and Big Business that generates, and is in turn generated by, the nation-state. In the modern nation-state, power is simply too abstract and too remote from the people.

Government as a Necessary Evil

Deadwood is filled with anti-government comments that are almost libertarian in spirit. The federal government especially comes in for criticism, because it is the furthest removed from the people it tries to rule and therefore lacks the crucial knowledge of local circumstances needed to rule well. With regard to the United States' treatment of the Indians, Swearingen sarcastically remarks: "deep fucking thinkers in Washington put forward that policy" (1,3). Even one of the corrupt politicians from Yankton, Hugo Jarry, speaks with contempt of the federal government, specifically its attempts to hide its own corruption and incompetence: "Washington harasses us for our difficulties in distribution to the Indians, thereby distracting the nation at large from Washington's own fiscal turpitudes and miasms" (3,9). Jarry also complains about the ignorance of his fellow federal bureaucrats in Yankton:

"They're too busy stealing to study human nature" (2,5). Milch clearly shares his characters' skepticism about the federal government: "I'm always amazed when people say, 'Congress has adjourned and they have accomplished nothing.' A congressional term that accomplishes nothing is what the Founding Fathers prayed for. They wanted to keep the government canceling itself out, because it's in the nature of government to fuck people up."[30]

Deadwood shows how predatory government is on all levels. Nothing Swearingen can do on his own to rob the people of the camp can match the ambitious plans of the new municipal government to fleece them. The leading citizens get together under Al's leadership to raise the money to bribe officials in Yankton to let their mining claims stand. The first thing that the newly "elected" mayor, E. B. Farnum, proposes is a scheme to extract money from the unwitting townspeople: "Couldn't our informal organization lay taxes on the settlement to pay the bribes?" Farnum hits the nail on the head when he defines the nature of government: "Taking people's money is what makes organizations real, be they formal, informal, or temporary" (1,9). With government activity being epitomized by raising taxes to pay bribes, it is no wonder that politicians acquire a dubious reputation in *Deadwood*. Wolcott is the most repulsive character in the entire series, and yet even he insists on dissociating himself from the public sector: "I am a sinner who doesn't expect forgiveness, but I am not a government official" (2,10).

Perhaps the most eloquent discourse on the nature of government in *Deadwood* is delivered by Swearingen's rival saloon keeper, Cy Tolliver, on the occasion of Yankton's attempt to question the validity of the town's mining claims: "Who of us here didn't know what government was before we came? Wasn't half our purpose coming to get shed of the cocksucker? And here it comes again—to do what's in its nature—to lie to us, and confuse us, and steal what we came to by toil and being lucky just once in our fuckin' lives. And we gonna be surprised by that, boys, government being government?" (2,5). Despite such negative views of government in *Deadwood*, Milch seems to acknowledge its necessity, and even the idea that the town must be incorporated into the nation-state. Civilization, after all, requires some sacrifices, even of our natural freedom. In the most Rousseauian comment in the series, Swearingen tells his henchman Dority: "From the moment we leave the forest, Dan, it's all a givin' up and adaptin'" (3,2). But even with this concession, Milch, like Swearingen, gives a less than ringing endorsement of the power of government: "The politicians will always screw you, but there are circumstances in which we would rather have them around."[31]

This quotation from Milch seems to sum up the attitude of *Deadwood* toward government, especially the nation-state. Government is at best a necessary evil, but we must be skeptical about its claims to serve the public interest, and always remain vigilant to resist its perennial tendency to increase its power and encroach upon personal freedom. The closer power can be kept to a local level, the better. We see how Milch's faith in order without law ultimately puts him in the camp of those, like Locke, who believe in limited government, maybe even radically limited government. Perhaps the dilemma of freedom versus law can be resolved after all, along the lines of the U.S. Constitution, which attempts to limit government powers, secure the freedom of its citizens, and impose the rule of law upon the government itself. But there is enough of Rousseau in David Milch to raise doubts about the viability of this solution, and leave us wondering if living under government, especially in a large nation-state, requires too much of a sacrifice of our freedom. Perhaps in the end the Wild West is preferable to the Tame East. If *Deadwood* fails to resolve the freedom/law dilemma, at least it explores the issue with genuine philosophical depth. Such is the remarkable result when John Locke and Jean-Jacques Rousseau meet Wild Bill Hickok and Calamity Jane in the Black Hills of South Dakota.

Notes

1. Television is a collaborative medium, and Milch himself would not claim sole responsibility for creating the whole of *Deadwood*. In the cumulative screen credits for the three seasons the show ran, a total of 14 different directors and 16 different screenwriters are named. In his commentaries, Milch makes it clear that he worked closely with the individual actors in creating the characters they were playing. Nevertheless, all the evidence suggests that *Deadwood* is essentially the product of David Milch's imagination; he maintained creative control over all aspects of the production. Therefore throughout this essay I will refer to Milch as the author of *Deadwood* in the sense in which French film theorists use the term *auteur*.

2. I have transcribed all quotations from *Deadwood* from the DVDs. I will cite them by the season number and episode number in parentheses (so that this citation would read: 1,1).

3. David Milch, *Deadwood: Stories of the Black Hills* (New York: Melcher Media, 2006), 121.

4. The quotation from Milch at the beginning of this sentence is taken from the bonus feature commentary "The New Language of the Old West" in the first season set of DVDs of *Deadwood*.

5. Thomas Hobbes, *Leviathan*, ed. C. B. MacPherson (Harmondsworth, UK: Penguin, 1968), 223-24.

6. For Hobbes's basic indifference on the issue of forms of government, see *Leviathan*, 238-40.

7. Hobbes, *Leviathan*, 186.

8. On the artificiality of the state, see Hobbes, *Leviathan*, 226.

9. Ibid., 185.

10. Ibid., 184.

11. Ibid., 185.

12. Ibid.

13. See Leo Strauss, *Natural Right and History* (Chicago: University of Chicago Press, 1953), 234-35 and Robert A. Goldwin, "John Locke," in *History of Political Philosophy*, ed. Leo Strauss and Joseph Cropsey (Chicago: Rand McNally, 1963), 492.

14. Hobbes, *Leviathan*, 188; see also 234. The word *propriety* meant the same as "property" when Hobbes was writing.

15. For Hobbes on property, see Richard Pipes, *Property and Freedom: The Story of How Through the Centuries Private Ownership Has Promoted Liberty and the Rule of Law* (New York: Alfred Knopf, 1999), 32. This book gives an excellent overview of the issue of property throughout history.

16. John Locke, *Two Treatises of Government*, ed. Thomas Cook (New York: Hafner, 1947), 134.

17. Ibid., 184. For Locke on the sanctity of property, see Pipes, *Property*, 35.

18. Ibid., 186.

19. Ibid., 134.

20. Ibid., 136.

21. Ibid., 139.

22. Ibid., 130.

23. See Thomas L. Pangle, *The Spirit of Modern Republicanism: The Moral Vision of the American Founders and the Philosophy of Locke* (Chicago: University of Chicago Press, 1988), 308, note 5, where he speaks of "the truly amazing speed with which Locke's conception of property permeated and radically transformed English common law. By 1704 (six years after the publication of the *Two Treatises!*) Locke's notions begin to appear as the standard or orthodox notions in legal commentary. I believe it is safe to surmise that Locke's influence on the legal and hence political thinking of the American colonists in subsequent years, by way of this transformation in legal thinking, was enormous."

24. Milch, *Deadwood*, 213.

25. Jean-Jacques Rousseau, *The First and Second Discourses*, ed. and trans. Roger D. Masters (New York: St. Martin's, 1964), 140.

26. Ibid., 150-51.

27. For Rousseau's negative view of property, see *Discourses*, 141-42, 151-52, 156-57.

28. See especially the important discussion in note i of the *Second Discourse*, 201-203.

29. Jean-Jacques Rousseau, *The Social Contract and Other Later Political Writings*, ed. and trans. Victor Gourevitch (Cambridge, UK: Cambridge University Press, 1997), 41.

30. Milch, *Deadwood*, 143.

31. Ibid., 135.

CHAPTER THREE

~

Political Assassination in Popular Fiction and Political Thought

Trotsky, Arendt, and Stephen King

Charles C. Turner

Introduction

On December 30th, 2006, former Iraqi president Saddam Hussein was executed by hanging. The previous month an Iraqi Special Tribunal had found him guilty of crimes against humanity. Almost one year later, on December 27, 2007, former Pakistani prime minister Benazir Bhutto was killed by a bomb blast two weeks before an election many expected her to win. Groups linked to al-Qaeda claimed responsibility for the attack.

In what ways are these two events similar and in what ways are they different? Both involved political leaders from Muslim nations dying at the hands of their political enemies, although the former case, importantly, included a trial while the latter did not. It is not difficult to see how students of contemporary politics can become confused by the use of political violence. When, if ever, does it serve the ends of justice? Is assassination ever morally justifiable? For present purposes, I will use both assassination and political killing as synonyms to refer to either the killing of a political figure, or the killing of a non-political figure for specifically political purposes.[1] As previous scholars have noted,[2] assassination "can never be separated from the political context in which it occurs; its impact, public and systemic, is political."[3]

Political thinkers and novelists alike have pondered the moral dilemma of eliminating evil for the greater good. In the modern world of politics only the most radical thinkers have advocated assassination, whereas fiction writers have tended to find the practice more acceptable—witness the ratio of fictitious accounts of assassination to actual political murders. In short, there is an assumption in popular fiction that it is okay to kill the bad guy, though doing so may come at a steep price.

This chapter confronts these assumptions by examining the moral boundaries of political assassination in Stephen King's *The Dead Zone* and "Everything's Eventual" and comparing the moral decisions of King's fictional characters to the positions taken by Leon Trotsky in "Their Morals and Ours" and Hannah Arendt in *On Violence*.[4] As many have explored political violence from both theoretical and fictional positions, the first question to address is, why these three? The major reason for concentrating on Trotsky and Arendt is that they both take the issue of justified political violence seriously, rather than setting it aside as many modern theorists have done. Moreover, their conclusions differ in a significant respect. While Trotsky argues that violence can be justified when the resulting consequences are sufficiently *transformational*, Arendt argues instead that violence can be justified only when the resulting consequences are sufficiently *certain*. Such distinctions are important, but hard to envision given both the—thankfully—small number of actual assassinations and the taboo nature of political violence as a practical choice in public discourse.

To best explore the potential morality of political violence and the importance of the above-mentioned philosophical distinctions we need the proxy of fiction. Again, examples abound, yet the ubiquity of Stephen King makes him, in some ways, one of the best conveyances of American popular culture.[5] More importantly for present purposes, King tells stories in which the extent and certainty of transformational consequences are precisely the issues at stake, presented in a quasi-magical realist style that, in effect, permits thought experiments regarding these conditions that are not possible in real life. In other words, it is difficult for us to remove our political worldview from our thoughts on Hussein or Bhutto, but we may find it easier to have more wide-ranging thoughts about the actions of King's fictional characters.

In order to properly address these topics, I begin with an examination of Trotsky and Arendt's positions on assassination in an effort to identify the crucial components of just political violence—to the extent that such a concept exists. I then consider King's work and how the violent actions of his characters might be evaluated by moral philosophy. Do they meet the moral criteria established by either Trotsky or Arendt? If so, how does this inform our understanding of the relationship between moral action and contemporary popular culture?

Trotsky and Arendt on Assassination and Political Violence

Though political thinkers have confronted assassination and weighed its merits for millennia, two twentieth-century theorists—Leon Trotsky and Hannah Arendt—addressed the moral issue more directly than most, and with emphases that are new in the contemporary world. Historically, philosophers and religious leaders found assassination justifiable, if at all, only if it was the sole means by which a society could end a tyranny.[6] Trotsky and Arendt each offer distinct arguments for why such an approach is too limiting in the modern world. Products of an age that no longer relies on absolute moral foundations, Trotsky and Arendt each take on the challenge of re-creating new foundations for human morality. Trotsky, a revolutionary Marxist writing in the midst of Stalinism and just prior to World War II, constructs his moral world from the perspective of dialectical materialism. This perspective on history causes Marxists to re-examine traditional morality and, at the very least, redefine tyranny in ways that make political assassination a more significant part of the conversation than it had been previously. Arendt writes in the post-Marxist tradition over three decades later, with Stalin and Hitler behind her and the political unrest of the 1960s in her immediate present. Her observations of totalitarianism and genocide lead her to develop a framework of humanity—the human condition—that mistrusts violence, but acknowledges its theoretical potential as a tool for preventing even greater violence. It is these re-conceptions of the role of violence in the modern world that make Trotsky and Arendt an interesting focal point for an examination of the morality of political assassination in popular culture.

Leon Trotsky, a key architect of the Bolshevik Revolution, approaches assassination most directly in "Their Morals and Ours," an essay originally published in *The New International* in 1938. In this essay, Trotsky takes on the criticism that revolutionary Marxism defies conventional morality. In particular, he addresses the charges that Trotskyists believe the ends justify the means and that they are no different from Stalinists.[7] Trotsky responds to these charges by first exposing the class basis of traditional morality:

> The bourgeoisie, which far surpasses the proletariat in the completeness and irreconcilability of its class consciousness, is vitally interested in imposing its moral philosophy upon the exploited masses. It is exactly for this purpose that the concrete norms of the bourgeois catechism are concealed under moral abstractions patronized by religion, philosophy, or that hybrid which is called 'common sense.' The appeal to abstract norms is not a disinterested philosophic mistake but a necessary element in the mechanics of class deception.[8]

Trotsky demonstrates that most religious and moral systems are subject to some form of the argument that the ends justify the means. For example, not only do the Jesuits uphold this maxim when they focus on ends as the locus of moral justification, but Martin Luther did as well when he called for "the execution of revolting peasants" and the utilitarians do likewise when they say "that those means are moral which lead to the common welfare as the higher end."[9] Next, Trotsky presents the Bolshevik basis of morality, distinguishing it from Stalinism in the process. As its first task, Trotskyist morality must completely separate itself from bourgeois morality. It must have an ethical foundation resting on materialism rather than on existing bourgeois notions, because "whoever fawns before precepts established by the enemy will never vanquish that enemy."[10]

This foundation leads to a morality in which "that is permissible...which really leads to the liberation of mankind."[11] And, of course, liberation can be messy. Even though the end result will be peaceful, Trotskyist morality requires breaking some big eggs to get there. Trotsky's world is one where tyranny is not merely one form of government, to which an unfortunate handful of nations are subject; it is the defining characteristic of all governments that have not experienced a successful and complete socialist revolution. Trotsky describes the post-revolutionary state as "a society without lies and violence" but warns that "there is no way of building a bridge to that society save by revolutionary, that is, violent means."[12]

Trotsky distinguishes this morality on one side from the centrists who cannot fathom a complete break with existing morality and on the other side from the conservative reactionaries such as Stalin who are willing to engage in violence and deceit that goes well beyond class liberation. The former group he calls the "petty pick-pockets of history" for their unwillingness to engage in true revolution.[13] As to the excesses of the latter, he suggests that "boundless intellectual and moral obtuseness is required to identify the reactionary police morality of Stalinism with the revolutionary morality of the Bolsheviks."[14] Trotskyist morality accepts violence solely as a vehicle for transforming society, not as a tool for keeping citizens in check. Moral violence works in only one direction; it is for liberation, not oppression. The act must rest on a widespread sense of class consciousness, else risk "becoming subordinated to the bourgeois ideology."[15]

So, where does the specific case of political assassination fit into this moral framework? Trotsky's moral system suggests assassination *can* be moral if it meets one important condition and one caveat.[16] The critical condition is that the act must serve to advance the class struggle (and, thereby, achieve a more just society) rather than further alienate the workers from each other.

The caveat is that Trotsky is far less convinced that individual acts will meet the condition than acts brought about by groups of revolutionaries.[17] Thus, the epitome of moral violence becomes an act like the assassination of the Romanovs—an act by the vanguard of the proletariat to foment class solidarity, sever ties with a bourgeois regime, and enhance the chances for a successful socialist revolution. Living in the founding generation of Russia's experiment with socialist revolution, Trotsky's view toward violence is both instrumental and immediate. His morality may not say that the ends justify any means, but it certainly holds that purpose matters; the nobler the goal, the wider the scope of permissible action.

In retrospect, the contemporary reader may find Trotsky's morality too urgent, too willing to accept the claimed consequence of action in place of the observable result. The passing of a generation will provide a broader vantage point for observing not only socialist revolution, but its fascist and nationalist offshoots as well. For many, the empirical reality of the first half of the twentieth century became an important lesson in reining in the scope of new moralities and retesting the footing of new foundations. Thus, from Trotsky's emphasis on class struggle and revolution we turn to an emphasis on democracy and the human condition, offered most clearly by the post-Marxist thinker Hannah Arendt. Having witnessed revolution gone wrong at the hands of men such as Stalin, and new modes of morality perverted by Hitler, Arendt rejects the sweeping consequentialism she sees in moral visions like Trotsky's and favors a more cautious and limited approach to moral violence. Although, like Trotsky, she values eliminating tyranny and establishing freedom, her skepticism regarding the predictability of consequences leads to a tighter rein on violent action.

Arendt considers political violence most directly in *On Violence*, though the ethics of killing human beings is a frequent topic of her inquiry in other works as well.[18] Arendt's main concern in this work is to distinguish the term violence from power, as she feels contemporary theoretical usage has improperly linked the two as synonyms. Arendt defines power as the ability of a group to "act in concert" and violence as a tool that is sometimes used to increase strength.[19] Thus, violence might be used as a tool in a political act, though it might not be necessary and violent acts can also be apolitical and certainly immoral. On one hand, she accepts that violence is an inevitable—if sometimes irrational—part of the political world because we have not yet found a proper substitute for it.[20] On the other hand, she critiques the use of violence—particularly as a tool of the new left—for its overwhelming reliance on particular ends to justify it as a means. There is only one sure outcome of violence as political action, Arendt warns: "the practice of violence, like all action, changes the world, but the most probable change is to a more violent world."[21] Put another way, Arendt seems to say that violence as a means for creating a new political order, while common in the modern age, is suspect.[22]

In spite of this risk, Arendt explicitly condones some violent acts, particularly those with symbolic force that send a clear message beyond the mere perpetuation of violence. Arendt accepts, for example, the state violence of capital punishment as a just symbolic act. In approving of the death penalty for Adolf Eichmann, she declares:

> Just as you supported and carried out a policy of not wanting to share the earth with the Jewish people and the people of a number of other nations—as though you and your superiors had any right to determine who should and who should not inhabit the world—we find that no one, that is, no member of the human race can be expected to want to share the earth with you. This is the reason, and the only reason, you must hang.[23]

Though the certain result is death for one man, here Arendt's scales of justice favor the value of the lesson such an act of public violence has to offer. The eyes of the world were focused on the actions of a Jerusalem courtroom in 1961-1962. And, because of this, the violent act was justifiable; it taught the dangers of violating the human condition.

Despite the Eichmann example, Arendt is far more skeptical of the certain results of violent acts in most cases. In the process of critiquing violence as political action, Arendt makes an important claim that calls into question the validity of political assassination.[24] Violence, Arendt argues, is a suspect political tool because it relies on a prediction about the future, which is always a doubtful prospect and is therefore easily abused. Taking social science (and, in particular, game theory) to task, Arendt observes:

> Only in a world in which nothing of importance ever happens could the futurologists' dream come true. Predictions of the future are never anything but projections of present automatic processes and procedures, that is, of occurrences that are likely to come to pass if men do not act and if nothing unexpected happens; every action, for better or worse, and every accident necessarily destroys the whole pattern in whose frame the prediction moves and where it finds its evidence.[25]

Despite these imperfections of social science, Arendt does allow for the possibility of positive outcomes to violent acts:

Since when we act we never know with any certainty the eventual consequences of what we are doing, violence can remain rational only if it pursues short-term goals. Violence does not promote causes, neither history nor revolution, neither progress nor reaction; but it can serve to dramatize grievances and bring them to public attention.[26]

Assassination, therefore, runs a great risk by using violence in the present to prevent some anticipated future evil. It is a risky gamble with uncertain consequences. In the end, Arendt concludes that political violence "can be justifiable [an appeal to the future], but it never will be legitimate [an appeal to the past]. Its justification loses in plausibility the farther its intended end recedes into the future."[27] In other words, assassinating a political leader moments before they launch a nuclear attack is more likely justifiable than assassinating a politician whom one believes will take such action at some undefined point in the future, an issue that will come to bear later in this essay. Of course, for Arendt, part of being human—of the human condition—is *not* knowing the future. The limitations of our foresight are part of what we have in common and any violation of that commonality risks the loss of our humanity.[28] It is Stephen King's ability to deftly handle fictional consideration of both of these types of situations that makes him an ideal focal point for the consideration of moral violence in contemporary popular culture.

The Dead Zone

Turning from political philosophy to the world of popular culture, there are nearly limitless opportunities to observe the theory of assassination in fictional practice. One finds two cogent examples in the fictional world of Stephen King, quite possibly the best-selling American fiction writer of all time.[29] As King, like all of us, is a product of his times, it should come as no surprise that the ethical quandary of taking action against an oppressive leader surfaces in a number of King stories.[30] Indeed, the period from 1918 to 1968—which includes King's formative years and the era preceding them—saw over 1,500 assassinations worldwide, including the assassination of sixty-eight heads of state.[31]

Not only are King's stories often preoccupied with the relationship between morality and violence, they also push the limits of the human condition, via characters who have inhuman knowledge of the future and abilities to shape it. In *The Stand*, for example, all of the central characters are haunted by dreams of their own near futures. The characters are drawn to visions of either a "good" community or an "evil" one. The choices they make during the day determine the vision that draws them at night, thus shaping their future. The final visions draw the two communities together and culminate in an act of apocalyptic violence that destroys the evil city, effectively assassinating its leader.[32] *The Dark Tower*, likewise, features a main character who spends a lifetime—perhaps several lifetimes—in pursuit of an evil leader whom he feels compelled to assassinate. These themes of the moral boundaries of violence and the (possibly malleable) limits of the human condition place King's fiction in dialogue with modern moral philosophy.

King's most thorough exploration of assassination comes in *The Dead Zone*. In typical King style, there is a supernatural twist; the novel examines the issue of precognitive tyrannicide. The story centers on Johnny Smith, a young high school teacher in a small New England town who spends nearly five years in a coma after a serious car accident. When he wakes he finds he has a special ability—he can see into the past, present, and future of others' lives by touching them. This ability leads Smith through many adventures—medical tests, crime solving—but the ultimate showdown comes when he shakes hands with a populist candidate for Congress. Living in an early primary state, Smith had made a habit of meeting the various candidates who came through to see if he would pick anything up by shaking their hands. Though it starts as a hobby, he eventually must admit to himself that he'd been "looking for a wild card in the deck all along."[33] He finds his wild card in Greg Stillson, an up-and-coming politician whose "single most important goal . . . is the accumulation and preservation of power."[34] Smith sees Stillson becoming president and starting a worldwide nuclear war.[35] Stillson wins his race in 1976 as an independent and is reelected after forming his America Now Party in 1978.

As Stillson's populist rise builds in momentum, Smith must take more and more seriously the possibility that his vision will become a reality. He struggles with the idea that he is able to step outside the boundaries of the human condition and wonders whether this also allows him—even forces him—to go beyond the boundaries of human morality. He repeatedly asks himself the time honored cliché of ethics: "*If you could jump into a time machine and go back to 1932, would you kill Hitler?*"[36] At first his answers are adamant: "No. . . . That's never an answer. *Never.*"[37] As time passes, though, and Stillson becomes more powerful, Smith's answers begin to change. He goes through the exercise of weighing his options. He could try to sabotage Stillson's party from the inside, but this might not work and he fears he will be recognized from his earlier contact with the man. He could hire someone to dig up dirt on Stillson. This seems like a less certain approach, as Stillson could always scapegoat one of his underlings, and the last person to investigate Stillson, an FBI agent, ended up dead. He also considers merely wounding Stillson, as Arthur Bremer had done to George Wallace, but worries that this might not end Stillson's career and may actually win sympathy for him. This leaves him with assassination as the only sure option for preventing a Stillson presidency and the catastrophic war that would follow.

The question remains theoretical, though, as Smith believes Stillson won't become president for another ten to fourteen years. But this all changes at the end of 1978, when Smith learns he has an aggressive brain tumor. Knowing he will soon be dead regardless, Smith decides to act. He holes up in the balcony of a small village's town hall and waits for Stillson to arrive for a speech. As Stillson enters to loud applause Smith fires his rifle. In the end, Stillson is undone by the cowardice of his own actions—he uses a child as a shield to avoid being shot at. Smith's shots miss the mark, but he is himself gunned down by Stillson's bodyguards. Before he dies he touches Stillson's ankle and has one last vision of the future. Things have changed. He failed to assassinate his target, but he succeeded in averting large scale disaster.[38]

The strength of this book as an exploration of political violence lies in the ambiguity of the answers it provides. We know Smith has had accurate visions in the past—but are they all guaranteed to be accurate? Do we know with certainty that Stillson will start a nuclear war? Or that killing Stillson will prevent one? The brain tumor as well is a complicating factor—is it affecting Smith's interpretation of events and his ability to act rationally? Is Smith right that the alternatives he rules out would not have been effective? Is Smith, as his mother believed, fulfilling a destiny God intended for him?

These questions point to the unknowability of the consequences of violent action. Even a character like Smith, who circumvents some limitations of the human condition, has his doubts. In the end, he acts violently and believes himself moral in doing so, but he only acts when he does because an aspect of the human condition which he cannot escape—his own mortality—has forced his hand. Smith's decision is a rebuttal to the Arendtian caution against the unknowable: sometimes our humanity forces us to make a choice.

"Everything's Eventual"

Turning to a more recent example of King's fiction, the short story "Everything's Eventual" is the first person account of Dinky Earnshaw, a nineteen-year-old whose special abilities lead him from a life of delivering pizzas to the role of psychic hit man.[39] Though the story begins with the line "I've got a good job now, and no reason to feel glum," the reader is given plenty of reason to doubt this optimistic claim.[40] Within a few pages Earnshaw has changed his tune: "I'm not going to spend my life in Columbia City, I can tell you that. I'm leaving, and soon. One way or the other."[41] Thus, the reader knows early on that the story's narrator is both dishonest (either with himself, the reader, or both) and determined to act in a manner that will change his present circumstances.

As a child Earnshaw discovered that he could cause death by drawing a complex (but otherwise meaningless) set of shapes, symbols, and words and then sending them to the victim as a "special letter."[42] A mysterious Mr. Sharpton finds out about this ability and offers Earnshaw a job using his ability with the equally mysterious Trans Corporation—either a classified arm of the government or the tool of powerful elites. Sharpton tells the naïve Earnshaw that Trans will use his ability "for the betterment of all mankind" and that while "it was about killing people. . . . the targets were bad guys, dictators and spies, serial killers . . . people did it in wars all the time."[43] Earnshaw's willingness to accept Sharpton's claims with no demands for proof seems to flout Arendt's concern with the uncertainty of knowledge about the future and blindly accept Trotsky's consequentialist ethic. He does not bother asking Sharpton to define "betterment of all mankind."

Earnshaw accepts the job and now all of his needs are taken care of by "cleaners" he never sees. He gets anything he wants by just writing it on a list. All he has to do in return is work with the names or addresses he's given. At first, he thinks little of the consequences, but a chance reading of a newspaper headline one day is the beginning of the end for Earnshaw's innocence. He sees the obituary of one of his hits and goes to the library to investigate further. Earnshaw concludes that the target, a newspaper columnist, had probably been a decent person and had been marked for death due to his opposition to military spending. For the first time, Earnshaw considers his victims as real human beings: "He was funny. He was charming. And I had killed him."[44] Hit with the harsh reality that he is responsible for the deaths of hundreds, Earnshaw realizes the Trans Corporation may have a much broader definition of "bad guys" than he does. Further investigation reveals more about his victims: one was a leading AIDS researcher; another was a Senate candidate who has been an outspoken critic of war. Earnshaw realizes he has become a mass murderer. He is not making the world a better place after all. As a naïve teenager who saw no better future and no way out of his dead end life, he accepted the job of just assassin without bothering to ask who was defining the terms. The rub is that there is no way out of his present predicament; the Trans Corporation holds all the cards and his own life and that of his mother may be the price for insubordination. In the end, he makes plans to send one of his special letters to Mr. Sharpton—a further act of assassination, but one with very different moral dimensions.

"Everything's Eventual" asks the reader to consider the moral dimensions of assassination when the killer has a high degree of certainty that he will be successful in killing his target without being caught, thus succeeding in the immediate sense, but a very low degree of certainty (and indeed, indifference) regarding the longer term consequences of his actions. Though the story confronts political morality, it is not itself moralizing. The main character is obviously conflicted about what he does, and he invites the reader to "take that any way you want. Any old way at all."[45] In addition, and perhaps even more importantly, King does not provide clear answers, but leaves the reader to puzzle over the story's ethical concerns. Earnshaw never questions the act of political killing itself, just whether the company has drawn the line too far out. The reader is left with the same questions Earnshaw asks himself: "Good of mankind? Bad of Mankind? Indifferent of Mankind? Who makes those judgments? Mr. Sharpton? His bosses? *Their* bosses? And does it matter?"[46] Earnshaw ends his narrative by answering these questions in the form of action. He decides to assassinate Sharpton as a way of escaping his situation and showing solidarity with a resistance movement. In effect, this tells the reader that morality does matter, and that decisions about the good of humanity should not be left to the elites.

Assassination in Theory and Action

How, then, might one critique the actions of King's characters Smith and Earnshaw in light of the political theories of assassination offered by Arendt and Trotsky? I suggest that the moral acceptability of each act hinges upon overcoming the human limits of knowing the consequences of our actions for the former and the potential for class transformation for the latter.

One can see a clear point of distinction between Smith and Earnshaw regarding Arendt's concern with predictability. King confronts this conundrum with each character, taking very different approaches. With Johnny Smith, the limitations of predictability in the social sciences are obviated by introduction of the fantastic. Smith does not have to rely on hunches or data or analysis of the past to predict future actions, he *knows* Stillson will cause a nuclear holocaust because he has had a psychic vision telling him so: "I have to do something about Stillson. I *have* to. I was right about [the restaurant burning down], and I'm going to be right about this. There is absolutely no question in my mind."[47]

In one sense, this is an easy out because it avoids the type of problem Arendt presents. In another sense, King merely replaces doubt in science with doubt in the supernatural.[48] Despite seeing vision after vision become reality, for years Smith avoids taking the only action he believes will guarantee a change. Only fatal illness forces him to eventually act. Though his dying vision shows him he has succeeded, ironically, he has done so in spite of failing to assassinate Stillson. Smith merely exposes the politician's cowardice. In the end, the act of violence that changes the course of the world is not one that kills a political figure, but one which, in Arendt's words, "serve[s] to dramatize grievances and bring them to public attention."[49] Ultimately, the reader is left to trust in Smith's precognition for assurance that this change will, indeed, make the world a better place. Arendt, for her part, warns that such outcomes are not guaranteed when she observes the outcomes of the French student protests: they acted against the establishment—only to see it replaced by de Gaulle.[50] Indeed, Smith fears Stillson's destructive impact because of his psychic vision, but in a world where weapons of mass destruction continue to exist, Smith's act has merely eliminated one potential actor, not the tools of destruction themselves.

As he becomes obsessed with politics, and Stillson in particular, Johnny Smith devotes himself to Arendt's conception of action, the *vita activa*—"a life devoted to public-political matters."[51] He follows the news constantly, in an effort to use normal human channels to deduce what his inhuman abilities have foretold. In this sense, Smith is a complicated figure for Arendt. He embodies a rejection of the human condition through his super-human ability, but the knowledge he gains from that ability leads him to confront some of the central issues of humanity—the sharing of human life on the earth, mortality, and violence as action.

On the whole, Arendt opposes violence as a violation of the human condition. This opposition is not universal, however, as can be seen from her support of particular violent acts. For one, she endorses resistance to tyranny. For another, she endorses the symbolic value of the death of one who has orchestrated crimes against humanity. Indeed, in both examples the justification seems to rise from the refusal by political oppressors to share in humanity with the oppressed. It is this refusal to "share the earth" that typifies Stillson's character as well. From his brutal killing of a dog to his willingness to risk the life of a child, Stillson makes clear his devaluing of human life. Though Smith's vision is silent regarding the specific reasons for Stillson's nuclear holocaust, the action is clearly one that could only be taken by an individual like Eichmann, one who refuses to share the earth with those he considers unworthy.

The problem of predictability in Dinky Earnshaw's case is even more severe, as the young man assassinates via a supernatural power, but relying on, presumably, more prosaic forms of data. The reader does not know for certain the reason particular targets are chosen for assassination, but it seems doubtful that they fit the scenario of immediate threat to peace. The occupations of the targets Earnshaw describes—a journalist, a biologist, a Senate candidate—suggest that the individuals may have simply possessed too much specialized knowledge or expressed too much criticism for the Trans Corporation's comfort. As the Trans Corporation is clearly the bad guy in King's story, it is not surprising that the type of assassinations it commissions are utterly unjustifiable in the eyes of Trotsky, Arendt, or likely any other non-fascist political thinker.

The interesting moral question, then, addresses the action Earnshaw contemplates at the end of the story—killing his boss, assassinating the head assassin.[52] Earnshaw does not change his position on the use of violence in general, only on when he should use it. This assassination might satisfy Arendt's critique, since it does not rely on long-term assumptions, only on the immediate outcome of freeing Earnshaw from his trap. Indeed, King's depiction of a bureaucrat standing up to the evil of his superiors depicts a reverse image of the case of Adolph Eichmann. Arendt condemns Eichmann for failing to stand up to the Nazi regime, arguing that the just actions of even a single individual will always make a difference.[53] Thus, it seems likely that a bold act of violence on Earnshaw's part in this case might be the type of rational, justifiable violence of which Arendt would approve. On the other hand, Earnshaw knows almost nothing about his chances of success. His extra-human ability will likely make his assassination attempt on Sharpton successful in the immediate sense, but Earnshaw does not know whether such an act will lead to a less violent future. The fact that he intends it to be the first volley in a revolution makes it more likely that killing Sharpton will instead lead to the outcome Arendt cautions against: "the most probable change is to a more violent world."[54]

Turning to a Trotskyist critique, the acts of Earnshaw and Smith are both *potentially* moral, with the key difference lying in the possible results of their actions. Smith is by no means either a revolutionary or a Marxist, but he is confronted with a Stalinesque enemy. Greg Stillson's cadre of bodyguards, a collection of former criminals beholden only to their boss, has a habit of violently silencing hecklers and anyone else interfering with the momentum of Stillson's candidacy. Stillson himself is clearly a demagogue and Smith's visions suggest he will rule as a fascist. But even though all of humanity may be better off without Stillson in power, there is nothing of class struggle in

Smith's violent attempt to end the politician's career. For Trotsky, Smith's act would "hardly evoke moral indignation" but as its result would not bring the workers closer to triumph, it would also not be the type of act he would consider morally obligatory either.[55] Revolutionary Marxism would merely heave a sigh as Smith's efforts led to one bourgeois leader being replaced by another.

Earnshaw, on the other hand, is preparing to act on behalf of a revolutionary movement. He hints that his plan to assassinate Sharpton has come about through association with others like himself who want to end their own oppression.[56] Unfortunately, as one of the keys to success for a network of revolutionaries is secrecy, Earnshaw is willing to write down very little about his co-conspirators. The reader only knows that they have sent Earnshaw an invitation to join them in revolt against the Trans Corporation and that they communicate via coded messages. The reader has only Earnshaw's own faith in the organization on which to rely. In this emphasis on a common struggle, Earnshaw behaves much more like a Trotskyist than Smith does in his inescapable isolation. As Trotsky observes: "only in the mass movement can you find expedient expression for your heroism….The liberation of the workers can come only through the workers themselves."[57] Earnshaw is a poorly paid worker whose job serves to further entrench those in power. When he and his co-workers decide to turn this process on its head by executing the executioner, the same act of sending deadly letters takes on a very different moral meaning. In Trotsky's frame: "even in the sharpest question—murder of man by man—moral absolutes prove futile. Moral evaluations, together with those political, flow from the inner needs of struggle."[58] Earnshaw's killing of scientists is morally impermissible, but killing his boss as part of a class struggle becomes a moral obligation.

To be sure, Earnshaw's actions, in solidarity with unknown other workers, are a step in the right direction. But without knowing the extent of his collaborators' organization and the theoretical basis of their actions, Earnshaw risks participating in a "purely spontaneous movement" that revolutionary Marxism might see as representing "the class struggle in embryo, but only in embryo."[59] The key questions to understanding the revolutionary nature of Earnshaw's act are twofold: Does Earnshaw act from a broad-based class consciousness? And, is his act part of a larger, theoretically grounded movement that could have transformational consequences? The text suggests that the answer to both questions may be yes.

First, though it is Earnshaw's nature to belittle his own worth, his reaction when reading about the lives of individuals he has killed suggests some sense of common humanity. Despite their differences, all of these individuals—like Earnshaw himself—suffer from class oppression. And the oppressive class, Earnshaw comes to realize, is the mysterious corporation that has hired him.[60] It is this realization that makes Earnshaw at least a potential revolutionary Marxist—one who has an understanding of not only his own class oppression, but of the oppression of all classes.[61]

The answer to the second question, regarding the extent of the movement Earnshaw decides to participate in, is less certain, though there are hints. Earnshaw himself, even if one accepts his growing class consciousness, is by no means a member of the vanguard of the proletariat. This role is left to an entirely unseen group, known to Earnshaw only through a cryptic note tucked inside an advertising circular.[62] Symbolically, Earnshaw's allies have communicated via the newspaper. And, perhaps not coincidentally, Earnshaw initially learns about his victims via a chance encounter with a newspaper.[63] Historically, newspapers have been the medium of choice for communication between Marxist intellectuals and the workers.[64] Though not dispositive, the use of a newspaper to communicate offers a symbolic connection to class consciousness and the revolutionary nature of Earnshaw's action.

Conclusion

So, where do political theory and the literature of Stephen King leave us on the problem of assassination as political action? The most accurate answer, but also the most dangerous, seems to be that they have left the door open, at least a crack. Had they been novelists themselves, Arendt and Trotsky would likely have written very different characters to personify the just assassin. Arendt would emphasize the act of the just individual, struggling against a tide of oppression via a highly certain action, whereas Trotsky's hero would lead the masses in a socially transformative worldwide revolution.

King, though, is the novelist here, and the bottom line is that Trotsky and Arendt would likely applaud the fact that both Smith and Earnshaw decide to act against oppressors. But their praise would not be without qualification, particularly in Smith's case for Trotsky and in Earnshaw's case for Arendt. Though the casual reader of King's fiction is more likely to sympathize with Smith's effort to prevent a madman from becoming president, Trotsky would find dubious his decision to act as a lone individual. Arendt's position is more complicated. On one hand, she would approve of the certainty of Smith's knowledge of the future. On the other hand, she would be discomforted by the super-human source of that knowledge.

Trotsky would be more likely to accept the morality of Earnshaw's decision to kill his boss. The effects are immediate and the solidarity of the action means it will have transformative consequences. Arendt, though, would likely challenge the likelihood of Earnshaw's act producing a less violent future. In a world where political violence remains all too common, it is important that we continue to seriously examine its moral value, or lack thereof. Contrasting worldly philosophies with fictional acts is one useful way of accomplishing this task.

Notes

The author would like to thank Margaret Hrezo, Susan McWilliams, John Michael Parrish, and Travis Smith for helpful comments on earlier drafts of this chapter.

An earlier version of this chapter was delivered to the American Political Science Association Annual Meetings, Boston, Massachusetts, August 28-31, 2008.

1. As an example of the latter case, consider the murder of a religious leader who has advocated that his or her followers take a particular political stance. For a discussion of political crime more broadly, see Ross (2003) and Kittrie (2000).

2. Murray Clark Havens, Carl Leiden, and Karl M. Schmitt, *The Politics of Assassination* (Prentice-Hall, 1970), 3.

3. A standard dictionary defines *assassinate* as: "1: to murder by sudden or secret attack usu. for impersonal reasons <~ a senator> 2: to injure or destroy unexpectedly and treacherously" (Merriam-Webster 1986, 108). More to the point, see Joseph R. Nolan and Jacqueline Nolan-Haley, *Black's Law Dictionary* (West Publishing Company, 1990), 14. *Black's* denotes assassination as: "murder committed, usually, though not necessarily, for hire, without direct provocation or cause of resentment given to the murderer by the person upon whom the crime is committed; though an assassination of a public figure might be done by one acting alone for personal, social or political reasons."

4. Of course, it goes without saying that the books and authors discussed here are merely examples. Arendt, Trotsky, and King are, I believe, particularly effective vehicles, but certainly not the only ones. Plato, Thomas More, Friedrich Nietzsche, John Rawls and countless others present interesting questions of the ethics of political violence. Political violence also arises in many works of literature: William Shakespeare's *Julius Caesar*, Charles Dickens's *A Tale of Two Cities*, and Albert Camus's *The Just*, to name a few. Rather than ignore other good examples of the themes explored here, I will reference them in notes.

5. King himself would likely not object to being considered as a mere conduit of ideas. He refers to himself (or at least to a character named Stephen King) in a similar vein in *The Dark Tower* series (Pocket Books, 2004) and in the Author's Introduction to *Lisey's Story* (New York: Scribner, 2006).

6. For a history of assassination, see J. Bowyer Bell, *Assassin!: The Theory and Practice of Political Violence* (St. Martin's Press, 1979). For more recent coverage from

the perspective of international relations, see Ward Thomas, "Norms and Security: The Case of International Assassination," *International Security* 25.1 (Summer 2000): 105-33.

7. In the realm of socialism, fine distinctions abound. As Trotsky himself describes them, Trotskyists (sometimes interchangeably called Bolsheviks or revolutionary Marxists by Trotsky) occupy the left end of the spectrum, social democrats the center, and reactionaries like Stalin the right.

8. Leon Trotsky, "Their Morals and Ours," *The New International* 4.6 (June 1938), 7.

9. Ibid., 4-5.

10. Ibid., 20.

11. Ibid., 22.

12. Ibid., 15.

13. Ibid., 14.

14. Ibid., 13.

15. V. I. Lenin, *What is to be Done? Burning Questions of Our Movement* (Peking, China: Foreign Language Press, 1975), 49.

16. Of course, Trotsky had no way of knowing that he would become a victim of political assassination himself just two years after the publication of his essay. One suspects he would have found that act immoral.

17. Trotsky, "Their Morals," 23.

18. See Hannah Arendt, *The Human Condition* (University of Chicago Press, 1989) and *Eichmann in Jerusalem* (Penguin Books, 1994).

19. Hannah Arendt, *On Violence* (Harcourt, Brace, and World, 1970), 44-46.

20. Ibid., 5, 82.

21. Ibid., 80. Social science seems to bear out this claim; scholars have observed that, in practice, assassination "rarely accomplishes" its ends (Havens, Leiden, and Schmitt, *The Politics*, 9).

22. Hannah Arendt, *The Human Condition* (University of Chicago Press, 1989), 228.

23. Arendt, *Eichmann*, 279.

24. To be sure, Arendt is largely interested in the violent uprisings of groups rather than in individual acts because she is critiquing contemporary New Left politics and assassination, with a few exceptions, has largely been a tool of the right. Marxism, she argues, sees revolution as the result of material circumstances in society, not as the result of individual acts (Arendt, *On Violence*, 11-12).

25. Ibid., 7.

26. Ibid., 79.

27. Ibid., 52.

28. Arendt, *The Human Condition*.

29. Publishing rankings are not an exact science. Though King has often been spoken of in this capacity, so have Earl Stanley Gardner and John Grisham. It seems safe to say with some certainty that King is *among* the best-selling American authors of all time.

30. See, for example, *The Dark Tower* series and *The Stand* (New York: Signet, 1991), in addition to the two stories explored at greater length here.

31. Figures include both attempted and successful assassinations. (Havens, Leiden, and Schmitt, *The Politics*, 21-22)

32. To be sure, Randall Flagg, as the embodiment of an immortal evil does not die, per se. In fact, he is at times the same evil leader that Roland pursues in *The Dark Tower* series.

33. Stephen King, *The Dead Zone* (Signet, 1980), 296.

34. Tony Magistrale, *Landscape of Fear: Stephen King's American Gothic* (Popular Press, 1988), 35.

35. King, *The Dead Zone*, 303, 390.

36. Ibid.

37. Ibid., 313.

38. Though Magistrale argues (*Landscape of Fear*, 36) that Stillson's "political career is foiled by an accident of fate," this seems to be an oversimplification that misses the mark. It is not merely an accident, but Smith's deliberate and willful action, which has the ultimate consequences that he intended, that ruins Stillson. Many a failed assassination attempt has had an effect on world history. It is the action, as opposed to inaction, that has made the difference. Moreover, Havens, Leiden, and Schmitt (*The Politics*, 15n) note that failed assassination attempts are "as important as successful" ones, the difference being only "the result of largely fortuitous circumstances."

39. Confusingly, the short story "Everything's Eventual" is one of fourteen stories that appears in King's short story collection titled *Everything's Eventual*. In the main character's vernacular, "eventual" is a synonym for "cool" or "awesome."

40. Stephen King, *Everything's Eventual* (Pocket Books, 2002), 253.

41. Ibid., 259.

42. Ibid., 278. In using this power, Earnshaw becomes the personification of the violence-as-creativity/art concept popularized by Sorel and others in the post-Nietzschean tradition. See, for example, Georges Sorel, *Reflections on Violence*, trans. T.E. Hulme (New York: Peter Smith, 1941), 291-5.

43. King, *Everything's Eventual*, 278.

44. Ibid., 310.

45. Ibid., 254.

46. Ibid., 315.

47. King, *The Dead Zone*, 353.

48. For another exploration of this theme, see Philip K. Dick's short story "The Minority Report," in *The Minority Report* (Pantheon, 2002).

49. Arendt, *On Violence*, 79.

50. Ibid., 49-50. Here Arendt's position is in clear contrast to Trotsky's. To be sure, from her vantage point, Arendt has had the opportunity to observe more revolutionary failures than did Trotsky.

51. Arendt, *The Human Condition*, 12.

52. Another interesting exploration of the morality of assassinating the assassin is Jack London's *The Assassination Bureau, Ltd.*

53. For example: "under conditions of terror most people will comply but some people will not. . . . Humanly speaking, no more is required, and no more can reasonably be asked, for this planet to remain a place fit for human habitation" (Arendt, *Eichmann*, 233).

54. Arendt, *On Violence*, 80.

55. Trotsky, "Their Morals," 22-23.

56. King, *Everything's Eventual*, 321.

57. Trotsky, "Their Morals," 23. Social science lends support to Trotsky's claim. Data suggest that the impact of an assassination is lower when committed by a lone individual than when carried out by an organized group (Havens, Leiden, and Schmitt, *The Politics*, 148).

58. Trotsky, "Their Morals," 23.

59. Lenin, *What is to be Done?*, 36.

60. King, *Everything's Eventual*, 319.

61. Lenin, *What is to be Done?*, 86.

62. King, *Everything's Eventual*, 320.

63. Ibid., 306.

64. See, for example, Lenin, *What is to be Done?*, 208.

Bibliography

Arendt, Hannah. *On Violence*. New York: Harcourt, Brace, and World, 1970.

———. *The Human Condition*. Chicago: University of Chicago Press, 1989.

———. *Eichmann in Jerusalem*. New York: Penguin, 1994.

Bell, J. Bowyer. *Assassin!: The Theory and Practice of Political Violence*. New York: St. Martin's Press, 1979.

Havens, Murray Clark, Carl Leiden, and Karl M. Schmitt. *The Politics of Assassination*. Englewood Cliffs, NJ: Prentice-Hall, 1970.

King, Stephen. *The Dead Zone*. New York: Signet, 1980.

———. *The Stand: Expanded Edition*. New York: Signet, 1991.

———. *Everything's Eventual*. New York: Pocket Books, 2002.

———. *The Dark Tower*. New York: Pocket Books, 2004.

———. *Lisey's Story*. New York, Scribner, 2006.

Kittrie, Nicholas N. *Rebels With A Cause: The Minds and Morality of Political Offenders*. Boulder: Westview Press, 2000.

Lenin, V.I. *What is to be Done? Burning Questions of Our Movement*. Peking, China: Foreign Language Press, 1975.

Magistrale, Tony. *Landscape of Fear: Stephen King's American Gothic*. Bowling Green: Popular Press, 1988.

Merriam-Webster. *Webster's Ninth New Collegiate Dictionary*. Springfield, MA: Merriam-Webster Inc., 1986.

Nolan, Joseph R., and Jacqueline M. Nolan-Haley. *Black's Law Dictionary*. 6th ed. St. Paul, MN: West Publishing, 1990.

Ross, Jeffrey Ian. *The Dynamics of Political Crime*. Thousand Oaks, CA: Sage, 2003.

Sorel, Georges. *Reflections on Violence*, trans. T. E. Hulme. 1915. Reprint, New York: Peter Smith, 1941.

Thomas, Ward. "Norms and Security: The Case of International Assassination," *International Security* 25, no. 1 (Summer 2000): 105-133.

Trotsky, Leon. "Their Morals and Ours." *The New International* 4, no.6 (June 1938): 163-73. Marxists' Internet Archive. Accessed: 14 November 2007 <http://www .marxists.org/archive/trotsky/1938/morals/morals.htm> (14 Nov. 2007).

PART II

DILEMMAS OF
PUBLIC LEADERSHIP

~

CHAPTER FOUR

On Hobbits and Hoplites

Dilemmas of Leadership in Aeschylus' The Suppliants
and J. R. R. Tolkien's Lord of the Rings

A. Craig Waggaman

Introduction

The essays in this book examine how different works of literature and popular culture shape our moral selves by asking us to vicariously participate in decisions that involve moral choices and more specifically, moral dilemmas. How should leaders handle instances when any decision they make is likely to have bad consequences? This is the situation faced by the leaders in both of the works of literature discussed in this chapter: Aeschylus' *The Suppliants* and *The Lord of the Rings* by J. R. R. Tolkien. Since these stories illuminate the qualities of mature moral leadership, they each represent the ability of popular culture to be a positive part of the moral education of both leaders and citizens.

We have seen very recently how the character of individuals and nations is revealed by decisions made under difficult circumstances. When al-Qaeda terrorists succeeded in their dramatic attack on symbolic targets in the United States, the primary lesson for the world should have been the immorality of deliberately targeting innocent civilians to pursue political or military objectives. The use of religion to kill the innocent only adds to the moral perversity of the act. Unfortunately, political ideology or a devotion to a single-minded justice grounded in vengeance are frequent substitutes for moral wisdom. In deciding how to respond to these attacks, American leaders faced a number of dilemmas, some strategic, some moral. The prudence of the Bush Administration's strategies in response to the attacks is still being debated in the United States and around the world. The legacy of the

Bush Administration's moral leadership clearly is a deeply divided country that even began to see torture as just a means to an end and a world which came to see the United States as an arrogant and messianic superpower. The effects of the actions and rhetoric of President Bush and Vice President Cheney remind one of Thucydides' eloquent description of the corruption of the Greek city-states that came as a result of the "greed and ambition" fueled by the circumstances of the Peloponnesian War.

> Words had to change their ordinary meanings and to take that which was now given them. Reckless audacity came to be considered the courage of a loyal ally; prudent hesitation, specious cowardice; moderation was held to be a cloak for unmanliness; ability to see all sides of a question, inaptness to act on any. Frantic violence became the attribute of manliness; cautious plotting, a justifiable means of self-defence. The advocate of extreme measures was always trustworthy; his opponent a man to be suspected.[1]

These same criticisms are now being made about President Obama's foreign policy and highlight the need for reflection by both citizens and leaders on the requirements of moral decision making.

Moral leadership requires rational decision making undertaken by an individual with a balanced consciousness. Moreover, even a leader with these qualities must be willing to engage herself in "deep-pondering" in order to discover right action in difficult circumstances. When the qualities of the mature and responsible political/moral leader are put into action, further evidence of good leadership will show itself in the transparency (honesty) of communication between leaders and citizens/subjects, a willingness and ability to listen to others and sort through opinions, and a mind able to examine and weigh a large number of factors before making a decision. These are qualities that are important for leadership in both domestic and international politics. This essay will examine these characteristics of moral leadership and how they are put into practice in The Suppliants and The Lord of the Rings.

The understanding of rational decision making used in this chapter is grounded in a definition of reason developed by Eric Voegelin in his essay "Reason: The Classic Experience."[2] Reason (nous) is both the weighing of means and ends with regard to pragmatic action, and the examination of ends in the light of the summum bonum, or highest good. The highest good in this sense is not an object of knowledge; it is an orientation of the soul of a mature and responsible person, and it forms the basis of a balanced consciousness. Such a consciousness is aware of our existence as creatures that engage in dual (metaleptic) participation in the Platonic metaxy.[3] Plato's idea of the *metaxy* (or middle) argues that human beings have a place in both a physical and a spiritual reality. We participate in both realities, hence the idea of dual participation. Another way to think of this is to say that we live an in-between existence: between life and death, time and eternity, earth and heaven. A balanced consciousness is balanced because it accepts both the fullness[4] of reality and our incomplete understanding of it. It does not try to escape that condition by narrowing reality to something that can be fully comprehended or reducing it to a specific ideological or religious orthodoxy. A balanced consciousness, therefore, is evidenced more by humility than arrogance.

The examination of means and ends as illuminated by the love of the Good itself requires what Aeschylus calls "deep-pondering" and what Voege-lin refers to as "deep-diving" or the descent into one's own psyche to make choices consistent with *dike* or right action. Good choices can be conditioned by the quality of laws and customs that are the product of wisdom, experience, and divine revelation. But Aeschylus and Tolkien tell us that such fixed standards, while very important, are not enough to guide human beings through dark and difficult times. There is no substitute for the anguish and soul searching of the individual who seeks justice or righteousness in specific and hard circumstances. This is the meaning of deep-diving.

In the literature discussed in this chapter, transparency and participation show evidence of mature moral leadership. I combine these two concepts because together they form a key part of the relationship between leaders and their citizen/subjects. When actions undertaken by a political community are likely to have painful consequences, it is particularly important that the decision to risk those consequences be made in the right way. To lie to or mislead people who may have to sacrifice themselves for their community is morally wrong, even if it is often considered politically expedient. If the cause cannot be articulated in a way which calls forth such courage, it is likely not worthy of that sacrifice. The cooperation and support of a crucial portion of the community will usually be needed in any case for a long-term successful outcome. Some sort of consultation with those who must give that cooperation will help to cement the unity needed to face challenges and risks such as those found in *The Suppliants* and *The Lord of the Rings*.

There is an underlying condition of moral leadership that has not yet been identified. A good decision is not an isolated event. It is part of the history of a civilization that includes moral advance and decline. A political community can decline to a point where it is unlikely to bring forth a rational leader in the sense described above. Even if it does by some fortuitous accident, the community is unlikely to listen to him. In the latter case, some deception might become a necessity to encourage people who are attuned only to self-interest not to grossly violate common standards of justice, thus precipitating further decline.[5] In short, the moral health of a political community is a fragile thing and needs to be cared for by leaders and citizens alike. The literature discussed in this chapter is not simply about the heroic actions of moral kings and leaders. It is about surrounding cultures and civilizations which permit the action or speech in question to be understood and acted upon by other characters in the stories.

The fictional drama of *The Suppliants* and the *mythopoesis*[6] of The *Lord of the Rings* were both produced for popular audiences of their respective time periods. They each demonstrate decisions made by communities which are willing to accept that they participate in a world of meaning of which they form only a part. This cosmos contains ordering principles which allow them to make moral choices, though these choices are not always obvious ones prescribed by ancient texts, customs, or laws. They require profound reflection and often terrible anguish—deep-diving. Further, the leaders portrayed in these stories are intensely aware of the importance of their choices and of their own limitations in trying to make them. They must seek to do what is right, but they also have the problem of involving their communities in these decisions in full knowledge of the physical and moral dangers they carry. They must resist those who would oversimplify the content of these decisions with appeals to security or patriotism or expediency and they must be able to use honest persuasion to bring a sufficient number of their followers along with them in their process of deep-diving. To the extent that this is done, the community retains its role as an historical actor in a drama of meaning. Absent this, it falls into oblivion—the meaningless rise and fall of power shells that lead the thoughtful or sensitive soul to search beyond such a history for a source of order in their own lives or sometimes to various forms of despair.

The Suppliants

The Greek playwright Aeschylus was a "Marathon Man." He had been present at one of the most glorious military victories in history when an outnumbered Athenian army defeated the army of the Persian Empire on an empty plain north of the city of Athens. If the Second World War was our "good war," the campaigns that made up the Persian Wars were the equivalent for Athens. Plato tells us in *The Laws* that the Athenians at Marathon (490BC) were bound together by fear of the Persians, friendship for their fellow citizens, and a reverence for the law and for the gods.[7] Later, Thucydides tells us that by the time of the Peloponnesian War (431BC), the binding forces of the now-imperial Athens had changed to fear, honor, and interest.[8] The friendship of citizens bound by fear of the laws and of the gods was replaced by the pride, paranoia, and self-interest of an imperial people and their leaders. As the "father" of Greek tragedy, Aeschylus' plays explored the foundations of spiritual order and disorder in the actions of his characters. This chapter uses one of his plays, *The Suppliants*, to show us how a mature and responsible King engages his people with the moral dilemmas surrounding war, justice, and piety as they decide whether to grant asylum to a group of fifty women fleeing forced marriage to their cousins.

"Tragedy as a form is the study of the human soul in the process of making decisions."[9] This definition of Aeschylean tragedy given by Eric Voegelin differs from more common understandings of tragedy, like that of Aristotle. The suffering of the tragic hero is not put forward for the pleasure or emotional catharsis of the audience. Instead, it shows us a mature and responsible soul in action under a variety of difficult situations. This could not have been done, according to Voegelin, until the development of Greek philosophy differentiated the soul as a independent source of order—a place where the divine and the human meet: the Platonic *metaxy*.[10] Maturity and responsibility now become not only social virtues, but spiritual ones. The well-ordered soul is a necessary condition for a fully human and happy life and thus a practical and a political concern of the community and its leaders.

In *The Suppliants*, King Pelasgus of Argos is asked to grant asylum to the fifty daughters of Danaus who have sailed from Egypt with their father, after being on the losing side of a war for control of part of the Nile Valley. They are fleeing forced marriages with their fifty cousins who, as part of their victory in the war in Egypt, have claimed the right to marry the fifty daughters of their uncle Danaus. The women liken the situation of the forced marriage to "unholy rape."[11] The justice of their desire not to be forced to marry men they do not love is tarnished somewhat by the fact that they seem to be against the institution of marriage itself, a less defensible position in the law, custom, or morality of their time. Their request for asylum is grounded in a claim to distant kinship with the people of Argos through their ancestor Io, a human lover of Zeus, who fled to Egypt to escape the jealous anger of Zeus' wife Hera. There Zeus found Io and she bore him a son, Epaphus, who was the ancestor of Danaus.

In order to strengthen their case for asylum, the fifty women threaten to despoil the temple where they have taken up residence by killing themselves if they are not taken in by Pelasgus and given sanctuary from their pursuing suitors.[12] Finally, they claim the protection of Zeus, who is defender of suppliants.

The King questions the women and their father, making it clear that he isn't at all sure that the claims of the men are not reasonable, especially under the laws of Egypt. He acknowledges the story which allows them to claim kinship but also points out how little the women resemble the women of his country.[13] Finally, he chastises the women for their impertinent speech.[14]

Knowing that allowing the women to settle in Argos might lead to a costly war, King Pelasgus tells them that he must consult with his people before deciding whether to grant their request. He and Danaus return to the city to take counsel with representatives of the people. A short while later Danaus returns to his daughters with the good news that the King has defended their cause and helped to persuade the people to give them protection. The women heap praise and blessings on the King and on Argos for defending their cause, but their celebration is cut short by the arrival of a herald sent by the sons of Aegyptus (their cousins) who have arrived to take back the women, by force if necessary. The play ends in uncertainty after the King has rebuked the herald who goes off with the threat that the real judge in this case will be Ares (god of war) "who decides such causes, not with damages in money, but with heavy toll of fallen men, and limbs convulsed in bloody death."[15]

As in many ancient tragedies, much of the action of the play that is of interest to us takes place off-stage, so we are left with the original audience to imagine the scene when Pelasgus discusses the situation with representatives of his people. Yet this is what makes the play so useful as a teaching tool. We are involved in the decision and must explore our own thoughts and assumptions about necessity and justice as we reflect and discuss the action of the play. What is most interesting for our purposes in this short play is the process of decision making used by King Pelasgus and the people of Argos in deciding to grant the request of the daughters of Danaus for political/sexual asylum. After hearing the story of the women, he bemoans the difficulty of the choice he faces:

> To save us all, our need is for deep pondering;
> An eye to search, as divers search the ocean bed,
> Clear-seeing, not distracted, that this dilemma may
> Achieve an end happy and harmless; first for Argos
> And for myself, that war and plunder may not strike
> Us in reprisal; and that we may not surrender
> You who are suppliants at the altar of our gods,
> And so bring Vengeance, that destroying spirit, to plague
> Our lives, who never, even in death, lets go his prey.
> Is it not clear we must think deeply, or we perish?[16]

Like many important decisions in political life, this decision is complicated. It requires clear knowledge of the facts of the case and prudence (the ability to choose appropriate means), but it also requires "deep-knowing" or wisdom concerning the purpose of the political community and its obligation to itself, to others, to the gods, and to justice. Pelasgus must be concerned with the consequences of his decision for the interests of Argos, but he has the wisdom to understand that the ultimate good of his city depends on its place in a larger order of existence in which it participates but which it does not control or fully understand.

One could simplify the decision of Pelasgus, but only by some form of reductionism. The realist reduction, for example, would examine the effect of the decision and its consequences on the power and the wealth of Argos. If a decision in favor of the women would not add to these, it would not be in the "interest" of the city to support their cause. Others might think only of the justice of their claim and argue in favor of helping them. Yet if a war ensues in which Argos might be destroyed, surely one would want a leader who could balance justice with necessity for the good of his city. A priest might look at the entrails of an animal and pronounce the will of the gods. But which of the gods is speaking? Are we sure we read the signs correctly? One can worry about the gods without assuming their commands are always clear and their prophets always trustworthy. In other words, piety is not a simple substitute for justice. What of one's own laws and customs? Decisions do not take place in an historical and cultural vacuum. But if one is aware of one's own history, should not one show some respect for the laws and customs of other peoples? If in Egypt the claims of the male suitors are socially acceptable, does that diminish the arguments of the women?

This is a proper moral dilemma—virtually any decision that Pelasgus makes will have some consequences which are bad. *The Suppliants* was the first play of a trilogy, and scholars piece together that the decision of the citizens of Argos to grant asylum to the daughters of Danaus leads to many bad consequences—a war, the King's death, and the murder of the men by the women on their wedding night. The problems are resolved (though this involves some speculation) by the intervention of Athena who defends the decision by one of the women to break her word with her father and sisters and not to murder her husband (she has fallen in love with him) and reconciles the women to marriage as an institution.[17]

So why should one view the process by which the original decision was made as a model of mature and responsible action, as this chapter argues? King Pelasgus engages at least a portion of his citizens (we are unsure as to how many or how exactly they are consulted) in a process of deep-diving to find *dike* (justice) in a difficult situation. Such diving would remain shallow in immature or disordered souls. In a city which aspires to moral excellence, however, depth is necessary because the difficulty of the situation requires many factors to be considered and weighed in order to make a just decision. Those participating do not turn their back on the interests of Argos in accepting the complexity of the decision. In fact, the costs of war weigh heavily on their minds.[18] But the interests of a well-ordered city are themselves complex if its citizens are interested in right action as well as prosperity and peace. According to Danaus, father of the suppliant women, the King uses "every subtle and persuasive turn of the orator's art" in his persuasion of his citizen/subjects. Danaus adds: "Zeus brought the issue to success."[19] The King and a critical number of the citizens of Argos are concerned not only with the city's prudential interests but also with what is just and also with the opinions of the gods, or with piety. Deep-diving in search of justice is an act of participation which includes both human beings and gods. Lastly, Pelasgus is aware that the laws of Egypt may be different from those of Argos regarding the rights of the suitors, and while their laws are not decisive in resolving the matter, they should be acknowledged as having some effect on how the actions of the men are viewed.[20]

So we are presented in *The Suppliants* with a leader who engages his citizen/subjects honestly in a dialogue about what is best for their community. This dialogue is open to the broadest possible understanding of reality—of the forces upon which the fate of souls and of nations are ultimately grounded. Customs (ours and theirs) are recognized and respected, justice and necessity are given their due, and the judgment of Heaven hangs over the proceedings, illuminating the actions of human beings as part of a larger drama of being which encompasses the mystery of existence in a cosmos that is too large for our complete comprehension.

There are two primary elements to this decision making process that make it worthy of emulation. The first is that it does not artificially narrow the factors to be considered in order to make the decision easier or to mask a decision made on the basis of emotion or selfish interests. "National interest"[21] here refers not just to the physical survival of Argos and its citizens or to an increase in their power and wealth at the expense of another political community, but also to its existence as a moral community that ultimately will be judged by its piety and the character of its justice. In other words, a rational decision requires a morally mature decision-maker. More simply, a rational decision *is* a moral decision because it takes into account the existence of the individual and the political community as participants in a drama of meaning whose source is the world-transcendent ground. Every fully developed moral or political philosophy rests on some ground of being that helps to illuminate the human condition. Sometimes this ground is firmly rooted in the world we see around us. Hobbes, for example, made the will to power the ground of being because he viewed survival and security as the primary human goals. For both Tolkien and Aeschylus, however, the ground of being is world transcendent in that it originates in a reality that transcends the physical world. Thus, a world-transcendent ground is a basis for moral decision making that requires individuals and political/cultural communities to move beyond individual or collective passions and self-interests, accepts the existence of a world of meaning that makes moral choice possible and essential, and involves citizens and decision-makers in dialectic about moral action that extends to other individuals and communities by way of their existence within the same transcendent ground of meaning. Such a world-transcendent ground—regardless of its spiritual, religious, or philosophical content—then serves as a foundation for human choice. Returning to our original argument about the meaning of rational decision making, it is reason (*nous*) in this sense of an orientation to the ground of being that keeps a people playing a part in the history of order. When action is reduced to "a struggle for power that takes place at all levels of life" we fall back into the Herodotean *kyklos* (wheel or cycle), the meaningless rise and fall of power shells over time.[22] If human existence at all levels is no more than the result of the random turning of the wheel of time or fate, then, under the view of reason in the classical sense, moral decision making (whether individual or political) is not relevant, meaningful, or possible.

The second element worthy of emulation is the participation and transparency of the process of decision making used in *The Suppliants*. It is especially important that when a decision is made that may have consequences that are harmful to all or even some citizens, the citizens should in some way or another embrace that decision as their own. As Pelasgus says to the women, "May my citizens never, if some mischance befell us, say to me, 'You destroyed Argos for the sake of foreigners.'"[23] People should not be scared or bribed or fooled into following their leaders into war. Nor should the decision be made based on passion, particularly the passions of the moment. Those most affected should be told the truth. They should understand the moral hazards associated with their choices and accept the responsibility attached to the probability that there will be bad consequences to any decision that they make. These actions and considerations are what give depth and maturity to the character of a society which has become conscious of itself as a moral actor on the historical stage.

In an age of mass communications and constant and sophisticated public opinion polling, it would seem very possible that a democratic political
community (or some interested portion of it) could engage itself in a similar
process of thinking through important political decisions. For a process like
this to work, however, several prerequisites would have to be met. A critical
mass of citizens (or their representatives) would have to be educated in a way
that making such decisions was important to them. They would have to be
willing to listen to arguments from their leaders and consider the evidence
presented to them. They would have to trust that they shared with their leaders a similar idea of what was good for the community. Finally, both leaders
and citizens would have to have prudence, meaning that they understood the
relationship between means and ends.

If diversity in a large commercial republic[24] means that all are entitled to
their own opinion and that opinions can legitimately come from anywhere,
including (perhaps even encouraging) the basest of passions and the most
simplistic ideological thinking, it is unlikely that a process like the one
defined in the last paragraph could ever be used to describe politics in a
community like the United States. If liberalism continues to be elaborated
along these lines, then any new sort of "virtue" that may be needed to fight
the next battle will have to be manufactured by moving the passions of the
citizens in such a way as to create the appearance of that desired virtue. But
if real virtue, however defined, comes out of the fabric of a *whole* culture,
such attempts are, at best, parlor tricks. The Athenians at Marathon had a
genuine virtue that had been lost by the time the Athenians used their crude
notions of *realpolitik* as a prelude to their massacre of the neutral Melians.
Aeschylus and Socrates both tried, but failed to prevent the civilizational
decline of imperial Athens.

As unlikely as it is to be realized, the model of a political community
engaging in an honest debate about the common good remains a compelling
one because there is no good substitute. *The Suppliants* does not propose a
hard and fast content to the idea of the common good; in fact doing so bor-
ders on a form of *hubris* that poses great dangers in foreign affairs, as we have
witnessed in the policies of imperial democracies from Athens to the United
States. Instead, it suggests that good regimes do not try to oversimplify reality
in order to make their lives easier or to master the tides of time and fortune.
The recovery of an understanding of reason that allows us to remain open
to (and aware of) as wide a swath of existence as possible is a check against
such *hubris* as well as a realistic way to proceed in making decisions that will
have a lasting effect on the political community.

For contemporary students, *The Suppliants* shows a style of leadership and a process of decision making that takes seriously both the particular and the universal without turning either into a fixed object of knowledge possessed by one nation or one party or one church or one ideology. We have been warned for a number of years of the dangers of relativism and nihilism to our civilization. But we seem to have forgotten the equivalent (perhaps greater) dangers of fundamentalism and ideology as attempts to evacuate the mystery from existence and identify truth as a thing, attainable within history.[25] Aeschylus is a small example of how one can hold onto a balanced consciousness without tipping inevitably toward these undesirable, if tempting, alternatives.

The Lord of the Rings

J. R. R. Tolkien modestly calls the writing of fantasy an act of "sub-creation" but emphasizes that this sub-creation is grounded in true experience and may even give us a glimpse of reality itself. Tolkien notes that one of the characteristics of the fairy tale is what he calls "recovery," and this recovery has to do with a "re-gaining of a clear view."[26] One might argue that an epic fantasy about good and evil is unlikely to have many realistic moral dilemmas. To the contrary, the lack of a "clear view" of a complex reality is a constant concern of many of the characters in these books, because they are forced to act without complete knowledge and often face choices where none of the options are desirable. Like Aeschylus, Tolkien asks the reader to enter into the story and suffer with the characters, who don't know they are in a fantasy tale, as they confront a series of difficult choices that place them and others constantly close to death. Because of the beauty of Tolkien's writing and the intricacy of the history of Middle-earth that he creates for the reader, this is easy to do.

Characters in *The Lord of the Rings* make both good and bad decisions. The good decisions partake of the qualities discussed in the introduction—an ability to "see" a larger part of reality, a participatory (or democratic) nature that nevertheless honors wisdom and experience, and a transparency that doesn't see others as merely tools or instruments of war. The bad decisions made by characters in *The Lord of the Rings* often come from defensible, even admirable motives. But they reduce the scope of decision making in a way that betrays the absence of a mature (balanced, rational) moral consciousness. Thus in a story of the struggle between good and evil, we are also able to see the "in-between" in the shortsighted decisions of those with good intentions.

The Lord of the Rings is the story of the end of the Third Age of Middle-earth. An evil spirit, Sauron, seeks to dominate all of Middle-earth by the conventional stratagems of war and diplomacy and by finding and possessing a ring of power. This ring, thought to have been lost forever, is found by the hobbit Bilbo Baggins in an earlier Tolkien work called *The Hobbit.* At the beginning of the *Lord of the Rings* trilogy, the Ring is passed down as an heirloom to Bilbo's nephew and heir, Frodo Baggins. With the help of the wizard Gandalf, Frodo finds out that this ring is the "One Ring" made long ago to master other existing magical rings.[27] If Sauron can obtain this ring, his power will be unassailable and the peoples of the world will be reduced to his slaves.

What to do with this ring is arguably the most important decision of all those made in the three books that comprise *The Lord of the Rings.* In a council that represents the "free peoples" of Middle-earth, the delegates decide that the Ring must be destroyed by taking it to Mt. Doom where the Ring was originally forged and throwing it into the mountain's volcanic crater. The council meets in secret in order to hide its purpose from the enemy, but it is otherwise a very open decision making body. All major "nations" who have an interest in the fate of Middle-earth and who are not seen as allied with the enemy, have sent representatives to the Council of Elrond. They all are asked to tell their stories, and the stories are pieced together to form a narrative that forms the "working documents" of the Council.

The decision making body has a mix of democratic and aristocratic elements. As suggested in the introduction, good decision making is often evidenced by transparency and collaboration. This is the case here. But difficult decisions also require a mature and balanced moral consciousness, or wisdom. The Council of Elrond is participatory, but it works because the representatives are willing to acknowledge and listen to the superior wisdom of some of its members, like the wizard Gandalf and Elrond, the elf-lord who convened the Council. Both Gandalf and Elrond have an authority that comes from experience (they are very old and have participated in past struggles with the enemy Sauron) and both understand and care deeply about Middle-earth.

Frodo is chosen to be the "Ring-bearer" and he and his servant and friend Samwise Gamgee, another hobbit, make the long journey to Sauron's stronghold of Mordor to carry out the task. In the meantime, the other major characters that set out with Frodo and Sam from the Elven stronghold of Rivendell are involved with trying to check Sauron's power and schemes in a variety of settings in order to give Frodo the time needed to accomplish his seemingly hopeless quest. Frodo's task seems foolhardy to those who would prefer the power of the Ring to be wielded by someone who could challenge Sauron and defeat him.[28]

The primary characters in the book embark on a war that they have very little hope of winning, caught between the powerful forces which the Greeks called *ananke* (necessity) and *dike* (righteousness). Decisions made under such circumstances require a wisdom that does not flow backward from some plan of victory, but rather arises out of a series of meditations on loss and death tempered by suffering. Most of the major characters have this experience in a physical form. Gandalf "dies" in the caves of Moria but returns. Aragorn must lead his men through the "paths of the dead" before he can find himself and legitimately claim the throne of Gondor. Frodo and Sam must literally march through Hell (Mordor) to play their role in the story.

Most of the primary characters in *The Lord of the Rings* are struggling to discover their roles in the great events that surround them. They each have their own temptations that would draw them away from these roles. Sam is tempted by his love of hearth and garden, Aragorn by his destiny to be King or, alternatively, by his doubts that he is deserving of that destiny, Boromir by his pride and desire to win the battle at any cost. The elves have perhaps the greatest temptation to overcome—to turn away from the spectacle of an imperfect world and retreat to Elvenhome where things do not change or die.[29] At each stage in their respective journeys, the characters must engage in their own process of Aeschylean deep-pondering, a process made communal and political by their friendship and love for one another and by their shared desperate need.

As in *The Suppliants*, custom, laws, and institutions are important elements of order in *The Lord of the Rings*. Tolkien makes it clear, however, that they are not enough. In one key scene after another, characters decide against the laws or customs of their city based on a sense of what is right. These are characters whose own experiences have prepared them for such decisions and they are not taken lightly. Freedom in *The Lord of the Rings* is not the freedom of an autonomous self; it is the freedom to act in accordance with *dike*. As in the classical philosophical account of a moral dilemma, one does not go beyond custom and law in order to pursue one's interest or pleasure but rather as a result of a desire to figure out what constitutes right action in difficult circumstances. When Eomer, nephew of King Theoden of Rohan, finds Aragorn and his companions within his king's territory, he violates custom and the orders of his king in order to allow them to continue searching for their lost companions. When Faramir, brother of Boromir and son of the steward of Gondor, captures Frodo and Sam near the entrance to Mordor, he is supposed to bring them back to his father. He guesses that they have something of great value and power—the Ring that Boromir desired to take and use to defend his beloved city of Minas Tirith. Yet Faramir shows his wisdom by defying power, custom, law and interest to allow the Ring-bearer to continue his quest. He does this because he understands that his homeland, Gondor (the inheritor of Númenor and its traditions after the island becomes corrupt and is destroyed) at its best is linked to Númenor at its best and that this is the real source of its greatness, not its power or its wealth—not even its continued existence. Faramir explains:

> War must be, while we defend our lives against a destroyer who would devour all; but I do not love the bright sword for its sharpness, nor the arrow for its swiftness, nor the warrior for his glory. I love only that which they defend: the city of the Men of Númenor; and I would have her loved for her memory, her ancientry, her beauty, and her present wisdom. Not feared, save as men may fear the dignity of a man, old and wise. [30]

Númenor is the lynchpin of Tolkien's trilogy because it represents all the pulls experienced by human beings. To those fighting Sauron, Númenor symbolizes humanity its best. When at its pinnacle, the people of Númenor exhibited wisdom and the sort of reason this chapter calls "reason in its classical form." Aragorn is not the true king merely because of his bloodline; he is the true king because most of the time he embodies the qualities for which the people of Middle-earth continue to honor the long-lost island. Yet, all the story's characters who demonstrate any wisdom understand that the pull of the Good is not the only pull felt by the creatures of Middle-earth.

The tension between loyalty to the particular and loyalty to the universal is a common theme in the three books that comprise the *Lord of the Rings*. It is illustrated most clearly in the role of the wizard Gandalf. The origins of the wizards are obscure and they seem to have no permanent home in Middle-earth. They are seen often as "meddlers" in other peoples' affairs and are wanderers who move in and out of local politics according to some larger plan that is hard for others to understand or to trust. Yet as the story unfolds, it becomes clearer that Gandalf is the true leader of the enemies of Sauron because he can see the furthest and is a caretaker of the whole of Middle-earth. It is Gandalf's *eros philosophos* (love of wisdom) that is required to stand up to Sauron's *eros tyrannos* (love of power). This is especially true after Gandalf's death in Moria. Gandalf the Grey, a kindly wizard known for his wonderful fireworks, is "sent back" as Gandalf the White with a power befitting his large part in the events that are quickly moving to certain but still unknown endings. When Denethor, the steward of Gondor, reminds Gandalf that the good of the city is his highest concern, Gandalf responds quickly and pointedly in a way that exposes the limitations of Denethor's wisdom.

> But I will say this: the rule of no realm is mine, neither of Gondor, nor any other, great or small. But all worthy things that are in peril as the world now stands, those are my care. And for my part, I shall not wholly fail of my task, though Gondor should perish, if anything passes through this night that can still grow fair or bear fruit or flower in days to come. For I also am a steward. Did you not know?[31]

For Gandalf, his responsibility—and that of all those who oppose Sauron—is to all of Middle-earth, not just to one race or one place.

Gandalf's wisdom allows him to ask for tremendous sacrifices from those around him. But they are willing to make those sacrifices out of their love for him, a love that comes from recognition that he is a steward of a common good that gives meaning to a variety of private and local goods. Without that connection, these private and local goods can quickly dissolve into little more than temporary interests and assertions of a will to power. In a world where we were truly autonomous beings the mischief this would cause might be limited. But in a world where there is active evil that understands and uses private wills to its ends, the stakes are obviously higher.

In *The Suppliants*, we are shown the action of a King who is both mature and responsible. In Tolkien's much longer work, all of the characters must grow into their roles in the story, often as a result of the anguish of making difficult decisions and the suffering that these decisions bring about. No one better exemplifies this than Aragorn, the descendent of the Númenorean kings who must prove, mostly to himself, that he is fit to take the throne of Gondor. His virtue is sometimes shown in his capacity for leadership in a conventional sense, sometimes in his humility and self-doubt, other times in his openness to the wisdom of others. His last task before claiming the crown is to enter the city anonymously, not as a king or even as a soldier, but as a healer to tend to those wounded in battle. Aragorn is an intensely human character, always concerned that he can't see clearly enough, that he has made the wrong decision, or that he cannot save the ones that he loves. His humility encourages Aragorn to remain open to the advice of others, like Gandalf or Elrond, or Legolas, who keep Aragorn grounded in the best parts of his humanity rather than the worst. In the context of fantasy, Tolkien can bring all the parts of human nature into focus by placing them in other

sentient beings. The "moral hierarchy" of Middle-earth and its characters expand the Platonic understanding that the community is the "soul writ large."
Listening to these "parts" of himself allows Aragorn to avoid the very human
sins of pride or excessive attachment to the needs of the moment.

Though there are many moral dilemmas faced by characters in *The Lord
of the Rings*, Tolkien's story reinforces the same lessons that are found in *The
Suppliants*. Wisdom requires an orientation to right action and openness to
all parts of our being and to all of reality. This can only be suggested by the
sparse language and action of *The Suppliants*, but it is woven integrally into
Tolkien's mythic tale. The "free races" of Middle-earth that decide the fate
of the Ring represent all parts of the full human personality. The mostly
timocratic (honor-loving) cultures of Middle-earth worship power on the
low end and honor and tradition and courage on the top end. But the most
timocratic of all the men in the book, Boromir, would have chosen incor-
rectly regarding the Ring. He would have placed his love for his city above
the love of the Good itself and created splits in the alliance against Mordor
that would have been fatal. Honor and courage will always fail unless they
will listen to wisdom. Without this willingness on the part of the fellowship
of the Ring, their ability to make rational decisions would have been greatly
diminished. Reason leads to wisdom only if it retains the characteristics of
openness to the world-transcendent ground that can be more easily described
as a love of the Good. Rational decision making and moral decision making
in this sense are identical.

The second element of the decision making that we praised in *The Suppliants* is also present in *The Lord of the Rings*. Many decisions were made in
the open, and even when they were not, they were made collaboratively.
When politics is assumed to be about power and private interest, transparency does not really make any sense except as a tactic. But when human
relationships are grounded in friendship, when others are not seen as instruments for one's own pleasure or advantage, there is no need to disguise one's
motives. Thus when Aragorn decides that the remnants of the alliance that
won a temporary victory in the fields outside the walls of the city of Minas
Tirith must now march to the gates of Mordor to keep the enemy distracted
from the quest of the Ring-bearer, he asks for volunteers. This army has no
chance to defeat the power of Sauron in battle and merely getting close to
the cursed land of Mordor is enough to drive many men mad. So this is a
suicide mission meant to buy time. Aragorn doesn't hide this from the men
he commands and he shows compassion to those who cannot go forward all
the way to Mordor.[32]

Three examples of less than mature decision making help to further illuminate the argument of this chapter. Boromir's desire to use the Ring rather than destroy it has already been discussed. His love of his own country becomes Boromir's highest good. This is a natural virtue for a soldier, but it also suggests why soldiers may not make the best leaders unless they have acquired wisdom in some other way. Boromir's virtue is also his weakness and when he can't persuade the Council at Rivendell to keep and use the ring, he tries to take it by force from Frodo.[33] Boromir's father is Denethor, steward of Gondor. As steward his task is to protect the city until the kingship is claimed by a rightful heir. Denethor's ancestors have held the position for so long that he doubts that day will ever come, and in his pride believes he is a better leader than any pretender to the throne. Denethor has a "seeing stone" that allows him to see and communicate at great distances. He can even make contact with Mordor through his magical technology. While he believes he has the will to resist the power of Sauron, we find out that Sauron only allows Denethor to see what Sauron wants him to see. The result of having a seeing stone is a kind of blindness and it leads Denethor to despair. Like most political realists, Denethor ultimately measures his city's greatness by its power. When he sees that Sauron clearly has amassed an army that cannot be beaten on the battlefield, he slides into a suicidal hopelessness. Despite Gandalf's attempts, Denethor refuses to see a reality beyond that of armies and traditional military strategy. He falls out of the story and dies a dramatic, but ultimately pointless, death. Lastly, the wizard Saruman was once the head of the order of wizards. Like Denethor, he knows that Sauron's power is too great to be resisted. His narrow version of prudence suggests that he should temporarily join with Sauron in a complicated conspiracy designed to allow him to challenge Sauron at some later date. He convinces himself and others (his greatest power is that of persuasion) that he is acting in the best interests of all. When Gandalf discovers this strategy and tries to dissuade Saruman, Gandalf is imprisoned by him. Later, after he has escaped, Gandalf is forced to break Saruman's power and assume his leadership position. All three of these examples show how a too narrow understanding of reality leads to irrational and immoral choices. Power, pride, and love of the particular at the expense of the universal narrow the range of choices that we present ourselves in difficult times and often lead to mistakes at the level of tactics that make even those narrower goals less likely to be realized.

Thus far I have left out what is probably the most profound moral dilemma of Tolkien's trilogy. If the Ring of power is destroyed, the Elves suspect that much of what is permanent and beautiful in Middle-earth will pass away.

It will no longer be a middle ground between the "undying lands" and the mortal world of men, where things decay and die as a matter of course. It will become the world as we readers of the story know it, where the connections with permanent things are now based on faith—the evidence of that which can no longer be seen. Most of the main characters in the book end up leaving Middle-earth—this is the result of their decisions and their "victory" over Sauron. It is men who remain behind, temporarily ruled by a good King, but a good King who will someday die.

All moral dilemmas perhaps give us a taste of the essential sadness of the world of becoming where nothing is permanent. For Tolkien, this sadness is redeemed by the good news of the Gospels. Socrates makes a similar argument—a well ordered soul makes us friends with both human beings and the gods.[34] The love which flows out of that soul in search of the world-transcendent ground of being is what makes us human and is the authentic foundation of the reason that defines our humanity and of the friendship which binds us to our fellow men and women. The movement from instinct to calculation to reason is the movement from the child to the mature man. Yet these are individual consolations; their impact on the ebbs and tides of history are always contingent. Gandalf reminds Aragorn of this truth as they prepare their army for the last battle before the gates of Mordor.

> Yet it is not our part to master all the tides of the world, but to do what is in us for the succor of those years wherein we are set, uprooting the evil in the fields that we know, so that those who live after may have clean earth to till. What weather they shall have is not ours to rule.[35]

Gandalf's advice reflects the deepest wisdom of the story. Human beings have the responsibility to seek out and to fulfill their role as moral actors. But we play these roles without full knowledge of the end of the story or the identity of the playwright. This is why moral choice and leadership is an act of participation rather than the application of a law or a rule or a custom or a commandment. The best leaders not only understand this but are able to engage their citizens/subjects/friends/children as fellow actors in the drama of the human condition.

Conclusion

> The sphere of power and pragmatic rationalism is not autonomous but part of human existence which as a whole includes the rationality of spiritual and moral order. If the controlling order of spirit and morality breaks down, the

formation of ends in the pragmatic order will be controlled by the irrationality of passions; the co-ordination of means and ends may continue to be rational but action nevertheless will become irrational because the ends no longer make sense in terms of spiritual and moral order.[36]

The theme of this essay is that it is precisely when choices are made more difficult by the uncertainty or undesirability of outcomes that the framework of the decision making process becomes crucial. This is certainly the situation in which King Pelasgus finds himself in *The Suppliants*. All choices, including not deciding at all, have potentially disastrous results. The situation requires a deep and broad consideration of all the factors that inform a rational decision. Remember that reason requires an attempt to link the good of the individual with the good of the community and finally with the *summum bonum*, or the Good itself. In *The Suppliants*, this means considering the national interest (conventionally understood), the laws and customs of both your society and those with which you are engaged, and the requirements of justice. Justice here is not a "thing" to be discovered or found in a book or an ideology—it is an orientation toward a permanent moral ground—what has been called in this chapter the world-transcendent ground. Religion or piety can help us here and certainly "the judgment of heaven" is of great concern to King Pelasgus. Yet, as discussed in the introduction, dogma and ideology do not substitute for the soul-searching of the autonomous moral individual. The attempt to simplify life and politics by substituting rules for a life lived in the constantly moving tensions of the *metaxy* always degenerates into a closure of the individual or the society to the essential mystery of reality. The humility and uncertainty that participation in this mystery engenders in the moral consciousness of a mature soul is a necessary counterweight to the powerful human desire to escape the anxieties of existence by various attempts at oversimplification.

Argos is a city-state ruled by a king in a play written well over two thousand years ago. It might seem more than strange to present it to a contemporary audience as a model of good government. Yet the author of the play lived in a commercial democracy (Athens) and fought at Marathon where an outnumbered Athenian army marched out of the relative safety of their city's walls to meet the invading forces of the most formidable empire of the day—the Persians. Could the spiritual substance of Athens at that defining moment of its history be sustained by the public cult of tragedy? Aeschylus' tragedies asked citizen/spectators to engage in what Voegelin calls "representative suffering" as they are presented with a mature character who must decide on a course of action by diving deeply into his own soul to do the right thing.[37]

We have already emphasized the need for the boundaries of a difficult decision being delineated by a reason which is open to the full meaning of life in the *metaxy*. This is one element of the classical/Christian perspective on leadership found in these two works of literature. The other important part of the decision making process in *The Suppliants* that makes it a worthy model is the articulation by Pelasgus of the importance of involving his citizen/subjects in the decision of whether or not to grant asylum to the sup-pliant women. This certainly can be defended as a politically prudent course of action. An honest involvement of people in making difficult decisions that may significantly affect their lives helps to rally support and to diffuse responsibility if things go badly. What really makes this characteristic an important part of moral leadership goes much further than political pru-dence, however. In both the classic and the Christian understanding of the relationship between human beings and the divine ground, the primary "unit of analysis" is the human soul. The right order of the soul in a Platonic sense (or what is called a balanced consciousness in this essay) is the hard work of a lifetime. There are ordered or mature souls and there are disordered or immature souls. The former are ruled by reason in the classical sense of the word used throughout this chapter, the latter by passions. The good politi-cal community is concerned with the souls of its citizens and their mature development. The involvement of citizens in the deep-diving that Pelasgus refers to is an important part of the education of the soul.

In the *Lord of the Rings* the problem of depth and openness to the fullness of what is real and important is also a part of the problem involved in facing the dilemmas presented to the characters in the book. In Tolkien's work, however, we are shown more clearly how other characters attempt to avoid moral dilemmas before they become a problem in the moral consciousness of the decision maker. One sees a strong and natural tendency to avoid the problems posed by these difficult decisions by simplifying or reducing the factors that are considered important to making the decision. Boromir's patriotism and strategic prudence work well in most instances; in the most difficult ones, however, they are not enough. They lead both Boromir and his father, Denethor, to overestimate their capacity to resist the evil of Sauron and to place their hopes in the very instruments that Sauron has mastery over, like the Ring of power. Their love for their city blinds them and causes them to identify its power and survival with the good itself. Thus they resist the wisdom of Gandalf and Aragorn; first with regard to what to do with the Ring of power and then at the level of strategy in the war against Mordor.

The wizard Saruman's *realpolitik* is also inadequate, as it encourages him to cooperate with something that genuine reason would show can only be resisted and it masks his own will to power—a weakness which corrodes his reason and ultimately his ability to make even tactically prudential decisions. Gandalf's fall in Moria and his "resurrection" as a more confident leader of the forces arrayed against Sauron allows him to confront both Saruman and Denethor and assume the authority of command. It would be easy to say that he earned this position by way of his superior wisdom, but this would be true only if one saw his wisdom in the light of his suffering, his love for Middle-earth, and his clear-sightedness regarding both his allies and his enemies. Gandalf's wisdom would appear to be folly if there were not other major characters that saw reality in similar terms or were willing to follow him on faith, out of friendship or love.

Beyond Gandalf's wisdom, it is the unity of elves and men which is necessary for the project to succeed and to rebuild the kingdom of Gondor after the War of the Ring. In the story this is signified by the marriage of Aragorn and Arwen, daughter of Elrond who ruled the Elven stronghold of Rivendell. For Tolkien, both the spiritual and material aspects of our being are essential to our ability to make rational decisions. The physical territory of Middle-earth mirrors the landscape of the mature human soul, where all of the traits of human beings are personified in groups which become ordered or disordered depending on whether certain hierarchies and authorities are established and respected. The elves, with one foot in the immortal lands, overcome the tendencies of human beings to act only according to the short-term calculus of power and advantage. Yet men have their own virtue. They continue to love the world while acknowledging its lack of permanence and the contingent nature of justice, beauty, and order. They need each other's strength and counsel to choose wisely. Only this clear-seeing (or far-seeing) allows the fellowship to make the destruction of the Ring their overarching strategy.

The leaders of Tolkien's myth are truly heroic, though they each show weaknesses that temper their larger-than-life virtues. It is a fairy tale after all, but a complex one that has its origins in Tolkien's own beliefs as a Christian and his experiences fighting in World War I. King Pelasgus is not a fairy tale king, but he shows the same self-doubts in his ability to do what is right for his city as Aragorn does. His problem is smaller than the battle of good and evil, but the results of a bad decision can still lead to the destruction of his people. His ability to be seen as a model of a moral leader lies in his willingness to consider the good of his city as part of the problem of the Good itself. He does this even though it is dangerously inconvenient to do so. The willingness of his citizens to listen to argument and commit themselves to such a dangerous course of action contains the essence of the teaching of the play.

The audience must engage in a similar process of deep-pondering as they individually think and talk about what they might do in a similar situation.

Perhaps nowadays it takes stories to show us that the reduction of international relations to national interest and balance of power debases reason in the highest sense of that element of the human psyche that allows us to live as moral agents in a world of good and evil. Stories like *The Lord of the Rings* do reinforce somewhat conventional notions of right and wrong, heroism and villainy. This allows them to be dismissed as unrealistic. But they go further and show us that often the hardest and most important decisions require unconventional thinking, both tactically and morally. Old enemies must find common ground, and fidelity to old laws and customs do not always provide the answers we seek. This does not liberate us from law, custom, history, or piety. It does, however, force us to rethink their underlying foundations of meaning and sometimes to reformulate what the meaning demands in new and unforeseen situations. Both sides to this old argument are correct. Moral dilemmas force us to explore the nooks and crannies of our own moral consciousness and therefore provide opportunities for developing those habits of mind and heart that define the mature and responsible leader and citizen.

Notes

1. Richard Crawley, trans., *The Peloponnesian War* (New York: The Modern Library, 1951), 189.

2. Eric Voegelin, *The Collected Works of Eric Voegelin, Vol. 12: Published Essays 1966-1985* (Baton Rouge: LSU Press, 1990), 265-91.

3. Ibid., 279. "Man experiences himself as tending beyond his human imperfection toward the perfection of the divine ground that moves him. The spiritual man, the *diamonios aner*, as he is moved in his quest of the ground, moves somewhere between knowledge and ignorance (*metaxy sophias kai amathias*)." The *metaxy* is precisely that "in-between" referred to by Voegelin. A healthy moral consciousness lives in the tension created by our status as "in-between" creatures. To try and escape that tension by seeing ourselves as Gods or by living only in response to our natural human passions is to lose the balance of consciousness. Because that balance is part of my definition of rational decision making, moral wisdom (maturity) requires decisions that are made in light of this tension of existence that is here called life lived in the *metaxy*.

4. This is a somewhat awkward term for a difficult idea. I use it because it has a commonsense, if indeterminate, connotation. Here is a longer description of what the fullness of reality means within a classical and a Christian paradigm: "Only when the order of being as a whole, unto its origin in transcendent being, comes into view,

can the analysis be undertaken with any hope of success; for only then can current opinions about right order be examined as to their agreement with the order of being." Eric Voegelin, *Science, Politics and Gnosticism* (Washington, DC: Regnery Gateway, 1968), 18.

5. An example of this would be the speech of Diodotus in Thucydides' *Peloponnesian War*. After telling his fellow citizens that Athens has declined to a state where honest men must often lie to their fellow citizens to be believed, he tells them that he comes not to speak about justice but what is in Athens' interest. Using this argument, he barely convinces the Athenians to abandon a decision that would have been both unjust and against their larger interests.

6. *Mythopoesis* is used here to describe a form of storytelling in which a fictional world is structured and presented in such a way as to teach us truths about our own world that might otherwise remain hidden to us.

7. Thomas Pangle, trans., *The Laws of Plato* (Chicago, IL: The University of Chicago Press, 1980), 698b-699d.

8. Thucydides, *The Peloponnesian War* (New York, NY: Modern Library, 1951), 44.

9. Eric Voegelin, *Order and History Volume Two: The World of the Polis* (Baton Rouge: LSU Press, 1957), 247.

10. Voegelin, *World*, 220-40.

11. Aeschylus, *Prometheus Bound The Suppliants Seven Against Thebes The Persians* (London: Penguin Books, 1961), 64.

12. Aeschylus, *Suppliants*, 58.

13. Ibid., 62.

14. Ibid., 69.

15. Ibid., 82.

16. Ibid., 66.

17. See translator's introduction in Aeschylus, *Suppliants*, 10-13.

18. Or we assume they do, since the King is clearly worried about this and the citizens apparently know that they may be called to defend their choice with violence.

19. Aeschylus, *The Suppliants*, 73.

20. Ibid., 64.

21. The "national interest" is a vague, if popular, term used in contemporary politics and international relations theory. It usually is used to narrow a debate to immediate questions of security, power, and wealth.

22. The quote is a definition of politics from the well-known twentieth-century realist, Hans Morgenthau. "Power shells" refers to what is left in the study of history when a permanent ground of meaning is rejected. Meaning becomes simply the ideas associated with a dominant nation or civilization while it is supreme on the world stage. The question is whether there is another narrative of meaning across history that runs alongside the rise and fall of the great powers. It is this narrative that begins with the "discovery" of a permanent ground of meaning which is world-transcendent. The moral leader is thus responsible not just to the customs of her time and place, but

to the story of mankind itself as we seek to understand our role in this cosmic drama of meaning. The *kyklos* refers to the "wheel" of human affairs that "as it turns, it never suffers the same men to be happy forever." See Herodotus, *The History* (Chicago: The University of Chicago Press, 1987), 127.

23. Aeschylus, *The Suppliants*, 66.

24. I use the term large commercial republic to describe the United States because some would argue that such a place can only be held together by the satisfaction of the passions of the people. Thus a large republic must be a wealthy one (or maybe an imperial one) in order to survive. See, for example, Martin Diamond's article "The Federalist" in Leo Strauss and Joseph Cropsey, *The History of Political Philosophy* (Chicago: Rand McNally & Company, 1972), 631-51.

25. For a groundbreaking treatment of the religious foundations of modern ideologies, see Voegelin, *Science, Politics and Gnosticism.*

26. J. R. R. Tolkien, *The Tolkien Reader* (New York: Ballantine Books, 1966), 77.

27. Many have noticed the similarity to the story of the Ring of Gyges that can be found in Plato's *Republic*. Both rings make the wearer invisible and thus give them power which eventually corrupts them. Both stories ask the reader to consider how they would use such power.

28. The wisdom to resist the desire to use the Ring in the war against Sauron is, of course, an obvious theme of Tolkien's work. He notes in his introduction that if the work was really an allegory of the Second World War, as some had thought, the Ring would have certainly been used. The allies chose to use every weapon in their arsenal out of the "necessity" to defeat Hitler. Tolkien saw that there were indeed consequences to that decision. The singular dependence on power to maintain order and security is a corrupting force made powerful by the will to power that is a dominant flaw of human nature. The theory of political realism simply tries to make a silk purse out of a sow's ear. Power without wisdom leads inevitably to poor judgment and immoral action.

29. Elvenhome is an island in the sea west of Middle-earth and near Númenor, an island once ruled by good kings who were corrupted by their desire for the immortality of the Elves and destroyed by the gods. The story of Númenor shares many characteristics with that of Atlantis as told by Plato in *Critias*. A good remnant of the men of Númenor had fled the corruption and settled in Middle-earth, founding the kingdom of Gondor and its primary city—Minas Tirith.

30. J. R. R. Tolkien, *The Lord of the Rings* (London: HarperCollins UK, 1994), 656.

31. Ibid., 741-42.

32. Ibid., 862-68.

33. Ibid., 388-90.

34. Plato, *Gorgias* (Indianapolis: Hackett Publishing Company, 1987), 88.

35. Tolkien, *Lord of the Rings*, 861.

36. Voegelin, *World*, 363.

37. For a discussion of what Voegelin means by representative suffering, see *World*, 251-52.

CHAPTER FIVE

~

Defining Dilemmas Down

The Case of 24

John M. Parrish

Most studies in the now-growing field of "philosophy and popular culture" follow a familiar pattern: they employ a popular text (novel, play, film, or television program) as a means of illustrating an important philosophical truth.[1] This chapter differs from that pattern in at least one important respect: it employs a prominent and influential popular text (FOX's television drama *24*) to describe and then critique an important philosophical falsehood. My premise is that this kind of critical engagement with popular culture can be just as valuable as the more interpretive approach, and that in many cases it may indeed be more significant, since the impact of letting philosophical mistakes go unchallenged in our culture may well prove to be more consequential than any effect we could hope for positive philosophical truths to produce.

One of the most important concepts in the field of political ethics is the idea of a moral dilemma—understood as a situation in which an agent's public responsibilities and moral imperatives conflict in such a way that no matter what the agent does she will in some way be committing a moral wrong.[2] In the aftermath of September 11, 2001, there has been a profound reconceptualization of the commonsense notion of a moral dilemma in American political discourse, and one of the most important cultural forums for that conceptual revision has been the quintessential post-9/11 melodrama, FOX Television's *24*. Many regard Jack Bauer (Kiefer Sutherland), the hero of *24*, as a kind of avatar of the post-9/11 age. In the May 15, 2007, Republican debate in South Carolina, for example, presidential candidate Tom Tancredo had this to say about the question of torture:

> You say that nuclear devices have gone off in the United States, more are planned, and we're wondering about whether waterboarding would be a bad thing to do? I'm looking for Jack Bauer at that time! ... We are the last best hope of Western Civilization. When we go under, Western Civilization goes under.[3]

More generally, conservative voices have praised the show for its "political and moral toughness." According to this view, *24* illustrates such "enduring truths" as these: "that war affords few opportunities for moral purity; that we must still have the courage to make distinctions between unpleasant options, and act on our choices; that one does not have to be innocent to be right."[4] The same article goes on to describe Jack Bauer as "basically a superhero" and to argue that the show teaches valuable moral lessons for the post-9/11 era:

> *24* as a whole is patriotic in its honesty about the nature of our adversaries and its refusal to indulge in the moral equivocation favored by the most critically lauded television dramas. You never hear CTU [Counter Terrorist Unit] characters wondering while perched over their computers, "Why do they hate us?" or fretting that "we're just as bad as they are."[5]

In the public mind, Jack Bauer is, if not the exemplary man of his era, at least a leading and widely touted candidate for that role.

This attitude says something rather troubling about our society's ethical outlook, and we can see this perhaps most clearly through considering how *24* as a narrative proposes to revise the traditional philosophical notion of a moral dilemma for the post-9/11 age. Such an examination is what I undertake in this essay. Several recently published academic essays on *24* have suggested that the show is an especially promising forum for studying the concept of a moral dilemma.[6] I want to argue that on the contrary, given the show's implicit account of what a moral dilemma is, *24* is an exceptionally *bad* forum for considering what moral dilemmas are or how we should approach them. Focusing specifically on *24*'s Season Five (the year the show won the Emmy for Best Dramatic Series), this chapter will show how *24* relies implicitly on a false philosophical account of what constitutes a moral dilemma. Instead, *24*'s creators have substituted in the public mind almost a parody of the traditional philosophical account of a moral dilemma. Their methods for this conceptual revision have included both an extravagant, even baroque portrayal of the grand dilemmas which confront Jack Bauer and his fellow patriots, on the one hand, and on the other, a subtle de-valuing of the moral stakes in the more pedestrian variety of ethical conflicts Bauer and company must overcome in their quest to keep America safe, whatever the cost. Furthermore, since Bauer and CTU are the agents and defenders of the United States, *24* also seems to imply that the ethical permissions these agents possess are merely a particular instance of a more general range of moral rights and privileges which America itself possesses in the post-9/11 age. If so, then *24*'s account of moral dilemmas may have profound consequences: for if *24*'s effect is to systematically deny that there are serious moral dilemmas inherent in many or most of the choices its characters make, it may be misleading not just Bauer and CTU, but America as well, about the ethically problematic dimensions of similar choices in the real world.

The Ethics of *24*

When *24* premiered in the fall of 2001, a few weeks after 9/11, its chief novelty was its unconventional narrative structure. Nothing like its gimmick of twenty-four episodes, each containing one hour's worth of action in "real-time," had ever been attempted before on television, and this aspect of it engaged the most critical comment at the time. But from the long view, *24*'s most novel contribution was not an innovation of style but rather of character. In Jack Bauer we find perhaps the first character on television (and one of a very few in literature more generally) who is both ready to perform torture and other atrocities at a moment's notice if necessary, *and* still meets the conventional standards of "hero" rather than "antihero."[7] Jack Bauer is not Tony Soprano: he is meant to receive not merely our empathy but also our admiration.

In some ways Bauer's approach to the moral dimensions of his actions implies that we are meant to regard him as the ultimate utilitarian.[8] Repeatedly Bauer shows an unhesitating willingness to sacrifice the few—especially himself—to save the lives of the many, with no residual moral qualms.[9] Perhaps Bauer would not be such a thoroughgoing utilitarian in private life, but the scale of consequences for which he is responsible in the recurring crises of his world contrives to push utilitarian considerations relentlessly to the fore. The life or death of a president, the threat of nuclear holocaust in Los Angeles, viral outbreaks, impending wars, coups d'etat in the American government—these are the consequences he must reckon with on an hourly basis. It is an appeal to the good of the many, therefore, that grounds Bauer's willingness to break all the familiar moral rules—murder, torture, threatening and even killing innocent bystanders. "That's the problem with people like you, George," Bauer says to a squeamish superior. "You want results, but you never want to get your hands dirty. I'd start rolling up your sleeves," he continues, before reaching for a hacksaw to cut up the body of the man he has just killed in cold blood (2, 8am). [I employ the following method for referencing the episodes: (2, 8am) meaning the episode portraying the events that occur between 8am and 9am on Day 2, or more conventionally, in Season 2.] If Bauer were an unwavering utilitarian, we might expect that his utilitarianism would lead him to discount entirely the possibility of the existence of a true moral dilemma. After all, if utility is the only value that truly matters, then by definition it cannot conflict irresolvably with rival values. But this is not the whole of the story.

Bauer is decidedly, even chillingly open to transgressing the traditional norms of morality when necessary, relying on ostensibly utilitarian jus-tifications when he does so. But in addition to his apparent utilitarian commitments, Bauer nevertheless also lives by a code of strict (if rather unusual) ethical principles that do not seem to map onto utilitarianism so neatly.[10] Indeed, early in the series Bauer is viewed by his fellow CTU agents as almost priggishly high-minded, largely because of his willingness in the recent past to inform on colleagues engaged in corrupt practices. Bauer's explanation of his actions to his colleague Nina Myers in the se-ries' very first episode reveals the rigid moral code underlying what would otherwise seem to be his extravagant claims to ethical permissions and excuses.

> BAUER: You can look the other way once, and it's no big deal, except it makes it easier for you to compromise the next time, and pretty soon, that's all you're doing is compromising because that's how you think things are done. You know those guys I blew the whistle on: you think they were the bad guys? 'Cause they weren't, they weren't bad guys, they were just like you and me. Except they compromised—once (1,12am).

In Bauer's world, ethical compromise inevitably leads to the loss of one's moral compass altogether. Sometimes it is clear that this moral absolutism of Jack's is enlisted in the service of utilitarian imperatives: utilitarianism is the right way to make moral decisions, but those decisions once arrived at acquire the unbending force of a categorical imperative, leaving no room for uncertainty or nuance.[11] Still, on other (though admittedly rarer) occasions, Bauer seems to invoke the same rigid absolutist ethics *against* utilitarian con-siderations, as when (in Season 5) he refuses to allow a nerve gas canister to go off in a shopping mall full of innocent civilians even though his refusal may cost CTU their best chance of locating the terrorists and the remaining nineteen canisters of nerve gas.[12]

Bauer, which translates from German as "peasant" or "farmer," is also the German word for "pawn." At many moments Bauer does in fact seem to be a mere pawn, moved about by menacing, unseen hands; but if so he is always a crucial pawn, fortuitously placed to check or block the most important square on the board. As its time-related gimmickry might suggest, 24 is pervaded by an almost palpable sense of urgency and desperation. Alfred Hitchcock famously argued that narrative suspense hinged on the pursuit of an ultimately arbitrary object—he called it the "MacGuffin"—which served as a focus for the characters' energies.[13] In 24, the consistent "MacGuffin" that organizes the story is at any given moment what Bauer and his co-workers invariably describe as "our only lead." Anything that a CTU agent can characterize as constituting "our only lead" to the threatening conspiracy justifies our investing that "lead" with all the moral weight of the worst possible outcome.[14]

What exemplifies this sense of urgency in 24 perhaps better than anything else is the case of the so-called ticking time bomb scenario about which much has been written in the popular press since the events of 9/11.[15] The familiar scenario is this: if you knew a captured terrorist possessed vital intelligence about the imminent explosion of a nuclear device in an urban area, and also believed that torturing the terrorist was likely (though perhaps not certain) to yield the vital information (and that no other technique was likely to do so), is it morally permissible to authorize the torture? This is a grave philosophical question, and no ethicist I know denies the difficulty of resolving it in a way that accords with all our important normative intuitions. Michael Walzer was the first prominent philosopher to discuss the ticking time bomb scenario in his seminal article on the concept of a moral dilemma.[16] In that article, Walzer held that the ticking time bomb case was a quintessential instance of a moral dilemma. But he also insisted that it was an unusual and extreme case, and therefore not to be trusted as a general guide to questions such as the moral permissibility of torture.[17] (Indeed, Jane Mayer has recently reported that throughout the thousands of interrogations since 9/11, the ticking time bomb scenario has "never actually occurred," according to "one of the few U.S. officials with full access to the details").[18]

The key to the ethical sleight of hand which 24 performs lies in recognizing its attempt to use the peculiarities of its real-time narrative structure to turn the ticking time bomb scenario into a constant state of being. Not only is the time bomb ticking, we even hear the ticking itself, audibly, in appropriately electronic digital tones, before and after each commercial break. The effect of this is to turn the extreme moral conditions of the ticking time

bomb scenario into an everyday operating environment—such that our conclusions about that scenario, once reached, can be taken as a given in any
future moral calculations without qualm, and without the necessity of having
to rethink the quandary itself from the ground up. This has the predictable
but nevertheless significant effect, as we will see further below, of making it
much easier to redefine the concept of a moral dilemma itself in a more accessible and user-friendly—and ethically permissive—style.

Varieties of Moral Dilemmas

In contemporary philosophical ethics, the concept of a moral dilemma
implies the existence of a choice in which some degree of wrongdoing is
unavoidable.[19] Like most philosophical concepts, the terminology is often
applied more loosely than this in popular discourse. Any morally troubling
or difficult choice may be described as a "dilemma": but this looser popular
sense of the term does not capture the interesting philosophical problem
which the stricter definition captures. Moral choice is often difficult: what
sets the concept of a dilemma apart is its requirement of a conflict of practical
ethical imperatives resulting from an underlying and irresolvable conflict of
moral values. It is this stricter sense of the term "dilemma" that is the focus
of the analysis that follows.

At the same time as I am employing a strict definition of a moral dilemma,
in seeking to trace the concept's exploration through a text like 24 there is
no way to employ a strict measurement as well as a strict definition. To some
degree dilemmas must always ultimately be dilemmas in the eye of the be-
holder: the dilemmatic character of a particular choice situation is always at
least partly agent-relative, since a dilemma is just an irresolvable conflict of
practical ethical imperatives for *this* agent in *this* choice situation. In studying
the treatment of moral dilemmas in a text like 24, then, one's identification
of specific choice situations confronting specific agents as dilemmas (or not)
will require judgments that are necessarily subjective (though not of course
arbitrary). Here I rely on Aristotle's injunction that the student of politics
can apply to any given question confronting him just as much precision as
the subject matter admits of, and no more.[20] We can study moral dilemmas in
a text like 24 only by recognizing that our identification of some choice situations as dilemmas, and others as non-dilemmas, will necessarily be subject
to contestation and disagreement.

Nevertheless, while our subject matter may not admit of objective measurement, we can still be analytically rigorous in defining the criteria we use.
So I want to begin by offering a distinction between a *moral dilemma* (strictly

speaking) and a broader category of problem which I want to identify as a *moral quandary*. I offer the following definitions of the two terms:

- *Moral dilemma* (strictly speaking)—a choice in which, no matter what an agent chooses, she will be in some important sense doing something wrong—that is, in which there remains a residual wrongness to the choice not fully made up for by its benefits.
- *Moral quandary*—a broader category than that of a moral dilemma, this is a choice which contains substantial moral difficulty, even if there is a right course of action available—a troubling moral choice, though not necessarily an insoluble one. Moral dilemmas are a subcategory of moral quandaries.

In the analysis that follows, I will be concerned with *24*'s portrayal of both moral quandaries and moral dilemmas, though my focus will be on how *24*'s approach to ethical problems tends to collapse the distinction and thus erode the status of a moral dilemma as a special and specially meaningful type of moral difficulty.

Let me illustrate what I mean with reference to a moral dilemma from the first season of *24* which the show itself clearly recognizes as such. In Season 1, Jack Bauer's daughter, Kim, is kidnapped by terrorists plotting to assassinate presidential candidate David Palmer. The terrorists credibly threaten to kill Kim unless Bauer uses his security credentials to gain entrance to a Palmer campaign event and assassinate Palmer himself (1, 5am-8am). Bauer faces an ethical choice in which no matter what he does, he will in some sense be committing a moral wrong.[21] In this situation, the intractable nature of the dilemma results from a conflict of moral duties, neither of which Bauer can rightly abandon: his duty to protect innocent life and serve his country, on the one hand, and his special obligation to do whatever he must to protect his daughter's life, on the other. This is not just a difficult ethical choice, requiring the moral agent to accept costs and make sacrifices, or to impose them on others. It is instead an insoluble dilemma, because there is no morally safe choice available to the agent: whatever Bauer does will, in some important sense, count as having done the wrong thing, and consequently he will, in some important sense, have become a morally guilty man.[22] As President David Palmer says of a moral dilemma he confronts later in the series, "Sometimes you have to do the wrong thing for the right reasons" (3, 4pm).

This, then, is how I conceive (and how most philosophers conceive) of a moral dilemma, strictly speaking. How then do we trace the treatment of this concept in a text like the television drama *24*? I think we will first want to have some standard for identifying what ordinary observers would standardly categorize as moral dilemmas and moral quandaries (as defined above), and then for comparing these standard dilemmas with the way they are characterized by the show *24*. I therefore first offer two definitions of dilemmas or quandaries as they would be perceived by ordinary observers, which I call *standard dilemmas* and *standard quandaries*:

- *Standard dilemma*—a choice which an impartial and virtuous spectator, sharing roughly the values, sensibilities, and responsibilities of the agent, would tend to regard as constituting a moral dilemma (strictly speaking).[23]
- *Standard quandary*—a choice which an impartial and virtuous spectator, sharing roughly the values, sensibilities, and responsibilities of the agent, would tend to regard as a moral quandary. (For example, I count every instance of lying and every instance of serious violence as a moral quandary, on the assumption that any impartial and virtuous agent would find any instance of lying or violence—excluding self-defense—to be at least morally troubling and a cause for hesitation.)

Since my use of these standards is inherently subjective, we should attach no great importance to the fact if we should discover that *24*'s treatment of moral dilemmas does not square exactly with my own identification of them. But if on the other hand we were to find that there are large and systematic variations between *24*'s treatment of dilemmas on the one hand and standard dilemmas on the other—that is, if *24* routinely characterized choice situations as dilemmas or non-dilemmas in ways that diverged dramatically from my own (or any impartial, attentive, and reflective reader's) identification of them—that would be a basis for supposing that some larger piece of conceptual or ethical revisionism was at work.

Finally, therefore, since I will be concerned in this chapter specifically with the portrayal of moral dilemmas by *24*—and since the situations *24* identifies implicitly as dilemmas may not be identical with standard dilemmas (indeed as we will see they are quite different)—I offer two additional categories of analysis, the *24 dilemma* and the *24 quandary*:

- *24 dilemma*—a choice which *24* as a text treats as if it were a moral dilemma—as indicated by the attention, tone, emphasis, and information given about the problem. (For example, a character's statements of regret would be one important indicator that a choice counts as a *24* dilemma.)

- *24 quandary*—a choice which *24* as a text treats as if it were a moral quandary—as indicated by the attention, tone, emphasis, and information given about the problem.

I employ these categories in my analysis of the show *24* in the subsequent sections of this paper.

What I find, in brief, is that *24* takes the tragic conflicts associated with true moral dilemmas and transposes them to a new register of melodrama that turns tragedy into farce. To characterize *24* as a farce in the technical sense, even loosely speaking, may seem perverse, since it is (overtly) among the most humorless shows in the history of television. (In six seasons, as best I can tell, no character has ever laughed, nor has any character ever made a joke.)[24] But *24* does in effect recast tragedy as farce, by taking the melodramatic core of tragedy—and on at least one prominent theory of tragedy, value conflict is itself the substance of that core—and making it into a kind of parody of itself.[25] The rare choice situations which *24* is willing to treat as authentic moral dilemmas are in effect parodies of the standard account of a moral dilemma—baroque, grandiose, insoluble dilemmas invoking conflicts and consequences on an incalculable scale. The effect of this, as we will see, is to remove the idea of authentic moral dilemmas further and further from reality, while in turn devaluing and delegitimizing standard dilemmas wherever they occur, and particularly whenever they can plausibly invoke "the good of the nation" as their justification.

To be fair, it is doubtful that *24* deliberately aims to promote any particular moral or political vision. Rather, the moral and political ideology it adopts is the necessary backdrop for the narrative and (for want of a better word) artistic work it is trying to do: namely, to carry the concept of melodrama through to its logical conclusion. Nevertheless, the moral and political backdrop which *24* requires for its narrative to work is a familiar and influential ideological picture of the world; and in making use of that picture as it does, *24* both refines and expands the potential significance of that picture as a backdrop for other, more consequential activities. As Plato warned us, the theater is our most powerful public teacher, and what is done there has far-reaching repercussions for who we are and for what characters and what actions we come to view as fine and just.[26] So it is fair for philosophers to render some judgments about the work of cultural revisionism that *24* is, deliberately or not, undertaking in effect. The fact that *24* does not portray moral dilemmas in a manner consistent with the standard account is not a necessary consequence of either the show's form or of its forum.[27] It is instead a deliberate narrative choice, one deriving from a distinct philosophical outlook. I turn in the remaining sections of the paper to the problem of describing and then evaluating 24's view of moral dilemmas in the post-9/11 world.

Standard Moral Dilemmas in 24

For this paper, I reviewed the first five seasons of 24 (and I can report that there is wide variation in the quality and enjoyment of the various seasons as drama). I also conducted a closer study of Season 5, which was the year that 24 won the Emmy Award for Best Drama, and is considered by most viewers to have been at least among the show's best seasons. I coded the events of the 24 hours of that day according to the criteria discussed in the last section, identifying as a standard quandary any morally troubling situation and as a standard dilemma any choice characterized by a moral conflict not fully resolvable (employing my own subjective but educated ethical judgment in categorizing the choices). I followed a few rules consistently in coding: for instance, I coded as a standard quandary any instance of deception or betrayal not directed against an enemy; any act of violence not directed against an enemy; and any lethal use of violence when not in self-defense.[28] Any instance of torture conducted by a protagonist I automatically coded as a standard dilemma, on the view that there is always something residually wrong about torture even if it may conceivably be the best thing to do on balance.[29] Beyond this, I simply employed my own best judgment. I then further coded as a "24 quandary" or as a "24 dilemma" any standard quandary or standard dilemma which I felt 24 itself, as a text, acknowledged to be such (through attention, tone, emphasis, and related narrative techniques).

My close study of Season 5 confirmed an impression I had gained while watching the other seasons more casually: namely, that there is a significant discrepancy between the number of situations that would qualify as a "standard quandary" or "standard dilemma" under the criteria developed earlier and the number of cases that 24 itself acknowledges to be true moral quandaries or dilemmas. I first want to detail this discrepancy and offer some examples of it, and then draw my conclusion: that the discrepancy uses a variety of narrative devices to mask its controversial (and mistaken) revision of the traditional philosophical notion of a moral dilemma.

The first thing to note about the presence of moral quandaries and moral dilemmas in the narrative of 24 is that they are vastly more plentiful on the show than one would expect to find in ordinary life. In traditional philosophical ethics, a moral quandary (that is, a standard quandary) ought to be the exception rather than the rule in ordinary life, while a moral dilemma (that is, a standard dilemma) should be a very rare occurrence indeed.

Table 5.1. Season Five Quandaries and Dilemmas

	Standard Model	24 Model
Quandaries	89	45
Dilemmas	39	10

Standard quandaries should confront most moral agents infrequently, and the large majority of moral agents might be expected to go their whole lives experiencing at most a handful of standard dilemmas. This discrepancy is of course partly a function of the various characters' roles and responsibilities in the story of 24: almost all of them work in the high-risk, high-consequence field of counter-terrorism or in the (notoriously) ethically problematic field of politics and governance. Even counting for this, however, the scale of the discrepancy is quite striking. In Season 5 of 24, for example, the characters experience (by my count) a total of 89 separate standard quandaries and 39 separate standard dilemmas in one 24-hour period. This comes to approximately 3.7 quandaries and 1.6 dilemmas per hour.

I provide an episode-by-episode accounting of my coding results in an Appendix (table 5.2).

To illustrate the point, let me offer now an example of how I coded the quandaries and dilemmas I observed in a representative hour of 24. The hour in question occurs from 1pm-2pm on Day 5 (that is, Season 5). In this hour, I identified three ethically significant choice situations, all faced by Jack Bauer:

- Jack Bauer Returns to CTU: President Charles Logan insists that Bauer—who has left CTU and is believed to be dead by everyone, including his daughter, Kim—must return to active duty to help stop an ongoing terrorist conspiracy that threatens thousands of lives across Los Angeles. Bauer knows that, given his training and experience, he can greatly increase the likelihood of foiling the terrorists and saving lives; but accepting Logan's charge also means that his daughter will likely have to go through the emotional trauma of learning he is still alive. *This choice situation I identified as both a standard quandary and a "24" quandary, since Bauer seems torn by the moral costs of the choice and deliberates about the trade-off. I do not identify the choice as either a standard dilemma or a moral dilemma, since there is no wrongdoing as such (though there are certainly costs and sacrifices involved) in the decision to let his daughter know he is alive.*

- Bauer Tortures a Conspirator: Bauer and CTU capture a terrorist conspirator who is now their "only lead" to a larger conspiracy to release nerve gas in multiple locations in Los Angeles. Bauer shoots the conspirator in the leg, refuses to allow him to receive pain medication, and begins applying direct methods of torture to elicit the needed information. *This choice situation I identify as a standard quandary and standard dilemma, and as a "24" quandary but not a "24" dilemma. On my criteria torture automatically qualifies for the status of a standard dilemma, since there is always something residually wrong about the use of torture even if its use may turn out to be the best available choice under tragically difficult circumstances. "24" does appreciate this choice as a quandary—there is hesitation by some CTU personnel over the decision to withhold pain medication—but not as a dilemma, as Bauer himself shows no hesitation to apply torture and expresses no hint of regret.*[30]

- Bauer Accepts a Troubling Deal: The conspirator, Rossler, makes a deal with CTU to turn over the microchip controlling the nerve gas canisters in exchange for full immunity and safe passage from the country. His deal also includes permission to take with him Inessa, a fifteen-year-old girl who has been kidnapped in order to be sold as a sex slave. Bauer tries to talk CTU out of making the deal, but in the end he accepts the deal and leads Inessa away to go with Rossler. *This situation I coded not only as a standard quandary and standard dilemma but also a "24" quandary and "24" dilemma. Like the previous choice, there is clearly something wrong about both failing to acquire the information needed to save thousands of lives and failing to protect a child from being sold into slavery. Whichever Bauer chooses, he will remain guilty of the other wrong. But in this instance, "24" recognizes the dilemmatic nature of the choice, as evinced by Bauer's arguing against making the trade before finally accepting its necessity.*

As Table 5.1 shows, there is a massive discrepancy between the number of (standard) moral dilemmas faced by the characters on 24 and the number that we would typically expect to be experienced by a small number of moral agents in reality in any 24-hour period, even in the high-stress, high-stakes world of counterterrorism. The scale of this discrepancy is concealed, however, by the fact that 24 itself, using a variety of narrative devices, recognizes only about half of the standard quandaries as 24 quandaries, and only about a quarter of the standard dilemmas as 24 dilemmas. Here are some examples of choice situations which I identified as standard quandaries but which 24 did not characterize as moral quandaries:

- Jack Attacks an FBI Agent (5, 8am)—Jack Bauer, wrongly suspected of murder and on the run from CTU, attacks an FBI agent (with non-lethal force) to obtain his credentials in order to search the crime scene. *This is a repeatedly used form of standard quandary through the series, as Bauer and others unhesitatingly use non-lethal violence against non-hostiles including law enforcement agents when it helps them pursue their objectives.*
- Chloe Helps Jack (5, 8am)—CTU analyst Chloe O'Brien assists Jack Bauer in pursuing leads and avoiding pursuit by CTU, in contradiction to the clear, lawful, and reasonable orders of her superiors. *This is another form of standard quandary that is repeatedly employed throughout the series, yet rarely if ever is perceived by the show or its characters to constitute an ethical issue.*
- Kim Cuts Herself Off from Jack (5, 7pm)—Kim Bauer has just learned that her father (Jack) is still alive and has been reunited with him. However, even though she loves her father, Kim Bauer declares that she will not see him anymore for the sake of her own emotional well-being. *Surely this is a kind of moral quandary, even if there is a best thing to do on balance without a residual moral wrong to complicate the choice.*
- Chloe Tasers a Suitor (5, 2am)—Though it may beggar belief to those not accustomed to following *24*'s rather odd moral compass, Chloe O'Brien actually employs a taser on a guy coming onto her in a bar because he is distracting her from providing online mission support to Jack (who is, incidentally, engaged in hijacking an airplane at the time). *No inkling of an ethical problem is raised about this choice, though there are non-overt indications that it is meant to get laughs.*

More significant are the cases in which *24* does not characterize as a moral dilemma a choice situation which meets the criteria of a standard dilemma. Here are some examples of choice situations I identified as standard dilemmas, but which *24* did not characterize as moral dilemmas:

- Bauer Tortures Rossler (5, 1pm)—Discussed above
- Bauer Shoots Miriam Henderson (5, 5pm)—Jack Bauer enters the home of Christopher Henderson, a former CTU operative who is now one of the terrorist collaborators, and his wife, Miriam. Bauer threatens to shoot or torture Henderson, but Henderson replies that with his training and experience he can withstand any pain and thus withhold the information Bauer needs. Bauer agrees, and instead shoots Miriam Henderson in the leg, threatening to follow up with a permanently

disabling shot to the kneecap, in an effort to convince Henderson to cooperate. *This may be the only way to acquire Henderson's cooperation, but surely, on any moral theory that would allow the possibility of a moral dilemma in the first place, harming an innocent bystander in this purely instrumental way counts as a wrong that is not made up for morally by whatever good ensues from a successful result.*

- Bauer Summons the LAPD (5, 11pm)—Bauer and associates break into a bank's safety deposit vault to acquire a recording which ties the terrorist conspiracy to the highest levels of the U.S. government. Before they can leave, some of the conspirators arrive at the bank. If found in the bank, Bauer may be killed or be deprived of the recording. So Bauer trips a silent alarm summoning the LAPD, anticipating that they will start a firefight with the conspirators that will endanger many officers but may provide Bauer and company with an opportunity to escape. *In essence, Bauer is leading unsuspecting police officers to their death in a fight they are unlikely to win, in an attempt to provide cover for him to pursue his admittedly vital mission. Since Bauer is at this moment a renegade CTU agent, the officers would presumably not consent to take part in the firefight if its true purpose was known to them. There is perhaps a kind of necessity to Bauer's action, but a seeming wrongfulness as well.*

The prevalence of standard quandaries and standard dilemmas in *24*'s narrative, on the one hand, and the discrepancy between *24*'s moral characterization of the situations and that dictated by the standard philosophical account, on the other, are in fact closely related: indeed they are essentially cause and effect. For it is the very proliferation of moral quandaries and dilemmas, I want to suggest, that helps to undermine the applicability of the standard philosophical account of a moral dilemma to the world of *24*. In a world in which moral quandaries and dilemmas present themselves to us in such abundant supply, how can we not come to see these as commonplace and, eventually, as less problematic, reserving our recognition of true quandaries and dilemmas for those cases that truly are beyond the pale? And perhaps in the world that Bauer and his associates "really" inhabit, this approach may make some sense as a psychological coping mechanism (though on the standard philosophical account it cannot be ethically permissible to simply move the goalposts in this way, as though the morally troubling aspects of these situations did not remain intact). But the danger is that *24* does not seem quite content to leave the matter there. The show's clear implication is that Bauer and company are emblematic of the endemic problems confronting America in the post-9/11 age, and that consequently what goes for *24* goes, equally well, for the agents of America wherever they struggle against its terrorist enemies.

24 Dilemmas

How has *24* been able to consistently succeed in defining dilemmas down in this way? The answer lies in two narrative strategies the show employs. One, which we have just considered, is the proliferation of morally problematic situations, which helps to desensitize the viewer to the moral stakes of any particular choice through the sheer numbness induced by constant exposure to exacting ethical challenges. The other key method *24* uses to define dilemmas down is its strategy of substituting for the standard dilemma what I call a "24 dilemma": that is, the kind of choice that *24* itself, as a text, is willing to acknowledge as being genuinely dilemmatic.

What we are interested in here are moral quandaries that *24* itself characterizes as genuine dilemmas. Sometimes the moral conflict at stake is between the vast public consequences of a proposed action, on the one hand, and its relation to one's private responsibilities on the other. Some examples of this kind of conflict include:

- Bauer Botches the Palmer Assassination—Discussed above (1, 5am-8am).
- Tony Almeida Chooses to Save Michelle Dessler (3, 8am-10am)—CTU Director Tony Almeida's wife, Michelle Dessler, is kidnapped by a terrorist mastermind seeking to release a deadly virus within the United States. He cooperates with releasing the terrorist's daughter from custody—CTU's only point of leverage for preventing him from releasing the virus—to ensure Michelle's safe return.
- One Doctor, Two Patients (4, 2am)—Lee Jong, a Chinese official with information crucial to stopping the launch of a nuclear missile, sustains a vital injury in a firefight at the Chinese consulate. Bauer rushes him to surgery in CTU's medical unit, but finds the only available doctor has already begun a critical surgical operation on Paul Raines, who is not only the estranged husband of Jack's lover Audrey but also sustained his injury while saving Jack's life. Bauer points a gun at the doctor and orders him to save Lee Jong's life rather than Raines's—knowing it will not only cost an innocent man his life but also may well cost Bauer himself a chance at happiness with Audrey, who still cares for Raines.
- The Mother with the Kidnapped Daughter (5, 10pm)—The First Lady's aide, Evelyn, has vital information about the complicity of

President Logan in the nerve gas conspiracy. When her daughter is kidnapped, however, her duty to reveal what she knows runs up against a strong countervailing moral pressure (though she ultimately chooses to risk her daughter's life to fulfill her public duty).

- Audrey's Life versus Evidence of Logan's Guilt (5, 12am-1am)—Terrorist collaborator Christopher Henderson holds Jack's girlfriend Audrey hostage in order to bargain for evidence of the conspiracy that Jack has acquired. Henderson cuts Audrey's left brachial artery, and forces Jack to turn over the evidence in exchange for allowing Jack time to call for medical assistance.

Another category of 24 dilemmas includes cases in which the moral conflict is between performing a presumptive moral duty (including, but not limited to, saving thousands of innocent lives) and refraining from some form of presumptively wrong conduct. Some examples include:

- Teri Substitutes Herself for Her Daughter (1, 8am)—Teri Bauer and Kim Bauer, Jack's wife and daughter, have been kidnapped by terrorists to compel Jack's cooperation in the attempt to assassinate presidential candidate David Palmer. One of the kidnappers tells Kim to come with him into the next room; his clear intent is to rape her. Her mother offers herself to the kidnapper instead, arguing that he will enjoy himself more with an acquiescent partner than with Kim, who will put up a fight. The kidnapper agrees.
- President Palmer Orders the Torture of Roger Stanton (2, 6pm-8pm)— President Palmer knows that a nuclear bomb is going to be set off in Los Angeles sometime in the coming 24 hours. He strongly suspects his national security advisor, Roger Stanton, of being complicit in the conspiracy. Palmer authorizes his personnel to torture Stanton to acquire whatever information he may have.
- The Trial of David Palmer (2, 2am-7am)—Persuasive but inconclusive evidence suggests that the plot to set off a nuclear bomb in L.A. was sponsored by a rogue Middle Eastern state. The Vice President strongly believes that any delay in attacking will cost thousands of lives due to the loss of the element of surprise, but President Palmer disagrees. Mike Novick, President Palmer's chief of staff, firmly agrees with the Vice President, but hesitates over whether to cooperate in the Vice President's plan to remove Palmer from office using the 25th Amendment so that the attack can be speedily launched.

• Letting the Child Abuser Go (with the Child)—Discussed above (5, 1pm).

A third category of *24* dilemma involves cases where the lives or wellbeing of a comparatively few innocent persons are traded to preserve a substantially greater number of lives, but by means of a deliberate choice to cause (or fail to prevent) the deaths of the few in such a way that they are deliberately (and usually fatally) wronged by the choice. Examples of this include:

• The Pre-Pardon of Nina Myers (2, 4pm-5pm)—Terrorist collaborator Nina Myers has information vital to stopping a nuclear attack on Los Angeles. She is offered immunity from prosecution for her information, but she feels she will never be safe as long as Bauer (whose wife she murdered) is still alive. She asks the President for a pardon for her own prospective murder of Bauer, effective before she commits it. The President must decide whether to include this unusual pardon provision in the immunity deal.[31]

• The Execution of Ryan Chappelle (3, 5am-6am)—A vital lead developed by CTU regional director Ryan Chappelle promises to locate a money trail that will help capture terrorist Stephen Saunders, who is holding the country hostage with the threat of releasing a deadly virus. Only Chappelle possesses the expertise to follow up the lead effectively. Saunders informs the president that if Chappelle's body is not delivered to a specified location in one hour, he will release the virus. The president must decide whether to order the execution of a loyal and innocent CTU agent to buy time to prevent the virus's release.

• Nerve Gas in the Shopping Mall (5, 2pm)—Jack Bauer is following a group of terrorists to their hideout when he observes them entering a suburban shopping mall. The terrorists as a whole are in possession of twenty canisters of nerve gas, and Bauer and company fear that they plan to release one canister in the mall. They consult the President, who must decide whether to prevent the release of nerve gas in the mall, or permit it in order to follow the terrorists back to their headquarters to hopefully forestall the release of the other nineteen canisters. ("The terrorists are forcing us to make a tragic choice," the President observes.)

• Permitting the Assassination of the Russian President (5, 3pm-4pm)—Terrorist leader Vladimir Bierko, in possession of twenty canisters of nerve gas, threatens to release the canisters in populated areas unless

President Logan discloses the motorcade route of visiting Russian President Suvarov and his wife (to facilitate an attempted assassination). On learning that her husband plans to turn over the motorcade route details, First Lady Martha Logan enters the limousine with her friends the Suvarovs in an attempt to force her husband to prevent the ambush. Secret Service Agent Aaron Pierce, unaware of the plot, insists on accompanying Mrs. Logan, and she is unable to prevent him from entering the motorcade with her.

- Bauer Shoots Miriam Henderson—Discussed above (5, 5pm).

What all these cases have in common are the grand scale of the incalculable consequences they engage, combined with the wild implausibility of the circumstances which put these values at risk. The combination of these two factors takes what according to the standard philosophical account is a moral tragedy and transposes it into the register of an ethical farce.

An important part of what enables 24 to succeed in its redefinition of the traditional notion of a dilemma is that it manages consistently, through the device of the 24 dilemma, to turn the standard dilemma (that is, the moral dilemma proper) into a parody of itself. 24 dilemmas are so extreme, so far beyond the familiar boundaries of sane moral choice, that when a standard dilemma appears alongside it—when, for example, you put next to any of the mad circumstances described above a standard dilemma such as the decision to torture to obtain information vital to saving lives—it begins to appear not only rather prosaic but indeed also rather silly by comparison.

There is, in addition, one more important reason why 24 contains so few observable instances of what it is willing to acknowledge as a moral dilemma, and this is to be found in the unusual temporal compactness and concision of the show's narrative.[32] Because events on 24 happen in real-time, there is very little opportunity for *deliberation* about the moral stakes and quality of the choice in question. But this in turn makes it much more difficult to generate an effective narrative representation of a moral dilemma. To recognize a moral dilemma as such in the actions of others, we need to be able to observe some aspect of their deliberation, either before or after the fact.

This does not mean, however, that a drama like 24 is incapable of representing a moral dilemma, as shown by the few but clear cases depicting a 24 dilemma. What it means instead is that the *scale* of the moral conflict or consequences engaged by a dilemma in 24 must be truly extraordinary, far beyond the bounds of the standard case, in order to engage our heroes' attention as containing any moral significance at all. And this in turn results in our gradual and subtle acquiescence in this redefinition of what counts as genuine moral conflict. It works a quiet magic over its viewers, one which incrementally redraws the boundaries of our moral outrage to make them more conducive to the moral extremism of a post-9/11 age.

The Moral of the Story

The first great book in the Western tradition to argue for a philosophically coherent politics, Plato's *Republic*, also argued that the most serious danger to such a politics lay in the power exercised over a community by its culture, and specifically by its modes of entertainment. In the *Republic*, Socrates famously declared that the poets and the tragedians would have to be banished from his ideal Kallipolis because of the threat their compelling arts posed to the virtue of its inhabitants. Notoriously, Plato went on to apply this principle to promote a wide-ranging censorship of seemingly innocuous beliefs and stories, giving Plato's arguments on these points a (largely deserved) reputation for puritanism and paranoia. Yet Plato is surely right about one key point: namely, his claim that there is a deeply political dimension to poetry and drama, since they claim to tell us important truths about the character of the good life and the qualities of fine and just actions.[33] Narratives—especially narratives about heroes and their deeds—are seductive: they invite not only our enjoyment, but our surrender to their spell. For any audience captivated by this spell of the narrative arts, "the pleasure they take in what happens to others necessarily carries over into what happens to them."[34] The myths in which we revel tonight gradually and insensibly become the practices we live out tomorrow.

Culture matters, and thus the various philosophical and moral lessons implied by our culture matter as well. They matter because they help to define our sense of the morally possible and impossible; they matter because they shift our ethical focus, and define our ethical blind spots. When a show like *24* helps to conceive, however casually, a vital philosophical concept like that of a moral dilemma, its effects may potentially be much wider (at least in the short term) than that of the most sophisticated academic argument. And there is considerable evidence to suggest that it is having such an impact both in the wider culture and specifically among those fighting the war on terror. *24* lead writer Howard Gordon comforts himself with the thought that "people can differentiate between a television show and reality," while star Kiefer Sutherland stresses that *24* is "just entertainment," merely a "fantastical show" that uses torture as "a dramatic device." But Brigadier General Patrick Finnegan, the dean of the U.S. Military Academy at West Point, disagrees: he recently flew to Hollywood to plead with *24*'s producers to alter their portrayal of torture, citing the corrupting effect on the legal and moral sensibilities of current officer cadets. Diane Beaver, the military's top lawyer at Guantanamo, has remarked that Jack Bauer and 24 gave U.S. interrogators "lots of ideas" regarding interrogation models.[35] (The show's effect on practice in the front lines of the war on terror was recently verified by a study by the U.S. Intelligence Science Board.) Former Homeland Security Secretary Michael Chertoff, a fan of the show, says that it "reflects real life" and that it accurately portrays how those fighting the war on terror must try to "make the best choice with a series of bad options." Popular talk-radio host Laura Ingraham has argued that the fact that Americans "love Jack Bauer" is "as close to a national referendum that it's O.K. to use tough tactics against high-level Al Qaeda operatives as we're going to get."[36]

24 is a frequently entertaining and occasionally riveting piece of political theater, and by itself that is all to the good. But when 24 contributes to making it more difficult for us to see hard ethical cases as *being* hard cases, when it makes it easier for us to see murder and torture and betrayal as nothing more than necessary acts of statesmanship and survival, when it helps to deaden our sense of moral tragedy by stretching melodrama to the point of parody and farce, it does us a grave disservice. Such ethical revisionism can over time help to impair, not just our aesthetic sensibilities, but also those ethically sensitive judgments and practices out of which true citizen virtue alone can emerge.

Notes

Sincere thanks to Paul Cantor, Joshua Dienstag, Margaret Hrezo, Joel Johnson, Wayne Le Cheminant, Susan McWilliams, Eric Rovie, Travis D. Smith, Charles Turner, David Williams and anonymous reviewers for helpful comments regarding this essay.

1. For a discussion of philosophical approaches to this subject matter, see William Irwin and Jorge J.E. Garcia, eds., *Philosophy and the Interpretation of Pop Culture* (Rowman and Littlefield, 2007). For examples of practice, see Paul A. Cantor, *Gilligan Unbound: Pop Culture in the Age of Globalization* (Rowman and Littlefield, 2001) as well as the *Blackwell Philosophy and Pop Culture Series*, edited by William Irwin (Blackwell), one volume of which I rely on extensively in what follows, namely Jennifer Hart Weed, Richard Davis, and Ronald Weed, eds., *24 and Philosophy: The World According to Jack* (Blackwell, 2008).

2. On the concept of moral dilemmas, see the essays collected in Christopher Gowans, ed., *Moral Dilemmas* (Oxford University Press, 1987).

3. FOX News debate, May 15, 2007. Bauer's idolization is not uniform on the right. In response to a question on torture at a recent debate, Sen. John McCain admonished his fellow GOP presidential candidates that "… I would hope that we would understand, my friends, that life is not 24 and Jack Bauer." CNN debate, Nov. 28, 2007.

4. Paul Beston, "Getting Dirty in Real Time," *The American Spectator* (July/August 2005).

5. Ibid. It is unclear which critically lauded dramas Beston is referring to in his later comment; to my knowledge, no character on *The West Wing*, for example, ever exhibits either of the two worries he outlines.

6. See in particular Randall M. Jensen, "What Would Jack Bauer Do? Moral Dilemmas and Moral Theory in 24," and Stephen de Wijze, "Between Hero and Villain: Jack Bauer and the Problem of 'Dirty Hands,'" both in *24 and Philosophy*.

7. A few year's later, Sayid Jarrah on ABC's *Lost* would provide a second example, though Sayid is much more troubled by his acts of torture than Jack Bauer is. Bauer himself would probably realize the unusual narrative dimensions of his status as a protagonist, since (according to an official show handbook) he was an undergraduate English major at UCLA.

8. For an outline of utilitarianism as an ethical doctrine, see Jeremy Bentham, *An Introduction to the Principles of Morals and Legislation* (Dover, 2007) and John Stuart Mill, "Utilitarianism," in *On Liberty and Other Essays*, ed. John Gray (Oxford University Press, 1991). For applications of utilitarianism specifically to the problem of moral dilemmas, see R.B. Brandt, "Utilitarianism and the Rules of War," *Philosophy and Public Affairs* 1 (1972): 145-165, and R.M. Hare, "Moral Conflicts," in Gowans, ed., *Moral Dilemmas*. For more critical views, see Thomas Nagel, "War and Massacre," *Philosophy and Public Affairs* 1 (1972): 123-144, and Bernard Williams, "A Critique of Consequentialism," in *Utilitarianism: For and Against*, eds. J.J.C. Smart and Bernard Williams (Cambridge University Press, 1983).

9. In later seasons, Bauer does appear to suffer to a certain degree from greater misgivings about his vocation and the worth of the choices and sacrifices it forces upon him. I attribute this shift in tone primarily to two factors. First, there does seem to be a growth in the overall number of moral dilemmas faced from season to season in *24*: Season 5, for example, appears to be (on average) more rife with dilemmas than Season 1. Second, this may reflect a certain degree of psychological realism in how Bauer's character is written: having faced so many dilemmas over so many years, the toll they have taken on what Alasdair MacIntyre has called "the narrative unity of a human life" will plausibly be greater in later seasons than in earlier ones. See Alasdair MacIntyre, *After Virtue: A Study in Moral Theory*, 2nd. ed. (Notre Dame, 1983), ch. 15.

10. I do not think this disjunction conveys anything systematic about Bauer's underlying moral theory (such as some complex form of rule utilitarianism); rather, it seems to reflect a sort of moral particularism (or, less charitably, an eclectic inconsistency in his moral beliefs).

11. Bauer's absolutism is made somewhat easier to stomach, of course, by the fact that under conditions of uncertainty about results and consequences, Bauer's judgments invariably turn out to be right. On this point see further Rob Lawlor, "Who Dares Sins: Jack Bauer and Moral Luck," in *24 and Philosophy*.

12. See Randall M. Jensen, "What Would Jack Bauer Do?: Moral Dilemmas and Moral Theory in *24*," in *24 and Philosophy*.

13. Francois Truffaut, *Hitchcock*, rev. ed. (Paladin, 1978), esp. ch. 6, 191-195.

14. On the corollary doctrine in post-9/11 foreign policy, see further Ron Suskind, *The One Percent Doctrine* (Simon and Shuster, 2007).

15. See Alan Dershowitz, *Why Terrorism Works* (Yale University Press, 2002); Sanford Levinson, ed., *Torture: A Collection* (Oxford University Press, 2004); Charles Krauthammer, "The Truth About Torture," *Weekly Standard* (Dec. 5, 2005); Andrew Sullivan, "The Abolition of Torture," *New Republic* (Dec. 19, 2005); and Bob Brecher, *Torture and the Ticking Bomb* (Blackwell, 2007).

16. Michael Walzer, "Political Action: The Problem of Dirty Hands," *Philosophy and Public Affairs* 2 (1973): 160-180.

17. Walzer did not believe that true moral dilemmas were restricted to such extreme cases, however; he offers a more mundane example of a politician who accepts a contribution from a shady contractor in order to win an election the outcome of which carries vital consequences to the community.

18. Jane Mayer, *The Dark Side*, (Doubleday, 2008), 330.

19. On this point, compare Bernard Williams, "Ethical Consistency" with Alan Donagan, "Consistency in Rationalist Moral Systems," both collected in Gowans, ed., *Moral Dilemmas*. See also Michael Stocker, *Plural and Conflicting Values* (Clarendon Press/Oxford University Press, 1990).

20. Aristotle, *Nicomachean Ethics*, trans. and ed. David Ross, (Oxford University Press, 1980), 1094b12-1095a6.

21. Of course from the perspective of certain moral views, for example those which do not recognize special moral responsibilities to family separate from general moral responsibilities to humanity, or those which make a strong distinction between the moral status of actions versus omissions of action, it might appear that there is no moral *wrong* here. But *24* gives no indication that it holds such a theory, and certainly does not promote such a view consistently.

22. On guilt as a feature of moral dilemmas, see Walzer, "Political Action: The Problem of Dirty Hands," along with Suzanne Dovi, "Guilt and the Problem of Dirty Hands," *Constellations* 12: 128-146.

23. Here I employ a very old procedure of moral judgment recommended by Adam Smith in *The Theory of Moral Sentiments*, ed. D.D. Raphael and A.L. Macfie (Liberty Fund, 1984), esp. at III.1 and *passim*.

24. Of course, not many of the *characters* laugh in any television show. There was little actual laughter at the bar at *Cheers* or in Jerry Seinfeld's apartment or at the Bluth model home, though there were of course plenty of jokes. (The Simpson family does occasionally laugh, but almost invariably in ironic circumstances, as while

watching Itchy and Scratchy's murderous exploits—or they are laughed at, as by local bully Nelson Muntz.)

25. For exposition and critical discussion of the theory that this kind of value conflict constitutes the essence of tragedy, see Anne and Henry Paolucci, ed., *Hegel on Tragedy* (Griffin House Publishing, 2001), and Walter Kaufmann, *Tragedy and Philosophy* (Princeton University Press, 1979).

26. Plato, *The Republic*, trans. Tom Griffith and ed. G.R.F. Ferrari (Cambridge University Press, 2000), 376e-417b, 595b-608b.

27. For comparison, see the subtle and intricately wrought moral dilemma presented contemporaneously with *24*'s first season (and shortly after the events of 9/11) on NBC's *The West Wing*, Season Three, episodes 21 ("We Killed Yamamoto") and 22 ("Posse Comitatus").

28. Whether it is ever right to use such means even against one's enemies is a question as old as Book I of Plato's *Republic*. If (contrary to my own belief) it is always wrong to do so, then my own coding will be substantially *under*estimating the number of moral quandaries and dilemmas in *24*. (Who counts as an enemy is similarly tricky, but for simplicity's sake I count anyone who could reasonably be believed to be deliberately engaged in a crime or threat against the public as an "enemy" in the relevant sense.)

29. See Walzer, "Political Action: The Problem of Dirty Hands" for an argument supporting this presumption, along with Henry Shue, "Torture," *Philosophy and Public Affairs* 7 (1978): 124-143.

30. This is typical of Bauer's attitude toward torture throughout the series. Consider this representative quotation from Bauer interrogating a prisoner: "You probably don't think I could force this towel down your throat, but trust me, I can. All the way. Except that I'd hold onto this little bit at the end. When your stomach starts to digest the towel, I pull it out. Taking your stomach lining with it. Most people probably take about a week to die. It's very painful" (1, 10am). For more detailed discussions of the treatment of torture in *24*, see Jane Mayer, "What It Takes," *The New Yorker* (Feb. 19, 2007); Douglas L. Howard, "You're Going To Tell Me Everything You Know: Torture and Morality in Fox's *24*," in Steven Peacock, ed., *Reading 24: TV Against the Clock* (I.B. Tauris, 2007); and Donal P. O'Mathuna, "The Ethics of Torture in *24*: Shockingly Banal," in *24 and Philosophy*.

31. This case is treated in considerable detail in Georgia Testa, "Palmer's Pickle: Why Couldn't He Stomach It?" in *24 and Philosophy*.

32. On the narrative impact of these aspects of the show, see Paul A. Cantor, "Jack in Double Time: *24* in Light of Aesthetic Theory," in *24 and Philosophy*. Cantor's account of the use of Shakespearean "double time" in *24* reinforces my claim that *24*'s use of its time scheme to define dilemmas down is a deliberate narrative choice, since if the show wanted to use ethical deliberation as a device to signify the moral difficulty of a particular decision, Cantor's "double time" would presumably afford a convenient means of accomplishing it.

33. *The Republic*, 599b-601d.

34. *The Republic*, 606b.

35. Mayer, *The Dark Side*, 196.

36. Except where otherwise cited, all quotations in this paragraph are from Jane Mayer, "What It Takes."

Table 5.2. Appendix

Day 5	Standard Quandary	Standard Dilemma	24 Quandary	24 Dilemma
7am	3	2	1	0
8am	3	0	0	0
9am	2	0	2	0
10am	1	1	1	0
11am	0	0	0	0
12pm	2	1	2	0
1pm	3	2	3	1
2pm	2	2	2	2
3pm	4	2	3	2
4pm	3	2	2	1
5pm	2	1	1	0
6pm	3	2	2	1
7pm	3	1	3	0
8pm	6	2	2	0
9pm	5	2	1	0
10pm	3	2	3	1
11pm	4	2	1	0
12am	5	2	2	1
1am	6	2	4	1
2am	8	4	4	0
3am	4	1	1	0
4am	4	0	1	0
5am	7	3	3	0
6am	6	3	1	0
Total	89	39	45	10

PART III

DILEMMAS OF INSTITUTIONAL EVIL

CHAPTER SIX

~

Modes of Moral Reasoning in *Uncle Tom's Cabin*

Joel A. Johnson

Introduction

Harriet Beecher Stowe's *Uncle Tom's Cabin*—the best-selling novel of the nineteenth century[1] and arguably the most influential piece of political literature ever—receives little attention from modern social scientists. Even those who work at the intersection of politics and literature tend to pass by Stowe.[2] There are reasons for this, of course. In her account of southern slavery, Stowe relied heavily on secondhand reports; was prone to exaggeration; and seemed to accept and perpetuate certain racial stereotypes, even as she sought to undermine others. In addition, her work falls short of the standards of truly great literature, being overly long, occasionally repetitive, and even at times boring.[3] Others might object to the religious underpinnings of the work. (Julia Ward Howe noted that Stowe's religiosity "could hardly have been congenial . . . to one who read Emerson.")[4] Most importantly, though, as an antislavery tract *Uncle Tom's Cabin* is an historical artifact, addressing what is now to most people a dead issue. It is difficult to see the novel as thought-provoking, when the contemporary reader overwhelmingly agrees with Stowe's position from the outset.

Given these considerations, should political scientists consign *Uncle Tom's Cabin* to historians, to be studied only as a product of and shaper of its antebellum context? Or is there something about Stowe's work that makes it more than a mere time-bound polemic—perhaps as John Locke's *Two Treatises of Government* remain more than a deft hatcheting of Robert Filmer? Is there some timeless wisdom in *Uncle Tom's Cabin* that thoughtful students of politics still ought to consider? I believe this indeed is the case. George Orwell (the Harriet Beecher Stowe of the twentieth century) might have put it best when he wrote that *Uncle Tom's Cabin* "is an unintentionally ludicrous book, full of preposterous melodramatic incidents," but is nonetheless "deeply moving and essentially true."[5]

I argue that *Uncle Tom's Cabin*, despite its many flaws, is a strikingly good exercise in moral psychology. Specifically, I claim that Stowe provides an extensive and useful typology of the ways people react to serious moral dilemmas—including, but not limited to, the institution of slavery. In addition to explaining the causes of these various reactions, Stowe suggests (sometimes explicitly, sometimes implicitly) the factors that might change one's attitudes toward certain injustices. For an understanding of how arguments, passions, violence, and suffering interact at points of grave moral crisis, scholars would be well advised to give Stowe's classic novel a careful reading.

Uncle Tom's Cabin is a work of persuasion, to be sure, but its persuasiveness arises from Stowe's careful descriptive efforts. More than seventy characters appear in the novel, each of whom bears some relationship to the institution of slavery. Although many of these characters overlap in their attitudes towards slavery, there are remarkably few characters who react in exactly the same way. This lack of duplication in such a large cast makes for a highly complex novel of social mores. Even if one were to focus just on how *victims* of slavery tend to react, we find examples in *Uncle Tom's Cabin* of flight, blind submissiveness, subversion, armed resistance, and heroic self-sacrifice. However, for Stowe this only begins to delineate the variety of responses people have to slavery. We also encounter, at various points in the novel, wise reformers, foolish reformers, eager perpetrators of the injustice, unwilling accomplices, and unwitting accomplices. Although some rough handling is necessary to squeeze Stowe's characters into categories, imposing some such order is necessary to analyze the work effectively. As a first cut, one can divide the cast of *Uncle Tom's Cabin* into victims on the one hand, and perpetrators and their accomplices on the other. Further subdivisions can then be made within each category. After discussing Stowe's typology of victims and perpetrators, I will review her rhetorical tactics and offer some concluding thoughts about the broader applicability of her moral psychology.

Responses to Injustice: The Victims

Stowe implies that all Americans are victims of slavery in one way or another, much as most non-slaves are to some degree responsible for the perpetuation of the institution. Here, however, I will be focusing on the most obvious victims, slaves themselves. Although Stowe occasionally lapses into racial determinism, her depiction of slaves as they struggle to survive under the harshest injustice is nuanced and compelling. In *Uncle Tom's Cabin* there is tremendous variation in how slaves react to their bondage. Each response is, in its own way, understandably human, though not all are laudable and some require almost superhuman effort.

The first category of victims, for Stowe, includes those who respond to injustice by putting their heads down, gritting their teeth, and attempting to find some happiness amidst forced misery. For some this is easier to do than for others. The slaves owned by the Shelby family of northern Kentucky, for example, are treated reasonably well, are allowed to marry outside the plantation, and are almost considered members of the household. It is relatively easy for Aunt Chloe, Uncle Tom's wife, to serve as matriarch of her own family and of the other Shelby slaves, thanks to a considerable amount of autonomy, adequate living quarters, and the owners' respect for her cooking. The Shelby slaves are allowed to worship as they please (most choose Uncle Tom as their guide to Christian piety), and some are even confidants of their owners. Eliza and Mrs. Shelby seem to share a particularly close bond, almost that of a mother and daughter (601).[6] Under such circumstances, gentility and kindness mollify the formal injustice. Mr. Shelby's slaves are, as a result, not primed for revolt; their lives are much as the slavery apologists claimed most slaves' lives were.

Even those slaves with personal ambition can find some satisfaction within slavery. One of Mr. Shelby's slaves, Black Sam, proves he knows exactly how to advance his own interests when Eliza escapes from Mr. Haley, the slave trader: namely, organize a search party with much show of haste, but secretly work to delay it. "[K]nowing which side the bread is buttered," thanks to his vaunted "habit o' *bobservation*," Sam correctly concludes that the Shelbys actually wish Eliza to escape (97, 103). Sam, hoping to fill Tom's place as Mr. Shelby's favorite, engineers a hilarious and greatly successful delaying action, which plays upon Haley's willingness to view slaves as foolish, careless children. To be sure, Sam does not upset the institution of slavery, nor does he ever complain about it. He simply knows, as "politicians of all complexions and countries know," how to secure an advantage in an unfavorable situation (97). In this case, it means gleefully playing one white man off another. Such small victories ultimately change little, but compared to the rest of a slave's life, can provide just enough reason to stay in line.

Stowe knew the Shelby plantation was slave agriculture in its mildest form. More typical was life under a harsh overseer, with constant anxiety about one's future and that of one's family. *Uncle Tom's Cabin* is replete with horrifying episodes in which children are sold away from their parents, often to masters with cruel or lecherous designs. As property, slaves had little recourse, and most did not attempt to overthrow the system. They struggled as best they could to endure loneliness and grief, seeking solace in each other and in religion. Given her purposes, however, Stowe does not dwell on hopeful slaves. After all, portraying too many patient slaves might give her readers the mistaken impression that slavery was tolerable. Instead, Stowe shows us how cynicism—not just hope—can also motivate quiescence.

Cassy, Simon Legree's quadroon mistress, is a case in point. As Uncle Tom lay bleeding after one of Legree's brutal beatings, Cassy—whose "face was deeply wrinkled with lines of pain, and of proud and bitter endurance" (501)—advises him to submit: "[I]t's of no use, this you've been trying to do. You were a brave fellow,—you had the right on your side; but it's all in vain, and out of the question, for you to struggle. You are in the devil's hands;—he is the strongest, and you must give up!" (511). After learning Cassy's story, most readers would be hard pressed to disagree. As a beautiful young woman, fathered by her master, Cassy had originally been treated as a proper member of her family. She was pious and had even entered a convent. Through a series of misfortunes and devious acts, Cassy was sold off, became mistress to two subsequent masters, and bore two children who were secretly sold away from her. As a final insult, she now had had to survive five years under Legree's tyranny. Stripped of her religious faith, her purity, and her children, and "pursued by devils that torment . . . day and night" (522), Cassy nonetheless proudly endures. It is not entirely clear why she submits, especially since Legree has no control over her children. Yet Cassy does derive some satisfaction from mastering her job and from her ability to frighten others—both free and slave—with her eccentric behavior. Indeed, being both an expert at one's tasks and a dangerous mystery to others can provide at least some reason for enduring, even when hope is gone. No one, though, could ever use Cassy's submission as an argument for slavery.

Whether Sambo and Quimbo, Legree's black overseers, are better off than Cassy is open to debate. In some respects, they are fortunate, having been spared many of the worst torments of Cassy's life. Legree even entrusts them with the whipping of other slaves. With this power comes a greater ability to survive, of course, but at a terrible price. Sambo and Quimbo are little more than beasts, since "Legree had trained them in savageness and brutality as systematically as he had his bull-dogs" (492). In fact, Stowe points out that they are crueler than most white overseers, since they have been more "crushed and debased" (492). Regardless of race, Stowe notes, "the slave is always a tyrant, if he can get a chance to be one" (492-93). By "playing one off against another" and supplying them with women, Legree neutralizes Sambo and Quimbo, even as he gives them the appearance of power. Whereas Sam might reasonably expect a reward and genuine thanks from the Shelbys for slowing down Haley's pursuit, Sambo and Quimbo can expect no such kindly treatment from Legree. They submit to their master as trained fighting dogs do, not as the family puppy might. In neither case is full humanity displayed, since Sam, Sambo, and Quimbo are all victims of degradation, but not even full animality appears in Sambo and Quimbo. As Stowe puts it—in a manner reminiscent of Aristotle[7]—"brutal men are lower even than animals" (493).

As the foregoing suggests, Stowe provides a thorough catalog of the ways humans submit to and endure injustice. She also, however, depicts a great number of rebellious responses to the injustices of slavery. Again, each response is in its own way human, even though readers might find some more praiseworthy than others.

Several of the slaves in *Uncle Tom's Cabin* choose to attempt escaping. Eliza is the best known of these, fleeing Haley and his dogs and braving the icy Ohio River to reach the free states. For her, the duty to protect her son had suddenly overpowered the pious docility that previously had made her such a reliable slave. Others attempt flight, as well, each in a distinct way. Cassy, upon Tom's urging, is finally able to escape Legree through trickery, hiding in his attic while he hunts the woods for her. Eliza's husband, George Harris, also escapes, thanks to his light complexion, remarkable ingenuity, and flat-out courage. Of all the characters in the book, George is the most stridently independent, being prepared to use deadly force in effecting his escape and utterly rejecting the established order. As he puts it to Mr. Wilson, a kindly white man who used to employ him:

> [W]hat country have *I*, or any one like me, born of slave mothers? What laws are there for us? We don't make them,—we don't consent to them,—we have nothing to do with them; all they do for us is to crush us, and keep us down. Haven't I heard your Fourth-of-July speeches? Don't you tell us all, once a year, that governments derive their just power from the consent of the governed? Can't a fellow *think*, that hears such things? Can't he put this and that together, and see what it comes to? (185)

George, as Stowe depicts him, is a Lockean/Jeffersonian rebel, bent on securing his natural-born rights in independence from tyrannical masters. For him, submitting peaceably to slavery would be an inhuman act on *his* part. (Interestingly, three months after *Uncle Tom's Cabin* appeared in book form, Frederick Douglass made a strikingly similar argument in his famous Independence Day oration.)[8]

Perhaps the most controversial victim in *Uncle Tom's Cabin* is Uncle Tom himself. Depending on one's perspective, Tom is either the least or the most powerful character in the book.[9] In one sense, Uncle Tom is the ultimate "Uncle Tom," quiescent and eager to please, and generally content with his lot. He is no revolutionary, and critics would say he actually contributes to the injustice by not opposing it with his great moral authority. On the other hand, Tom is a man of the deepest Christian piety; for him, whether slavery exists or is destroyed, or whether he is free or in chains, is less important than holding to the tenets of his faith. Even Simon Legree cannot break Tom, since the sticks and stones of this world cannot reach his soul. Tom is not incapable of escaping (he even tells Cassy that under different circumstances he might try it [562]), but he believes his responsibility to the innocent, helpless, and lost trumps any concern for his own self-preservation. This sense of duty fortifies him as he leaves the Shelby plantation, as he endures Haley's and Legree's punishments, as he befriends Cassy, and—at the very end—as he helps re-humanize Sambo and Quimbo.

There are many other victims in *Uncle Tom's Cabin*, and there is not space here to recount all of their stories. Some are truly horrific, as when Haley steals and sells a slave woman's baby, driving her to suicide; or when Cassy overdoses her infant son on laudanum, in order to save him from a slave's life. In addition, there are almost as many kinds of responses as there are victims, as no two victims react exactly the same way. Indeed, because slavery is particularly horrific, it tends to call forth a greater variety of responses. Quiescence or mild protest might be suitable reactions when injustice is mild, but serious harm will provoke more determined reactions. In desperation, reasonable people can come to see flight, revolt, suicide, or even murder as a reasonable alternative to enduring deep injustice any longer. To her credit, despite her occasional biases, Stowe provides an appropriately complex depiction of these responses that serves as a lesson to any reformer expecting victims of injustice all to react to change in the same way.

Responses to Injustice: The Perpetrators

Stowe makes clear that there is also much variation among the perpetrators of injustice and their accomplices. From Mr. Shelby to Simon Legree, from Augustine St. Clare to Miss Ophelia, nearly everyone is implicated with the institution of slavery in some way—either actively advancing its cause or doing too little to undermine it. As with the victims, the perpetrators in *Uncle Tom's Cabin* can be categorized according to their responses to slavery, with each category containing complex subdivisions.

The first category is the most obvious: those who willingly and sometimes eagerly support slavery. The infamous Simon Legree is in this category, of course, as are the slave drover Mr. Haley and the slave hunters Tom Loker and Marks. Fancying himself a kind master amidst sometimes distasteful circumstances, Mr. Shelby is also a willing perpetrator, though occasionally an uneager one. Certainly, several members of Augustine St. Clare's extended family are eager supporters. Marie, Augustine's hypochondriac wife, is a brutal mistress to the household slaves, including Uncle Tom. Augustine's brother Alfred explicitly rejects the egalitarian platitudes of the Declaration of Independence, and Alfred's son Henrique treats slaves viciously. Each of these willing perpetrators (plus all the others portrayed in the novel) would agree, at some level, with Alfred's assertion that "we can see plainly enough that all men are *not* born free, nor born equal; they are born anything else. For my part, I think half this republican talk sheer humbug. It is the educated, the intelligent, the wealthy, the refined, who ought to have equal rights and not the canaille" (391). When this ideology is buttressed both by power and religion (Stowe emphasizes how ministers rarely made biblical arguments against slavery amidst their plantation congregations, and usually did quite the contrary),[10] the institution could not easily be made to collapse.

More interesting to Stowe—and to us—is the class of unwilling perpetrators. In his more progressive moments, Mr. Shelby is in this category. His wife certainly belongs here, for Mrs. Shelby expresses sincere regret for not successfully convincing her husband to economize and to free his slaves. The most intriguing example of the unwilling perpetrator, however, is Augustine St. Clare. Thanks to his wealth, St. Clare affords a large household of slaves, for which he provides little discipline or guidance. St. Clare despises slavery—and himself, for owning slaves. The result is "mismanagement" and overindulgence. St. Clare knows the evil institution must be abolished, but he can see no way of achieving that end. He considers himself powerless, except for his ability to free his own slaves. Yet even this would, in his opinion, not help his servants' plight, for they would be released into a hostile world with no protection, education, resources, or experience at being free. Wracked by guilt and indecision, St. Clare ultimately fails to do anything to undermine the institution he hates. When he dies suddenly, his servants are sold off as mere property, just like anyone else's.

The *unwitting* perpetrators of injustice are far more numerous. Usually, these are characters who find slavery distasteful, but do not realize the extent to which their own actions sustain the institution. When such thoughts *do* occur to them, they are quick to rationalize their action or inaction, to preserve the bliss of pretended innocence. With the possible exception of

Augustine's daughter Eva, who radiates pious egalitarianism, the upstanding characters of the novel are all contaminated by slavery. Stowe argues, quite forcefully, that geographical distance and lack of direct participation in slavery do not constitute innocence. The northern creditors who accept slaves as collateral for loans to southern planters do as much or more to sustain slavery as the planters themselves, even though they comfort themselves by using the morally neutral term "business" to describe the transactions (471-72).

In a similar position is Mr. Bird, a senator in the Ohio legislature. When we meet him in chapter nine, he has just voted for a law making it illegal to aid escaped Kentucky slaves. He explains to Mrs. Bird that he supported the law not because he approved of slavery but because "our brethren in Kentucky are very strongly excited, and it seems necessary, and no more than Christian and kind, that something should be done by our state to quiet the excitement" (142). Because "there are great public interests involved," he continues, "we must put aside our private feelings" about slavery (144). Senator Bird is a reasonable, public-spirited man, willing to subordinate his own beliefs—in the spirit of Daniel Webster, Henry Clay, and the other supporters of the Compromise of 1850—to the perceived common good. However, it is precisely Bird's fear of causing "a great public evil" (144) by pressing his own beliefs too forcefully that keeps him supporting the unjust status quo.[11]

Stowe challenges her northern readers by emphasizing how northerners can be worse than southerners when it comes to involvement with slavery—often without knowing it. Simon Legree and Alfred St. Clare—two of the hardest masters to be found in the South—are of northern stock, as is Mr. Stubbs, the ruthless overseer of the plantation owned by Augustine and Alfred's father. Northern capital and consumer demand makes slave plantations profitable, and northern apathy prevents reform. However, to understand the nuances of how the northern mind-set is an obstacle to abolition, one must examine the character of Miss Ophelia, Augustine St. Clare's Vermont cousin who comes south to live with him.

Stowe devotes several chapters to Miss Ophelia, and the discussions she portrays between Augustine and Ophelia contain some of the most telling arguments about the North's responsibility for slavery's perpetuation. We learn that Ophelia grew up in a small New England village, "where everything is once and forever rigidly in place, and where all household arrangements move with the punctual exactness of the old clock in the corner" (244). A "tall, square-formed, and angular" woman, Ophelia is "a living impersonation of order, method, and exactness" (247). The vice she hates most is "shiftlessness," which is the opposite of her most obvious virtue, conscientiousness (247-48). When word got out that she might be traveling to New Orleans, her fellow villagers buzzed with gossip, as if she were going as a missionary to some exotic land (245). Truly, to these New Englanders Louisiana was both culturally exotic and in desperate need of salvation. Some even questioned the wisdom of spending money on a new dress for Ophelia, for that might both show too much respect for the wicked ways of the South, and deprive genuine missionaries of a much-needed contribution.

Ophelia is properly anti-slavery in her attitudes. It would be unusual, given her upbringing, to have become anything else. Consistent with her principles, Ophelia begins expressing her dismay as soon as she arrives at Augustine's home. However, it soon becomes clear that Ophelia objects more to the household's disorder and Augustine's laziness than to slavery itself. Augustine's slaves, as mentioned earlier, are under few restraints, and some even dress up in their master's clothing. The kitchen is in complete disarray (notwithstanding that the cook, Aunt Dinah, prepares excellent meals), and Ophelia sets herself the task of banishing shiftlessness and instituting conscientious order. Her energetic attempts to "induce systematic regulation" (312) begin at four o'clock in the morning, prompting Augustine to chide her for placing such an "extravagant value on time" (317). Ophelia is undaunted, though, and with great energy she continues to eliminate waste and unnecessary expense, disciplining servants in the process. In doing so, however, she reveals her own prejudices—which are precisely those northern prejudices that prevent a workable solution to the slavery problem.

Ophelia is appalled by the easy familiarity among Augustine, his daughter Eva, and the household slaves. Eva even embraces them lovingly when she arrives home, which Ophelia later claims "fairly turned her stomach" (255). Having listened to Marie St. Clare prattle on about her many ailments and the difficulties of managing spoiled servants, all the while saying little and coldly attending to her knitting, Ophelia fairly bursts when Augustine begins to defend his indolent lifestyle:

> I think you slaveholders have an awful responsibility upon you . . . . I wouldn't have it, for a thousand worlds. You ought to educate your slaves, and treat them like reasonable creatures,—like immortal creatures, that you've got to stand before the bar of God with. That's my mind. (271)

St. Clare is quick to respond, and to point out Ophelia's hypocrisy regarding slaves:

> You loathe them as you would a snake or a toad, yet you are indignant at their wrongs. You would not have them abused; but you don't want to have anything to do with them yourselves. You would send them to Africa, out of your

sight and smell, and then send a missionary or two to do up all the self-denial
of elevating them compendiously. (273)

Ophelia concedes that Augustine might have a point, but then the matter
is dropped.

Just as she tries to reorganize the St. Clare household, Ophelia casts judgment on slave society as a whole, asking Augustine how he can sit and do
nothing to remedy the injustice. Augustine replies in a way that highlights
Ophelia's blindness:

Here is a whole class,—debased, uneducated, indolent, provoking,—put, without any sort of terms or conditions, entirely into the hands of such people as
the majority in our world are; people who have neither consideration nor self-
control, who haven't even an enlightened regard to their own interest,—for
that's the case with the largest half of mankind. Of course, in a community
so organized, what can a man of honorable and humane feelings do, but shut
his eyes all he can, and harden his heart? I can't buy every poor wretch I see.
I can't turn knight-errant, and undertake to redress every individual case of
wrong in such a city as this. The most I can do is to try and keep out of the
way of it. (328)

He adds, "[Y]ou've only seen a peep through the curtains,—a specimen of
what is going on, the world over, in some shape or other. If we are to be
prying and spying into all the dismals of life, we should have no heart to anything. 'T is like looking too close into the details of Dinah's kitchen" (328).
What Ophelia fails to appreciate is that people often do what they know is
wrong, simply because they think they have no choice in the matter (329).

To demonstrate to Ophelia the insufficiency of merely labeling something
evil, and stating what others ought to do, Augustine purchases a little slave
girl, Topsy, to be Ophelia's servant and student. Topsy is proof of St. Clare's
argument that oppression and degradation, especially when experienced as
a child, are responsible for most of the vices whites see among slaves. Topsy
lies, cheats, and steals, and does not fear Ophelia's reprimands or punishments, for she has received much worse in the past. Topsy baffles Ophelia,
who tries every method of instruction and discipline she can think of, and
then tells Augustine she plans to give up. Augustine is bemused and self-
satisfied, and asks Ophelia one final question:

Why, if your Gospel is not strong enough to save one heathen child, that you
can have at home here, all to yourself, what's the use of sending one or two

poor missionaries off with it among thousands of just such? I suppose this child is about a fair sample of what thousands of your heathen are. (408)

Ophelia has no answer.

Stowe would have surprised no one by pointing out that many Americans willingly supported slavery as a positive good or a necessary evil. Where she makes a greater contribution is in describing the helplessness that paralyzes certain opponents of slavery (such as Augustine St. Clare) and how seemingly innocent bystanders are often deeply complicit in the crimes they behold. As I discuss in the next section, Stowe is remarkably effective at exposing that complicity, thereby working to convert unwitting and unwilling perpetrators to the antislavery cause.

Modes of Persuasion in *Uncle Tom's Cabin*

As a work of description, *Uncle Tom's Cabin* is a valuable tool for understanding how people react to serious injustices. If this were all Stowe had done, her novel would be a useful corrective to the tendency to draw sharp lines between victims and perpetrators, and to view all victims as having similar experiences and motivations. Any conscientious reader of *Uncle Tom's Cabin* cannot fail to see how Stowe captures the variety among both victims and perpetrators. But Stowe's contribution does not end with her careful descriptions. Hers is a work of persuasion, bent on changing the beliefs and behaviors of the diverse members of a large audience, most of whom can be classed as perpetrators of the unwilling or unwitting kind. Insofar as she builds her case against slavery, Stowe provides much insight into how different groups of perpetrators might come to change their views and actions in ways that would effectively destroy the injustice.

Stowe might be termed a sentimentalist for emphasizing the emotional costs of slavery and for her ability to tug at readers' hearts. To some, this could be seen as a weakness, insofar as *Uncle Tom's Cabin* does not place strictly rational arguments for and against slavery in the forefront. Although such arguments do appear throughout the novel, it is the pathos of Tom's suffering and the thrilling desperation of Eliza's escape that stay in one's memory the best. Carl Van Doren once sneered that Stowe was "[t]he most effective of [the] sentimentalists, a writer whom, indeed, a profound passion once or twice lifted above sentimentalism though its flavor still clung to her."[12] Other scholars have disagreed, however, pointing out that "highly refined and pointed anger" motivates the narrative, not just cheap emotional appeals.[13] I contend that Stowe's sentimentalism is in fact what makes her work such a valuable analysis of how people actually think, feel, and behave amidst injustice, and a counterbalance to accounts that emphasize reason to the exclusion of emotion.[14] Stowe reminds us that moral reasoning is as much about the sentiments as it is about logic, if for no other reason than that moral reasoning is usually about the things we love, fear, and hate. Moral reasoning that fails to engage the affections will, more often than not, be unpersuasive.

Perhaps nowhere is this more evident than when Stowe employs ideals of gender and family to criticize the effects of slavery. The ideals Stowe invokes are in some ways traditional, but her understanding of gender and family duties cannot be reduced down to a crude stereotype of Victorian norms. Most of the white males in Uncle Tom's Cabin, for example, are brutish, effete, or incapable of effective action; while most of the women possess extraordinary strength and insight, and black men surpass their white counterparts in courage. Throughout the novel, Stowe challenges her readers to live up to their own ideals for gender roles, and sometimes to change those values.

Stowe does not provide a definition of manliness,[15] but she invokes norms of masculinity throughout her novel. In fact, the title of the opening chapter promises to introduce readers to "A Man of Humanity." Some confusion arises at first, since *two* men are mentioned in the leading paragraphs, Mr. Shelby and Mr. Haley. Casual readers will quickly conclude that the "man of humanity" must refer to the kindly, genteel Mr. Shelby. However, as the chapter proceeds, Stowe's intent becomes clearer. The second man, Mr. Haley, is—as a slave drover—also a man of *humanity*. Then the sarcasm of the title is doubled by what we learn of Mr. Shelby who, though he "had the appearance of a gentleman" (42), nonetheless is selling off his most trusted slave and the son of his wife's personal attendant—all to settle a debt. Both Shelby and Haley, then, are men of humanity in bitterly ironic ways. Neither, one might reasonably conclude, is even properly a man, much less a man of humanity.

Let us set Haley aside for the moment, and consider why Stowe draws Shelby as she does. As noted earlier, Shelby's plantation is about as idyllic a place as existed in the South: it has happy slaves, general prosperity, and the best of southern gentlemen heading the household. After conceding so much to the defenders of slavery, however, Stowe springs her trap: although Shelby has lived an "easy, even opulent" life (42), full of honor and dignity, he is emasculated as soon as his finances take a downturn. He is helpless to protect what is his own, and he is sullied by dealing with the gruesome realities of the domestic slave trade (which he can conveniently forget about when times are good). Haley, whom Shelby clearly despises, has the upper hand. (One sees this in Haley's overly frank manner, even towards Mrs. Shelby.) If Stowe had written only one chapter of *Uncle Tom's Cabin*, this first one would have effectively exposed the ideal of plantation gentlemanliness as the product of good fortune and little more. As long as he owns slaves and is answerable to the likes of Haley, Mr. Shelby cannot be free, and thus cannot be a true man. (Note how this argument differs from that of the slavery apologists, who claimed that masters were less free than their slaves, due to their constant regard for the slaves' wellbeing.)[16]

Unlike Shelby, Augustine St. Clare understands how slavery undermines manhood. However, he too is devoid of true courage and autonomy. As we have seen, Augustine sinks into lazy indolence, choosing to do nothing rather than strive without effect against that which disempowers him. He has no strength, no stomach for risk, and even no plan for protecting his own servants should he die. He lives in comfort and may in fact possess the sharpest mind of anyone in the novel, but he is thoroughly impotent.

These are the best of the southern men Stowe depicts. The rest often exceed them in power and the trappings of manliness (dominion over vast estates, physical strength, welcoming of risk, etc.), but are more like brutes than good republican citizens. The young George Shelby seems to approach that ideal as closely as anyone, but only after he has rejected slavery and done his part to end it. If there is hope for southern manhood, Stowe implies, it lies with southern women—not women like Marie St. Clare, of course, but rather like Mrs. Shelby. Mrs. Shelby sharply rebukes her husband for selling Tom and little Harry: "I have taught [our servants] the duties of the family, of parent and child, and husband and wife; and how can I bear to have this open acknowledgment that we care for no tie, no duty, no relation, however sacred, compared with money?" (83). Who needs abolitionists to say that slavery is wrong, she continues, when one has seen what she has of the institution?

> I was a fool to think I could make anything good out of such a deadly evil. It is a sin to hold a slave under laws like ours,—I always felt it was,—I always thought so when I was a girl,—I thought so still more after I joined the church; but I thought I could gild it over,—I thought, by kindness, and care, and instruction, I could make the condition of mine better than freedom—fool that I was! (84)

In the face of her persistent arguments for economy and the redemption of Tom, Mr. Shelby first patronizes her, then dismisses her ideas, and then finally just cuts off the discussion. Upon his death, however, Mr. Shelby shows that he had listened to his wife after all, entrusting to her—who had "a force of character every way superior to that of her husband"— all of the estate's finances. It is thanks to Mrs. Shelby's subsequent careful management and strident conscientiousness that Master George is able to go after Tom and eventually free all of the Shelby slaves.

In similar fashion, it is Ophelia who picks up Augustine's mess, exhorting him to action and notifying the Shelbys of Tom's location. Ophelia, in turn, inspired by Eva's simple goodness and democratic sympathies, comes to love Topsy, not hold her at arm's length like a repulsive beast. As David Grant puts it, Ophelia makes a "journey from coldness to a controlled warmth" that would later be "metaphorically reenacted in numerous Republican texts."[17] In the Bird household, the Senator's rationalization for aiding slavecatchers meets powerful opposition from Mrs. Bird who, though gentle in disposition, becomes fierce when witnessing cruelty. In all of these cases, fairly persuasive reasons were advanced to justify slavery's continuation. Mr. Shelby excuses his actions by noting that all other gentlemen do the same, Augustine by saying nothing good will come of his attempts at reform, and Senator Bird by saying that the social order will collapse if slavery is undermined. Each of these appears to be a defensible statement, but in reality each serves as a cover for fear. The men are hiding behind their cold logic, and the women in their lives know it. With more or less success, Mrs. Shelby, Mrs. Bird, and even Miss Ophelia challenge the men to be men: that is, to be courageous, face down fear, and dispense with cheap rationalizations for inaction. As Mrs. Bird tells her husband, who insists upon explaining his positions in terms of the "great public interests" at stake: "I hate reasoning, John,—especially reasoning on such subjects. There's a way you political folks have of coming round and round a plain right thing; and you don't believe in it yourselves, when it comes to practice. I know *you* well enough, John. You don't believe it's right any more than I do; and you wouldn't do it any sooner than I" (145). Later, when the senator proves his wife right by helping Eliza escape, Mrs. Bird approvingly notes that his heart is better than his head (153).

Why does Stowe place so much positive power in her female characters? For one thing, it is because she believes injustice is best appreciated when experienced directly, when one encounters "the imploring human eye, the frail, trembling human hand, the despairing appeal of helpless agony" (156). Mothers who have lost children, as Mrs. Bird has, know such pain more deeply than any legislature or moral philosopher could, and all mothers reading *Uncle Tom's Cabin* could empathize with Eliza. This is not untrue of men at the time (we see Senator Bird weeping at the memory of his lost child), but norms of childrearing were more gendered then than they are now, meaning that women could be relied upon to experience the grimy, bloody reality of domestic life more directly than men. Perhaps in consequence of this, Stowe's women do not simply seek escape from an unjust society, as Cooper's Natty Bumppo, Twain's Huckleberry Finn, and Thoreau do, but rather aim to "escape *into* some recovered or reconstituted social system more humane and nonviolent than that of Victorian America."[18]

In her depiction of the main slave characters, Stowe underscores the importance of sentiment—not just reasoned argument—in persuading her readers. Recall that Stowe's challenge was not so much to show that slavery was bad (most of her readers, including many in the South, would have conceded that—especially since the most aggressive defenses of slavery as a positive good had yet to appear in print),[19] but rather to mobilize people to action. To do so, she had to make slavery immediate and palpable, and draw emotional ties across the racial divide. Until Americans could see themselves in those whom they were enslaving, no end to the injustice could occur. As we have seen, Stowe's depiction of Eliza, as well as of Cassy, Madame de Thoux, and several other slave mothers, highlights the fundamental similarities among all mothers. Yet this was only one prong of her plan to excite the laudable emotions of her readers.

George Harris, by escaping bondage through pluck and sharp thinking, and then by defending his family as it flies to safety, serves as a race-transcending model of courage and fatherhood. Stowe even compares George, as he prepares to fire on his pursuers, to a Hungarian patriot defending a mountain pass (299). Readers could hardly overlook that George's spirit rivals that of any man of any race; this was precisely Stowe's intent in setting the plot as she did. However, George's manly heroism is not the only trait of his that would have disturbed readers out of their complacent toleration of slavery. George openly disavows his Christian faith, deeming it impossible to be both a slave and to embrace religious duty. All of a sudden, slavery appears to be doing nothing for George except robbing him of his family, his republican spirit, and his religion. Proslavery arguments based on expediency, stability, or the good of the slave would fail to persuade, once one has read about George Harris. Proslavery arguments calculating tangible costs and benefits would seem seriously deficient when placed against the image of such an impressive man as George, shackled and stripped of his dignity. Again, it is the intangible aspects of life that Stowe emphasizes and renders tangible through her storytelling: namely, the importance of honor, love, and the autonomy to craft one's life as one sees fit.

For those who find it impossible to empathize with either Eliza or George, and who care not whether slavery emasculates masters as well as slaves,

Stowe offers her portrayal of Uncle Tom. Tom is, in many respects, a feminine character, and interesting work has been done describing Tom as one of the novel's heroines.[20] While it is true that Tom does not appear to assert himself in a traditionally masculine way, he nonetheless cannot be reduced to purely feminine traits. In fact, Tom transcends gender categories, becoming not a masculine or feminine hero, but instead a martyr of Christian faith. Tom is no fool, and no collaborator. He knows exactly why he must go with Haley (if he does not, many others would need to be sold), and he knows that he must suffer at the hands of Legree and his thugs, because it is his proper duty to do so. In the process, he is beaten repeatedly—in the end, mortally so—but he remains faithful to his mission. All of Stowe's Christian readers would have been impressed by Tom's altruistic endurance, and more than a few would have wondered whether they could match Tom's almost superhuman faith.[21] Surely many would have been shamed into emulating Tom's self-sacrificing ways.

From reviewing her rhetorical strategies, we can see that Stowe certainly hoped to convince readers of the severe injustice of slavery and the need for resolute reform. To accomplish this, however, Stowe employed a myriad of characters that exposed the slave culture as a dangerous fraud, showed the importance of honor, dignity, and autonomy to a human life, and forged emotional attachments between white readers and black slaves. Judging from the book's immense popularity, Stowe was successful in her attempt. Yet Stowe is not sanguine about the likelihood of people immediately starting to rescue and free slaves upon reading her book. After all, for every person in the novel who does something to end slavery (e.g., the Shelbys, Miss Ophelia, the Birds), there are many who make no change—and would be unlikely to change even if presented with a persuasive argument to do so. A notable conversion in the novel is that of Tom Loker the slave catcher, but Loker only sees the error of his ways after he is shot by George Harris, abandoned by his fellow hunters, and nursed back to health by a Quaker community. Reading books and listening to anti-slavery disquisitions had nothing to do with his change of profession. More typical is Haley the slave drover, who changes not at all. Stowe explains that Haley and others like him are not the cause, but the consequence of slavery's existence. The slave economy makes such men necessary, so they arise and develop their cruel ways, as a matter of course. They cannot be wished away or persuaded to disappear. Until the basic economic structure changes, they will always be present. Still others might be more difficult to eliminate. Simon Legree, one of the most villainous characters in American literature, is—as Stowe describes him—not that unusual. He is a hard man with no use for books or rational argument. One suspects that he would hold on to his slaves even if men like Haley would find more profitable employment. Haley changes as the times change, but Legree is a rock of cruelty. He deals out only force, and it is probable that only force will make him change his ways. When George Shelby finally arrives at Legree's plantation and witnesses what Legree has done to Tom, he slugs Legree in the face. As Stowe notes,

> Some men . . . are decidedly bettered by being knocked down. If a man lays them fairly flat in the dust, they seem immediately to conceive a respect for him; and Legree was one of this sort. As he rose, therefore, and brushed the dust from his clothes, he eyed the slowly-retreating wagon with some evident consideration; nor did he open his mouth till it was out of sight. (592-93)

It is a hard truth that some perpetrators will only respond to being knocked down. Yet in this novel, when "knocking down" properly occurs (i.e., by George Harris and George Shelby), it is done by "a man" and "fairly." One wonders how the story would have changed, if the elder Mr. Shelby—to prove that he was indeed a man of humanity—had taken the chance to "knock down" Haley. (To be sure, this would not have ended slavery or slave trading, but it would have demonstrated the power of kindness when cleansed of timidity.)

Conclusion

Uncle Tom's Cabin is about slavery, but not just about slavery. Stowe's characters remain vivid today because they represent types that appear whenever there is serious injustice. Whether the issue is genocide, human trafficking, the subjection of women, animal rights, immigration, or sweatshop labor, analogues of most of Stowe's characters may be found. Temporizing politicians argue the same way Senator Bird does; perpetrators justify their actions either as Haley does (I'm just trying to make a living) or as Mr. Shelby and Augustine St. Clare do (everyone else is doing it, and besides, reform has little chance of success). Meanwhile, most people either turn a blind eye or, if they concern themselves at all with the injustice, judge without being helpful (like Miss Ophelia). Wisdom will usually be in short supply, and when present it will tend not to be joined with courage (Augustine's chief flaw). Courage itself will often serve the injustice, though sometimes not explicitly. (Most southerners, for example, saw themselves as repelling northern aggression and defending states' rights, not necessarily preserving slavery—though a southern victory would have had that result.)[22] Depending on the issue, one will also see victims responding in ways reminiscent of Eliza, Uncle Tom, George Harris, Sam, and even Sambo and Quimbo.

Stowe's book is, then, an excellent primer on the varieties of ways in which people perceive and react to injustice. However, as the latter part of this paper has shown, Stowe also helps us understand how and why people come to hold on to their views about controversial issues, and what might change their minds. Here Stowe's emphasis on the importance of intangible, sentimental factors (love, fear, hate, jealousy, prejudice) in either sustaining inertia or motivating change is particularly helpful to moral theorists and students of social action. It is remarkable how adept Stowe's characters are at turning the simple truth of slavery's injustice into a complex web of considerations that absolves the fearful and timid from any responsibility to act energetically. Without clear, instinctual thinkers such as Mrs. Bird, Mrs. Shelby, and Eva St. Clare, the simple truth would remain obfuscated.

Even when there is agreement that injustice is occurring and that something ought to be done, there are many constraints on collective action. Stowe was writing for a largely sympathetic audience, but she knew that to overcome their inertia she would have to push them in several ways at once (hence the simultaneous appeals to familial, religious, and patriotic duties). This is especially necessary given the sectional nature of the slavery controversy: the institutional design of federalism frustrated those who wished to make the South conform to the free market norms of the North. *Uncle Tom's Cabin* strikes the reader in multiple ways, each reinforcing the others (e.g., if Eliza's escape fails to excite the reader to action, then perhaps George's valiant fight for liberty or Tom's pious suffering will).

Stowe also disabuses us of the notion that those who are not eager perpetrators of injustice have clean hands. In fact, as with Wall Street financiers or even ordinary consumers, moral responsibility often lies substantially with those at a great distance from the victims. Stowe seems to implicate nearly all Americans in the evils of slavery, thus spreading around responsibility for the institution's continuation much as modern writers spread around responsibility for global injustices.[23] One need not conclude, of course, that all are equally culpable in Stowe's eyes, but few are completely exempt from blame. Miss Ophelia is not exempt, nor is Mrs. Shelby, who mistakenly believed that she could whitewash slavery by treating her slaves kindly. Strikingly, Stowe also implies that *ridding* the world of injustice will also require dirtying one's hands. By helping Eliza escape, Mr. Bird knowingly and willingly breaks the very law he had voted for in the legislature. Miss Ophelia has Augustine sign Topsy over to her, so that she can bring her to the North and release her—in essence, becoming a slaveholder in order to become a slave liberator. George Harris proves his willingness to fight and kill for his freedom. Each of these could be considered a significant moral compromise, but Stowe is rather untroubled by them. She understands the complexity of the decisions moral actors make, and she seems quite willing to overlook fingernail dirt in the service of justice.

Finally, Stowe illustrates the limits of persuasion, even as she demonstrates the extraordinary persuasive power of her art. Just as the full horrors of injustice often exceed what art can capture,[24] only some people will be receptive to artistic accounts of that injustice. Furthermore, not all of these will be persuaded to change their minds. As for the rest—the Haleys, Legrees, and Alfred St. Clares of the world—hard power might have to back up the soft power of artful persuasion. Although Abraham Lincoln famously credited Stowe with starting the Civil War, it took a Grant and a Sherman to win it. Nevertheless, scholars who wish to understand both how people react to injustice and how they come to change their opinions or become radicalized would be wise to give *Uncle Tom's Cabin* a full reading.

Notes

The author is grateful to Paul Cantor, Margaret Hrezo, Gregory Kaster, Susan McWilliams, John Michael Parrish, and Travis D. Smith for helpful comments on earlier drafts of this chapter, including the version presented at the 2008 Annual Meeting of the American Political Science Association.

1. See Harriet Beecher Stowe, *The Annotated "Uncle Tom's Cabin,"* ed. Henry Louis Gates, Jr. and Hollis Robbins (New York: W.W. Norton & Company, 2007), xliii, xlvi-xlvii.

2. Wilson Carey McWilliams mentions Stowe only once, in passing, in his magisterial *The Idea of Fraternity in America* (Berkeley: University of California Press, 1973), 228. Stowe does not appear at all in several other prominent books about politics and fiction, including Catherine Zuckert, *Natural Right and the American Imagination: Political Philosophy in Novel Form* (Savage, MD: Rowman & Littlefield Publishers, Inc., 1990); Martha Nussbaum, *Poetic Justice: The Literary Imagination and Public Life* (Boston: Beacon Press, 1995); Patrick J. Deneen and Joseph Romance, eds., *Democracy's Literature: Politics and Fiction in America* (Lanham: Rowman & Littlefield Publishers, Inc., 2005); and Edward B. McLean, ed. *The Inner Vision: Liberty and Literature* (Wilmington: ISI Books, 2006). Only a few scattered references to Stowe appear in the back issues of the sixty-two political science journals and sixty-six sociology journals indexed in JSTOR.

3. For a humorous example, see Gates and Robbins' confession that their eyes "tend to glaze over" during Augustine St. Clare's monologues (Stowe, *The Annotated*

"*Uncle Tom's Cabin*," 235 n. 19). For a succinct argument in favor of the book's literary value, see Josephine Donovan, "*Uncle Tom's Cabin*": *Evil, Affliction, and Redemptive Love* (Boston: Twayne Publishers, 1991), 11-12.

4. Quoted in Thomas F. Gossett, "*Uncle Tom's Cabin*" *and American Culture* (Dallas: Southern Methodist University Press, 1985), 166.

5. George Orwell, "Good Bad Books," in *The Collected Essays, Journalism, and Letters of George Orwell*, vol. 4, ed. Sonia Orwell and Ian Angus (New York: Harcourt, Brace & World, Inc., 1968), 21.

6. Parenthetical citations are from Harriet Beecher Stowe, *Uncle Tom's Cabin or, Life Among the Lowly*, ed. Ann Douglas (New York: Penguin Books, 1986).

7. Aristotle, *The Politics*, in *The Politics and the Constitution of Athens*, ed. Stephen Everson (Cambridge: Cambridge University Press, 1996), bk 1, chap. 2.

8. Frederick Douglass, "What to the Slave is the Fourth of July?" in *My Bondage and My Freedom* (New York: Miller, Orton, & Co., 1857), 441-45.

9. For a full discussion of this point, including a critical evaluation of James Baldwin's famous denunciation of Uncle Tom, see Gossett, *Uncle Tom's Cabin*, ch. 20.

10. See for example, the first minister's comments on the riverboat (200-202) and the sermon of Marie St. Clare's minister (279). Even Mr. Shelby is taken aback by the stridency of his minister's proslavery arguments: "I must say these ministers sometimes carry matters further than we poor sinners would exactly dare to do. We men of the world must wink pretty hard at various things, and get used to a deal that isn't the exact thing. But we don't quite fancy, when women and ministers come out broad and square, and go beyond us in matters of either modesty or morals, that's a fact" (85).

11. On Stowe's impatience with the cool rationality of laws that were helping to preserve slavery, see Alfred L. Brophy, "'Over and above . . . There Broods a Portentous Shadow,—The Shadow of Law': Harriet Beecher Stowe's Critique of Slave Law in 'Uncle Tom's Cabin,'" *Journal of Law and Religion* 12, no. 2 (1995-1996): 457-506.

12. Carl Van Doren, *The American Novel: 1789-1939* (New York: The Macmillan Company, 1945), 109.

13. Joan D. Hedrick, *Harriet Beecher Stowe: A Life* (New York: Oxford University Press, 1994), 216.

14. For a similar argument, see Catharine E. O'Connell, "'The Magic of the Real Presence of Distress': Sentimentality and Competing Rhetorics of Authority," in *The Stowe Debate: Rhetorical Strategies in "Uncle Tom's Cabin*," ed. Mason I. Lowance, Jr., Ellen E. Westbrook, and R.C. De Prospo (Amherst: University of Massachusetts Press, 1994), 14. For a valuable discussion of the complex relationship between emotion and reason in literature, see Nussbaum, *Poetic Justice*, ch. 3. Jane Tompkins, who makes one of the most compelling cases for Stowe's literary importance (*Sensational Designs: The Cultural Work of American Fiction 1790-1860* [New York: Oxford University Press, 1986], ch. 5), nonetheless concedes too much in stating that *Uncle Tom's Cabin* is not as psychologically subtle as the works of Hawthorne and Melville

(126). I argue that the novel is indeed psychologically subtle—and that this subtlety exists not in spite of, but largely because of the work's sentimental nature.

15. Stowe's conception of manliness is akin—though distinct in some particulars—to Harvey Mansfield's definition of a gentleman: "a manly man with polish and perfection" (*Manliness* [New Haven: Yale University Press, 2006], xii).

16. See, for example, George Fitzhugh, *Cannibals All! or, Slaves Without Masters*, ed. C. Vann Woodward (Cambridge: The Belknap Press of Harvard University Press, 1960), 16, 17.

17. David Grant, "Uncle Tom's Cabin and the Triumph of Republican Rhetoric," *The New England Quarterly* 71, no. 3 (Sept. 1998): 447.

18. Elizabeth Ammons, "Stowe's Dream of the Mother-Savior: *Uncle Tom's Cabin* and American Women Writers Before the 1920s," in *New Essays on "Uncle Tom's Cabin,"* ed. Eric J. Sundquist (Cambridge: Cambridge University Press, 1986), 157.

19. For example, Fitzhugh's *Cannibals All!* was published in 1857, and James Henry Hammond's famous "Mudsill Speech" was given in 1858.

20. See Elizabeth Ammons, "Heroines in Uncle Tom's Cabin," *American Literature* 49, no. 2 (May 1977): 170-75.

21. Susan Marie Nuernberg, following James Baldwin, argues that Tom is "too noble, meek, and forgiving to be a realistic character," and that "he is not a human being. Rather he is an inspiring myth" ("The Rhetoric of Race," in *The Stowe Debate*, ed. Lowance, Jr., Westbrook, and De Prospo, 268-69). I remain unconvinced that Tom is merely meek, and that his character has no tie to reality. Stowe herself addressed the latter issue: "The character of Uncle Tom has been objected to as improbable; and yet the writer has received more confirmations of that character, and from a great variety of sources, than of any other in the book." Harriet Beecher Stowe, *The Key to "Uncle Tom's Cabin"* (Boston: Jewett, 1854), 37.

22. See Drew Gilpin Faust, *The Creation of Confederate Nationalism: Ideology and Identity in the Civil War South* (Baton Rouge: Louisiana State University Press, 1988), esp. ch. 1.

23. For a useful synopsis of many such arguments, see Iris Marion Young, "Responsibility and Global Labor Justice," *The Journal of Political Philosophy* 12, no. 4 (2004): 365-88.

24. Stowe later wrote that *Uncle Tom's Cabin* "is a very inadequate representation of slavery; and it is so, necessarily, for this reason—that slavery, in some of its workings, is too dreadful for the purposes of art. A work which should represent it strictly as it is would be a work which could not be read; and all works which ever mean to give pleasure must draw a veil somewhere, or they cannot succeed." Stowe, *The Key to "Uncle Tom's Cabin,"* 1.

Bibliography

Ammons, Elizabeth. "Heroines in Uncle Tom's Cabin." *American Literature* 49, no.2 (May 1977): 161-79.

————. "Stowe's Dream of the Mother-Savior: *Uncle Tom's Cabin* and American Women Writers Before the 1920s." In *New Essays on "Uncle Tom's Cabin."* Edited by Eric J. Sundquist. Cambridge: Cambridge University Press, 1986.

Aristotle. *The Politics, and the Constitution of Athens.* Edited by Stephen Everson. Cambridge: Cambridge University Press, 1996.

Brophy, Alfred L. "'Over and above . . . There Broods a Portentous Shadow,—The Shadow of Law': Harriet Beecher Stowe's Critique of Slave Law in 'Uncle Tom's Cabin.'" *Journal of Law and Religion* 12, no. 2 (1995-1996): 457-506.

Deneen, Patrick J., and Joseph Romance, eds. *Democracy's Literature: Politics and Fiction in America.* Lanham: Rowman & Littlefield Publishers, Inc., 2005.

Donovan, Josephine. *"Uncle Tom's Cabin": Evil, Affliction, and Redemptive Love.* Boston: Twayne Publishers, 1991.

Douglass, Frederick. "What to the Slave is the Fourth of July?" In *My Bondage and My Freedom.* New York: Miller, Orton, & Co., 1857.

Faust, Drew Gilpin. *The Creation of Confederate Nationalism: Ideology and Identity in the Civil War South.* Baton Rouge: Louisiana State University Press, 1988.

Fitzhugh, George. *Cannibals All! or, Slaves Without Masters.* Edited by C. Vann Woodward. Cambridge: The Belknap Press of Harvard University Press, 1960.

Gossett, Thomas F. *"Uncle Tom's Cabin" and American Culture.* Dallas: Southern Methodist University Press, 1985.

Grant, David. "Uncle Tom's Cabin and the Triumph of Republican Rhetoric." *The New England Quarterly* 71, no. 3 (Sept. 1998): 429-48.

Hedrick, Joan D. *Harriet Beecher Stowe: A Life.* New York: Oxford University Press, 1994.

Mansfield, Harvey. *Manliness.* New Haven: Yale University Press, 2006.

McLean, Edward B., ed. *The Inner Vision: Liberty and Literature.* Wilmington: ISI Books, 2006.

McWilliams, Wilson Carey. *The Idea of Fraternity in America.* Berkeley: University of California Press, 1973.

Nuernberg, Susan Marie. "The Rhetoric of Race." In *The Stowe Debate: Rhetorical Strategies in "Uncle Tom's Cabin."* Edited by Mason I. Lowance, Jr., Ellen E. Westbrook, and R.C. De Prospo. Amherst: University of Massachusetts Press, 1994.

Nussbaum, Martha. *Poetic Justice: The Literary Imagination and Public Life.* Boston: Beacon Press, 1995.

O'Connell, Catharine E. "'The Magic of the Real Presence of Distress': Sentimentality and Competing Rhetorics of Authority." In *The Stowe Debate: Rhetorical Strategies in "Uncle Tom's Cabin."* Edited by Mason I. Lowance, Jr., Ellen E. Westbrook, and R.C. De Prospo. Amherst: University of Massachusetts Press, 1994.

Orwell, George "Good Bad Books." In *The Collected Essays, Journalism, and Letters of George Orwell.* 4 vols. Edited by Sonia Orwell and Ian Angus. New York: Harcourt, Brace & World, Inc., 1968.

Stowe, Harriet Beecher. *The Annotated "Uncle Tom's Cabin."* Edited by Henry Louis Gates, Jr. and Hollis Robbins. New York: W.W. Norton & Company, 2007.

————. *The Key to "Uncle Tom's Cabin."* Boston: Jewett, 1854.

————. *Uncle Tom's Cabin or, Life Among the Lowly.* Edited by Ann Douglas. New York: Penguin Books, 1986.

Tompkins, Jane. *Sensational Designs: The Cultural Work of American Fiction 1790-1860.* New York: Oxford University Press, 1986.

Van Doren, Carl. *The American Novel: 1789-1939.* New York: The Macmillan Company, 1945.

Young, Iris Marion. "Responsibility and Global Labor Justice." *The Journal of Political Philosophy* 12, no. 4 (2004): 365-88.

Zuckert, Catherine. *Natural Right and the American Imagination: Political Philosophy in Novel Form.* Savage, MD: Rowman & Littlefield Publishers, Inc., 1990.

~

CHAPTER SEVEN

The Problem of Slavery in *Harry Potter*

Susan McWilliams

Central to the appeal of J.K. Rowling's immensely popular *Harry Potter* series is its chief institution: the Hogwarts School of Witchcraft and Wizardry. Hogwarts, a boarding school for the most magically gifted children of the United Kingdom and Ireland, has much to recommend it. It is a place where every meal is a banquet. It is a place where adolescents are trusted enough to drink mildly alcoholic drinks. It is a place where a teenager could have suffered that greatest of childhood horrors—which is not dying, but living past the death of both parents—and still be loved, if not unscathed. Hogwarts is a place where magic, quite literally, happens.

From the first chapters in the first book of the *Harry Potter* series, the allure of Hogwarts is evident. When Hogwarts appears on the horizon, rising up over the foggy lake across which the first-year students are being rowed, its grandeur astonishes even the most cynical among them. They all gasp and go silent when they see, "perched atop a high mountain on the other side, its windows sparkling in the starry sky," that "vast castle with many turrets and towers."[1] Hogwarts is bewitching, and throughout the first few books in the series it is hard not to come to the conclusion that the magic of Hogwarts extends beyond its appearance—and beyond, even, the technical tasks of levitating and "disapparating" that students learn within its walls. Hogwarts seems to contain magic of a more intangible sort: a kind of *moral* magic. Particularly with Albus Dumbledore serving as headmaster, it seems that at Hogwarts, grievous moral errors do not occur. Dumbledore's mastery of spells and incantations appear to be bound up with a disarming moral clarity; Dumbledore always acts with a firm grasp of what is right. Dumbledore and the school he runs are charming in all senses of the word; they seem immutably *good*. Few are immune from coming to that conclusion: one eminent political scientist recently confessed to me that when he is faced with a problematic situation in the classroom, he asks himself, "What would Dumbledore do?" Hogwarts is, as Perry Glanzer has called it, an "exciting moral world," one in which students and faculty are enlisted "on the side of good in a cosmic battle against evil."[2]

It is not until the fourth installment in the series, *Harry Potter and the Goblet of Fire*, that we become aware that Hogwarts is not a perfect institution, morally speaking—when we learn with Harry's friend Hermione Granger that Hogwarts is sustained not just by magic but also by an enslaved class of house-elves. (Although Rowling introduces a single house-elf, Dobby, in the second book of the series, she does not let on until this fourth book that there is an entire class of those creatures, and that most of them work at Hogwarts.) In other words, the fact of an enslaved house-elf class only emerges in the *Harry Potter* series after Rowling has established the institution of Hogwarts in terms that are as enchanting as possible.

This means that Rowling makes her readers inhabit a critical theme of the story: it is easy *not* to see injustice. It is easy not to want to see injustice. It is easy not to see the house-elves, and most people—even most wizard people—don't. They neglect to, or they choose not to. Once you are accustomed to thinking of Hogwarts as an extraordinary and wonderful institution, whether the "you" is a character in the book or a reader of the *Harry Potter* series, it is frustrating if not dispiriting to see the school in this new, more imperfect light.[3] The simple thing to do is to pretend that the injustice does not really exist—or to claim that the enslavement is justified.

The argument that the enslavement of the house-elves is justified—that they are "happy slaves"—appears again and again in the *Harry Potter* series, particularly in the earlier books, and it is an argument advanced by sympathetic as well as unsympathetic characters. For readers of the books (as well as the characters in them), it is wholly tempting to adopt the position that the house-elves are in fact "happy slaves devoted to their masters"—despite the fact that perhaps no other argument is as unpalatable in the contemporary world as a defense, on any terms, of slavery.[4] Rowling's flirtation with the "happy slave" argument is in some ways a daring one; even though it is a claim the books ultimately reject, the *Harry Potter* series reveals exactly how appealing a claim it is.[5] It is an appealing claim not just for those characters in the series who have an immediate interest in perpetuating that particular oppression, but also for readers who would prefer not to think that characters they admire could be complicit in a great injustice.

The position of house-elves at Hogwarts demonstrates that it is easy to conceal or pretend away injustice when that injustice is an inconvenient truth. Not once, Hermione points out, does the definitive, thousand-page work on their school—the book, *Hogwarts, A History*, is a core text in the curriculum—mention that it has been and is responsible for the oppression of about 100 slaves. (When she recognizes this, Hermione becomes indignant, suggesting that "A *Revised History of Hogwarts* would be a more accurate title. Or A *Highly Biased and Selective History of Hogwarts, Which Glosses Over the Nastier Aspects of the School.*")[6] In fact, Hermione comes to learn, Hogwarts contains the largest population of house-elves in any single dwelling in Great Britain.[7] Apparently, Hogwarts has "owned" these house-elves for as long as anyone can remember, and the students at Hogwarts have been living with a massive injustice that no one acknowledges, discusses, or even realizes.

The enslavement of house-elves is a cruel hypocrisy in a wizarding school where the first of three "unforgivable" curses is the Imperius Curse—the curse by which one wizard enslaves another. Under the Imperius Curse, the victim feels compelled to do anything that the spell-caster wishes (although wizards with "real strength of character" may be able to shake off the worst of the directives).[8] The Ministry of Magic considers use of the Imperius Curse as horrific as murder; if one wizard uses this spell on another human being, he is punished with a life sentence in Azkaban, the prison under the charge of the soul-sucking Dementors. But use of the Imperius Curse is punished *only* when a wizard or witch uses it against another human being. Presumably, using it on house-elves would be acceptable—and surely it is no coincidence that the behavior of house-elves corresponds quite neatly with the behavior of those controlled by an Imperius Curse. The house-elves behave in such a way that it is difficult for outsiders to tell to what extent they are exercising free will, and to what extent they are being controlled: an enduring problem when dealing with sentient beings who are forcibly enslaved.

And Rowling makes clear, beyond any shadow of a doubt, that the house-elves are slaves.[9] They are unpaid. They are bound to masters whose claims upon them are predominantly ancestral. They are not permitted to choose against those masters. "House-elves," as one of their number says, "have no right to be unhappy when there is work to be done and masters to be served."[10] They can only be freed by the whim of the master—the person or family or institution—owning them. They have been a class enslaved for so long that most of them no longer understand what it would mean to be free. They have been enslaved so long that, for most of them, even the idea of freedom is terrifying. When Hermione shouts at a group of them that they have "just as much right as wizards to be unhappy," not to mention "the right to wages and holidays and proper clothes," they look at her as if she is "mad and dangerous." The house-elves are cowed, and the house-elves are "scared."[11] The first time Harry Potter asks him to sit down, the house-elf Dobby starts to cry. House-elves, he tells Harry, are never treated as equals. Rather, they are treated like animals; the Black family, for instance, beheads their house-elves in old age then stuffs and mounts their heads on the walls.[12]

Perhaps not surprisingly, most house-elf owners are somehow connected to Slytherin, the Hogwarts house associated with claims of ancestry, wealth and hierarchy—and the house which supplies the most steady stream of Death Eaters, the minions of evil Lord Voldemort. But it is not only Death Eaters who demonstrate callous disregard for the well-being of house-elves; even Professor Horace Slughorn, one of the few members of Slytherin who seems to have no prejudices against muggle-born or half-blood wizards, forces Hogwarts house-elves to "test" bottles of mead that he fears are poisoned. Regulus Black, though he is working against Voldemort, turns over his house-elf to the Dark Lord, a horrifying experience that haunts that house-elf for the rest of his life. Bartemius Crouch, Sr., a Ministry of Magic official, frames and punishes his house-elf for a crime he knows was committed by his son. And Harry's very likeable godfather, Sirius Black, regards his house-elf "impatiently" and "coldly," insulting his work and looking upon him with "disdain."[13] In fact, *each and every one* of the house-elves in the series who are discussed long enough to be named—Dobby, Hokey, Kreacher, and Winky—has suffered from significant abuse by human wizards.[14]

The house-elves are brutalized, both physically and psychologically. That horrifying reality is the first thing that Rowling lets on about house-elf life. Dobby, meeting Harry Potter for the first time, is disobeying his master in doing so. (Dobby comes to try to persuade Harry not to return for his second year at Hogwarts. Dobby knows that his master has plans to undermine or harm Harry, and Dobby has admired Harry from afar and so wants to protect him.) Meeting with Harry Potter directly contradicts the will of Dobby's master, and Dobby has been convinced that such contradiction merits punishment. So in between issuing warnings to Harry, Dobby is banging his head against the wall, ironing his fingers to a crisp, and promising to slam his ears in the oven door.[15] At first, Dobby's self-brutalization is so extreme that it seems almost comical. But as Harry realizes almost immediately, it is actually quite disturbing. The condition of enslavement has tyrannized Dobby in body *and* in mind. Even as he says he seeks freedom—and Dobby is rare among house-elves in that he verbally expresses the desire to be free from his master—he perpetuates the violence of his own enslavement.

With all this, Rowling makes it hard to miss the fact that Dobby, like all the house-elves, is a being like us. He is anthropomorphic, resembling a human more than any other creature. That is clear when Harry first sees him and thinks that Dobby looks like a "large and very ugly doll"—an unattractive variation on the human form, but a variation on the human form nonetheless.[16] Dobby uses our language, the same language that the witches and wizards around him speak—even though the speech of house-elves is just a little odd, as Brycchan Carey has discussed, characterized by pronoun and word-order mistakes, and in that way reminiscent of older English and American characterizations of black slave dialects.[17] From the moment Rowling introduces him, it is obvious that Dobby can reason and make independent choices; his first act in the books, as described above, is to make a choice against his master. He, like all house-elves, has the capacity to perform "powerful magic"—although the laws of the wizard world prevent him from exercising that power.[18] Later in the series, Dobby shows himself to be capable of the utmost loyalty and heroism; his actions in the final book save Harry, Hermione, Ron, and several others from certain death. Though his devotion to Harry can border on the obsequious, Dobby admires the young wizard because he thinks Harry stands for the marginalized and disenfranchised. Dobby is a house-elf of principle, someone who stands for serious things—even if his tics seem fit for a minstrel show. Dobby is no "natural" slave or inferior, despite what his comic appearances might suggest. With his abilities to reason, use language, make friendships, and choose on behalf of abstract principles, he fits well within Aristotle's definition of a political animal, capable of self-government.[19]

The problem of house-elves is a serious moral and political problem in the *Harry Potter* series, a problem so significant that it prompted one journalist to claim in the month before the final book's release: "The real question demanding resolution in *Harry Potter and the Deathly Hallows*, J.K. Rowling's seventh and final Harry Potter book, is what will happen to the house-elves—the underclass of slave labour that is the collective shame of the wizarding world."[20] Rowling took evident care in crafting this problem of slavery in *Harry Potter*. She introduces it halfway through the series, as a kind of benchmark in what Teresa Malcom has identified as the gradual "loss of illusions about the wizarding society that [Harry] joined with such wide-eyed wonder in the first book."[21] What do we do, Rowling asks us, about the presence of serious injustices—moral wrongs, even—in an otherwise admirable institution or community?

In the last four books of the *Harry Potter* series, once Rowling has intro-
duced the problem of slavery, we encounter multiple modes of response to
this injustice. Specifically, Rowling illustrates three kinds of reactions to the
problem of slavery at Hogwarts: *willful blindness*, *private action*, and *moral engagement*. Rowling demonstrates what each of those options looks like in the
respective actions of the series' three main characters: Ron Weasley, Harry,
and Hermione. Ultimately, Rowling indicates that moral engagement is the
most admirable of these responses to injustice, the mode of response that
corresponds to the greatest wisdom in both theoretical and practical terms.
But even that kind of engagement is not entirely complete on its own. This
teaching leads to further insights that Rowling offers about the nature of
good citizenship—a paramount concern of the *Harry Potter* books.

Ron's Willful Blindness

Ron offers what is perhaps the most tempting option to most people, most of
the time: *willful blindness* to an injustice. Throughout the series, Ron makes
the argument that the house-elves are happy. They like to work, he says.
"They. Like. It," he growls to Hermione. "They *like* being enslaved!"[22] Ron
rolls his eyes at the suggestion that there is something morally troublesome
about the house-elves' condition. He refuses even to admit the possibility
that the house-elves might benefit from better or more equitable treatment.

Ron's position seems to be the most common one in the wizard world;
as one commentator has written, his position "seems to be the sane, mainstream one."[23] His brothers Fred and George spend a lot of time getting the
house-elves in the Hogwarts kitchen to make them food. "We've met them,
and they're *happy*," George says. "They think they've got the best job in the
world."[24] Few students at Hogwarts are interested in fighting for the cause
of house-elf liberation. Even the loveable Hogwarts groundskeeper, Hagrid,
says much the same thing: "It's in their nature ter look after humans, that's
what they like, see? Yeh'd be makin' 'em unhappy ter take away their work,
an' insultin' 'em if you tried ter pay 'em."[25] Hagrid's position seems to be the
most surprising, since he—a half-giant who has been discriminated against
by human wizards for all of his life—tends to have sympathy for creatures
that most wizards find disgusting. But on this count, Hagrid's position is the
norm.

If willful blindness to the condition of the house-elves is the norm in
the wizard world, that may be because the majority of wizards come from
long-standing wizard families. They have not lived in any other way, on any
other terms, for generations. (Rowling emphasizes this in all seven books by

describing the many ways in which these wizards become incompetent in the world that is familiar to us: the "muggle," or non-magical, world.) The Weasley family is a typical wizard family, with connections in the wizard world that go back for generations. As such, they associate house-elves with wealth and standing. When Harry first asks about house-elves, the Weasley boys tell him right away that people who own house-elves are always rich and from old wizard families. "Yeah, Mum's always wishing we had a house-elf to do the ironing," says George Weasley. "House-elves come with big old man- ors and castles and places like that: you wouldn't catch one in our house."[26] When the Weasleys talk about house-elves, in other words, they focus on the conventional associations they have with house-elves—wealth, ancestry, history—and not on the status of house-elves in more fundamental terms.

The Weasleys, like most others in the wizard world, have accepted the conventional terms of wizard life. They take what is given by convention as what is right; they take what is as what should be. By describing this phenomenon, and by demonstrating how common the acceptance of the house-elves' condition is, Rowling points to an old truth: it may be easiest to overlook or neglect injustice—to inhabit a position of willful blindness— when it is familiar, when it is woven into the fabric of your everyday life. Convention is powerful. As the saying goes, "custom is king."[27] For humans, whether gifted with magical powers or not, what we see around us can seem to be more powerful or permanent or normal than it actually is. So it is easy to take what is given by convention and ascribe to that given a natural or fixed status—especially if you are not aware that things are done differently in other places. Tellingly, the only Weasley who says he agrees with the proposition that the house-elves need to be treated better is Mr. Weasley, the one member of the Weasley family who spends a significant amount of time investigating and exploring the non-wizard world.[28] But for most wizards, whose lives have a certain provincial quality, the ordinary course of action is to bow to established convention—and in doing so, to tolerate the enslave- ment of house-elves.

Harry and Hermione, both having grown up in the non-magical world, are more bothered by the status of house-elves than any of the Weasleys are. They see more clearly that there is something amiss about the way that hu- man wizards and witches treat house-elves, and about the way that the house- elves treat themselves. Neither is accustomed, by custom, to the anxiety and violence that surround house-elves, and so neither falls prey to the belief that the house-elves are happy in their situation. Neither is willfully blind to the house-elves' condition. Nor does either believe that even if the house- elves are unhappy, nothing can be done to undo such a long-established practice. Because they are both in the wizard world but not entirely of it, Harry and Hermione stand in a special critical position, a position similar to the one Dorothy occupies in *The Wizard of Oz*. As Bonnie Honig has observed, Dorothy's position as an outsider in Oz means that she is "unsocialized by the reign of terror that has molded the locals into servile abjection," which means that she is both more able to see the oppressions of Oz and to "(wittingly or unwittingly)" work to change them.[29] Harry and Hermione do not view the house-elves through the lens of custom, which means that they may see more clearly and lend some support to the undoing of that custom.

Oddly enough, then, Harry and Hermione resemble the ancient Greek *theoros*—the theorist—who gained wisdom about governance by traveling from his home city to other cities. The ancient Greeks saw the *theoros* as serving a valuable public function because they understood that it is often easier to see what is good and bad about a city when one has some outside basis for comparison.[30] Too, the *theoros* might—through exposure to multiple kinds of cities—have a better sense of what is conventional within a city versus what is natural. Where Ron Weasley and others who have never seen outside the wizarding world take house-elf enslavement as necessitated by nature, Harry and Hermione properly identify it as a matter of convention. But even though they share that basic recognition in common, Harry and Hermione respond to house-elf enslavement in very different ways.

Harry's Private Action

Harry is troubled by the way that Dobby mutilates himself—especially when he figures out that Dobby's self-flagellation is tied up with Dobby's attempts to help protect Harry from danger. Eventually Harry responds to that house-elf's repeatedly expressed desire to be free, and at the end of *The Chamber of Secrets* Harry liberates Dobby. To do this, he tricks Dobby's owner Lucius Malfoy—with some prompting by Dobby—into tossing aside a sock that the house-elf catches. According to custom, if a master gives a piece of clothing to his house-elf, that house-elf is emancipated. Dobby is overcome with gratitude, and for the rest of the series he is a fierce and passionate ally of Harry's.

But even though Harry cannot stomach the violent behaviors that accompany Dobby's enslavement, and even though he sees exactly how happy Dobby is to be free, and even though he knows that there are hundreds of other house-elves still living in bondage, Harry does not act further. His willingness to act on behalf of house-elves does not extend past that single house-elf who did him good service. He is not interested, for the most part, in liberating all house-elves—just the one who helped him out (and who happens to be in the charge of the Malfoys, a family that Harry despises more than all others).

Faced with the question of house-elves, Harry gives only a partial answer. He is willing, on certain terms, to manumit his own slaves but goes no farther. Harry is the leader who responds to slavery on the personal level but refuses to confront slavery as a moral or political matter. Harry responds to the crisis of slavery with *private action* but nothing more. He does not seem to see the problems of house-elves going beyond the problem of house-elves whom he happens to know and like. The fact that Harry lacks sensitivity to the plight of house-elves in thoroughgoing terms cannot be doubted, for in the fifth book of the series Harry comes into ownership of a house-elf, Kreacher. Harry does not like Kreacher and is convinced (largely by Dumbledore) that Kreacher, if freed, would become his adversary. So Harry decides not to disown Kreacher; instead, he sends him to work in the kitchens of Hogwarts. Although Harry has understandable reasons for worrying about what Kreacher would do if he were set free, his refusal to give up control of Kreacher suggests that he does not really see house-elf liberation as a moral imperative. (To be fair, he does not want anything to do with Kreacher, but that is because Harry does not like him—not because he objects to the idea of being a slave-owner.)[31] For Harry, the condition of house-elves is background noise, a frequency to which he only tunes in when it serves his own cause to do so. It is worth noting, too, that at the end of the series Kreacher, like Dobby, turns out to do great things for the people who show him kindness; he is not the inevitably hostile force that Harry assumes him to be.

Rowling links Harry's habit of seeing the house-elves in this highly privatized and episodic way with a broader lack of wisdom. More than once, Harry makes serious misjudgments about the house-elves. For instance, early on Harry fails to see that Kreacher's loyalty to the Black family is not entirely a matter of choice; more broadly, he does not understand exactly why the house-elves are the way they are. He only sees them on the surfaces. (Harry is not worried about Dobby's status on a moral level; he's worried about Dobby's surface-level, self-abusing behavior. He is merely interested in stopping the most evident, physical violence.) Harry neglects to see how long tradition and history have shaped the house-elves and their behavior.[32] Harry's understanding of the house-elves reveals his tendency to see only at the surface of things, neglecting more thoroughgoing modes of understanding.

For the most part, except when it benefits him personally to do otherwise, Harry avoids the problem of house-elf slavery.[33] Although many in the wizard world think of him as someone who is on the side of the downtrodden—and indeed, Harry does befriend some, like Hagrid, who exist at the margins of magical society—Harry's "sense of caring and willingness to side with the less fortunate are limited," as Rebecca Skulnick and Jesse Goodman have described.[34] As in other matters, Harry tends to be somewhat self-focused and "narrow-minded" when it comes to the question of house-elves, needing the wisdom of a friend to give him "any hope of getting a larger perspective on things."[35]

Interestingly, Rowling has said in interviews subsequent to the publication of the *Harry Potter* series that it was thinking like Harry's that brought house-elves to Hogwarts in the first place. As she tells it, one of the founders of the school, Helga Hufflepuff, was dismayed by the way certain house-elves were treated. So she took a few of them to Hogwarts, with the idea that she could at least make those few house-elves happier—by enslaving them at the school, where she could try to make sure those slaves did not suffer violent abuse. But Rowling dismisses what Hufflepuff did, saying that while it was progressive thinking "at the time"—and "we are talking about over a thousand years ago"—the Hogwarts founder should not be praised too much. "There was no kind of activism there," Rowling says, no vision or courage to say: "'Here's an idea. Let's, let's free them. Let's pay them.'"[36] Hufflepuff's way of approaching house-elf slavery, like Harry's, is inherently limited and—since it is clear in the books that even Hogwarts house-elves sometimes suffer physical abuse and mistreatment—is, on its own terms, not a success.[37] While such private and individualized approaches to injustice may achieve something on a small scale or in the short term, they do little to slow or halt the perpetuation of a generally violent and cruel order.

Hermione's Moral Engagement

Only Hermione sees the widespread injustice of house-elf slavery as a moral problem and confronts it with *moral engagement* and action. Hermione's astuteness on this matter may come from her much-discussed intellectual prowess; she is by far the best student at Hogwarts. It may come from the fact, as discussed before, that she did not grow up in the wizard world. It may also be that Hermione is particularly sensitive to those who are marginalized in the wizarding world; as the child of non-magical parents, she is often derided for being a "mudblood."

In any case, Hermione right away recognizes the enslavement of the house-elves for what it is. "You know, house-elves get a *very* raw deal!" she tells Ron. "It's slavery, that's what it is!" When Ron responds with his standard line—that the house-elves are happy—Hermione does not back down.

"It's people like *you*, Ron," she tells him, "who prop up rotten and unjust systems, just because they're too lazy." Also right away, Hermione understands that the enslavement of house-elves demands some kind of collective action. "Why doesn't anyone *do* something about it?" she asks.[38]

Once she realizes that no one else has taken or will take action to liberate the house-elves, Hermione does so herself. She forms the Society for the Promotion of Elfish Welfare (S.P.E.W.) and harangues Harry and Ron until they join. The short-term aims of S.P.E.W., Hermione explains, "are to secure house-elves fair wages and working conditions," and its "long-term aims include changing the law about non-wand use, and trying to get an elf into the Department for the Regulation and Control of Magical Creatures, because they're shockingly underrepresented."[39] Throughout the rest of the novels, Hermione is constantly working to expand the rolls of her organization and reminding people at every turn that the house-elves are enslaved—and that the everyday lives of Hogwarts students feed on that enslavement. She also articulates the important fact that since the house-elf enslavement is a moral problem, sustained by laws as well as custom, it demands a wholesale and total remedy—a remedy at the public as well as private levels. (Even if all house-elf masters privately liberated their house-elves, the laws allowing house-elf slavery would still be on the books, and the practice of house-elf slavery would likely continue.)

Implicit in the way that Hermione approaches the issue of house-elf enslavement is a rejection of the "happy slave" argument, or what might be the more nuanced version of that argument: that the problem isn't that house-elf enslavement is cruel in and of itself (because the house-elves do like to serve others), but rather the problem is that *some* masters treat their house-elves cruelly. Someone making that argument might claim that the solution to the cruelty of house-elf slavery is not to end that slavery, but rather—as Helga Hufflepuff did—take slaves out of the hands of cruel masters. At Hogwarts, George Weasley says, the house-elves "think they've got the best job in the world," and most of them are not mistreated, and as a result "they're *happy*."[40] For George and others, the case of the house-elf Winky proves their point; after Winky, the Crouch family house-elf, is punished for a crime she did not commit by being set free, she develops an addiction to butterbeer and spends all day "screaming with misery."[41] If Winky were really fit for freedom, George and others ask, why does freedom make her so unhappy? Wasn't she happier being a slave?

To that, Hermione insists that Winky has only become what she is because she is the product of long and unrelenting social conditioning. The house-elves are only "happy" slaves, Hermione argues, because "they're uneducated and brainwashed!"[42] It is hard to argue that it is in the *nature* of house-elves to be so servile, Hermione points out, since their service is enforced by *conventional* laws—the house-elves are forbidden to own wands; the house-elves are forbidden to perform their own "powerful magic"—that greatly restrict and restrain their natural abilities. It is hard to believe that "clause three of the Code of Wand Use," which prohibits house-elves from carrying or using a wand, would have been necessary if all the house-elves wanted to do was serve human masters kindly, without rights or pay.[43] (This argument even leaves out the obvious fact that not all the house-elves *are* happy: both Dobby and Kreacher resent, at times, the masters who own them.)

As Karen Brown writes, all signs in the *Harry Potter* series point to two conclusions: first, that the house-elves "were not always enslaved," and second, that "contrary to popular wizarding beliefs, it is not in their 'nature' to be as subservient as they are now."[44] If that is the case, Hermione's explanation—that, in Brown's words, house-elf slavery is a "social condition" based on a "mindset that is acquired and normalized over long periods of time by both the oppressed and the oppressor"—makes great sense.[45] But Hermione's argument is a daring one to put forth within the society where that conditioning and normalization have been taking place for more than a thousand years—and in the presence of house-elves like Winky, who resist her efforts on their behalf.[46] Hermione is not just morally astute; she is brave enough to be morally engaged.

It is Hermione's relentless and fearless speaking of truth to power—her capacity for Socratic *parrhesia* (speaking frank and honest speech, unintimidated by power)—that forces other wizards to confront the truth, again and again and again.[47] She knows that slavery, like any serious injustice, may brainwash both the slaves and the masters, both the recipients and the doers of injustice.[48] To confront such an embedded habit of self-delusion and illusion, Hermione demonstrates the need to call it out for what it really is, over and over again. Hermione is willing to become a nuisance to other people in service to a right cause, to continue to promote membership in S.P.E.W. even when many of her suitemates in Griffyndor House regard "the whole thing as a joke."[49] Hermione is willing to risk personal relationships for the sake of moral right. As Sarah Zettel has put it:

> Hermione publicly and unashamedly pursues the course she knows to be right, even when it costs her her friends or the regard of male authority figures. She is not deterred by the prevailing opinion of society. If she is not initially effective, she tries other methods to achieve her right ends. She is, in the main, highly confident in her own understanding, and that confidence frequently

pays off. She forcefully argues her points and does not back down when ignored. She brings every weapon she's got into her particular fight, and she succeeds, even if it takes a while.[50]

Hermione is the model of a morally serious citizen, who sees the connection between individual suffering and public rule, and who endeavors to make that connection evident to those around her. Her political engagement is guided by a serious and critical moral sensibility, not to mention passion and copious research.

Rowling makes clear that Hermione's willingness to confront house-elf slavery as a moral problem gives her multiple kinds of wisdom that other characters in the books lack. On this issue not only does Hermione have a kind of moral vision that escapes her fellow wizards, but also she has a kind of prudential vision that they do not. Hermione is the only character brave enough to see—and say—that the cruelty that wizards regularly inflict upon house-elves damages not only those elves but also their masters, and the cause for which their masters fight. Other people ignore her when she says this, but she turns out to be correct. After Harry's godfather, Sirius Black, is killed because his house-elf Kreacher tells his enemies where to find him, Hermione is tough but fair in her response. "I've said all along that wizards would pay for how they treat house-elves," she tells Harry and Ron. "Well, Voldemort did . . . and so did Sirius."[51]

When others, particularly Harry, do not understand why house-elves behave the way they do, Hermione does—precisely because she understands what it means for them to be enslaved. This is most clear as Harry tries to come to terms with Kreacher's behavior in the last book of the series. "I don't understand you, Kreacher," says Harry. "Voldemort tried to kill you, Regulus died to bring Voldemort down, but you were still happy to betray Sirius to Voldemort? You were happy to go to Narcissa and Bellatrix, and pass information to Voldemort through them ..." As Harry trails off in confusion, Hermione interjects, "Harry, Kreacher doesn't think like that. He's a slave; house-elves are used to bad, even brutal treatment; what Voldemort did to Kreacher wasn't that far out of the common way. What do wizard wars mean to an elf like Kreacher? He's loyal to people who are kind to him."[52] Hermione turns out to be right about this; in the last book of the series, Kreacher turns out to be nice to Harry—after Harry treats him well, less like a slave and more like a friend.[53] That Hermione sees the enslavement of house-elves in moral terms—and that she is willing to see all the terrible implications of that enslavement—means that she has insight that almost all other characters in the book lack. Hermione *notices* the house-elves in a meaningful way and understands them as fundamentally equal beings, a quality that throughout the series is linked not only to theoretical wisdom but also practical success.[54]

It is important to say, too, that when Hermione discovers to her horror that she is complicit in the enslavement of at least a hundred house-elves, she does not do what many morally sensitive people might do in her situation. Hermione, upon discovering that Hogwarts has slaves, does not leave the school. She does not try to wash her own hands of the problem by exiting. The only time Hermione even comes close to such a gesture is right after she finds out about the Hogwarts house-elves, and she refuses to eat the latest meal that they have prepared. But in general, Hermione chooses fight over flight—or in Albert Hirschmann's terms, she chooses voice over exit. Although it would not be difficult for her to exit Hogwarts—Hermione is smart enough to attend any other school she chooses—she does not withdraw from her relationship with the school. Rather, she chooses to voice her complaints, trying to repair and improve the school by speaking about what is wrong. In this way, as she is in other ways throughout the series, Hermione is a model of loyalty.[55] She is loyal to her friends and loyal to her community—but never wholly uncritical of either. She is loyal to those less fortunate and to the cause of justice. To that extent, she is a model of good citizenship.

And ultimately Hermione changes both Ron and Harry's minds about the situation of the house elves. The more Harry hears about house-elves, the more he feels "sympathy with the society Hermione had set up, S.P.E.W."[56] It is a significant testament to Hermione's efforts that Harry associates his changing feelings about house-elf slavery with *her* name and *her* society. It is also a significant change in Harry's way of thinking, an intellectual shift that Marc Bousquet calls his "most dramatic challenge" in the books. The "evolution of his feelings toward the situation of the house-elves," Bousquet writes, "takes place so slowly that for several installments of the series it is hard to credit Rowling with what appears to have been her ultimate intention, for Harry to move toward the greater sympathy with their situation evidenced by Hermione."[57] When eventually that change does happen, it is largely if not entirely due to Hermione's persistence.

In Ron's case, the change to Hermione's way of thinking is more sudden, but no less due to Hermione. When, in the battle at the end of the final book, Ron remembers the house-elves and says to Harry and Hermione that "we can't order them to die for us," it is clear that his recognition of the house-elves owes itself almost entirely to Hermione's incessant proddings and pleadings.[58] No wonder that this is the moment when Hermione finally chooses to kiss Ron, silencing him in mid-sentence.

Shortly thereafter, Kreacher leads a battalion of knife-brandishing house-elves into the final Battle of Hogwarts to join with Harry and his friends against the evil Lord Voldemort. The house-elves' willingness to fight is meaningful because it is freely chosen. Their actions are significant because they are self-governed. In the end, all the house-elves demonstrate that they are capable not merely of being free, but of using their freedom for great ends. In the end, they *choose* to take great risks on behalf of Hogwarts, echoing Dumbledore's teaching that "it is our choices ... that show what we truly are, far more than our abilities."[59] As Hermione understands, to deny someone the ability to make those choices is to deny them who they really are and what they really can be. It is also to deny yourself potential allies and friends. One must approach others, always, as equals—or even as beings who might have a kind of magic that you do not.

Rowling's Citizenship

The story of the house-elves is a story that J.K. Rowling has said she regards as crucial. (Among other things, she strong-armed the *Harry Potter* filmmakers to include Kreacher in the fifth movie, although they did not want to do so.)[60] That Rowling sees moral engagement as preferable to both willful blindness and private action seems evident and perhaps not all that controversial. But she also includes some important lessons about political action that get closer to the heart of things.

For one, it goes almost without saying that Ron, Harry, and Hermione are all fairly likeable people. Though each has their limitations—Ron can be whiny, Harry can be thoughtless, and Hermione can be self-righteous—they are all good-hearted young people who maintain strong friendships. But the fact that they respond unevenly to the crisis of slavery in the *Harry Potter* series signals an important political truth: being a likeable person does not make you a good citizen.

In fact, a constant theme in Rowling's work is that good citizenship often demands being unlikeable—or risking that other people will not like you. Good citizenship often demands being relentless, being unforgiving, being a nuisance to other people. The most conspicuous example of this is Dumbledore's insistence, in the fourth and fifth books of the series, that Lord Voldemort has returned. When Cornelius Fudge, the Minister of Magic, refuses to give credence to the Dark Lord's return, Dumbledore stops any pretense of being polite. "If your determination to shut your eyes will carry you as far as this, Cornelius," he says, "we have reached a parting of the ways."[61] When Dumbledore makes this proclamation, he knows that it will come at some cost to himself—placing oneself at odds with the Minister of Magic is surely an ill-considered career move—but he does so because he knows the grander cause is more important.

When it comes to house-elf slavery, Hermione is fearless in her quest, willing to annoy other people in the name of justice and truth. When all others—including the people she loves most—are begging her to tire of pursuing justice for the house-elves, she does not. At one point, Ron asks with evident exasperation when she will give up the cause. "I'm going to give it up when house-elves have decent wages and working conditions," she says. "You know, I'm starting to think it's time for more direct action."[62] Hermione stands firm, even when everyone around her—even when the people she loves—roll their eyes and treat her like a joke, even when she has to risk alienating her friends (and in this case her evident romantic interest). She exemplifies the bravery that Dumbledore lauds when he says, early in the series, that "it takes a great deal of bravery to stand up to our enemies, but just as much to stand up to our friends."[63]

That this is a paramount teaching of *Harry Potter*—being a "nice" person does not make you a good citizen—is made clear in one of the series' other great storylines. Severus Snape is the unctuous, scowling potions teacher at Hogwarts who never misses an opportunity to make Harry's everyday life more difficult. Snape is not a likeable or "nice" person, and it seems from the stories of his youth that he never has been. But by the end of the series we know that Snape is willing to make the ultimate sacrifices for justice. His actions call to mind the truth that for we social creatures, sometimes the ultimate sacrifice is not giving up your life, but giving up your good reputation—your "sacred honor," in the words of the signers of the Declaration of Independence—and your easy sociability with others.

One of the great mistakes in judgment that Harry makes—and he makes it over and over again—is thinking that because he and Snape do not like each other personally, they must also be political enemies. He assumes that because Snape is not nice to him, Snape must be on the side of evil in the cosmic battle—even when Dumbledore assures him, and he does so in virtually every book, that Snape is on the side of good.[64] (Many readers, before the last books in the series came out, made the same error.)[65] But Harry neglects to understand that in politics, just because you do not like someone does not mean that she is not on your side. So, too, is the opposite true. Just because you are close with someone does not mean that they are on your side when it comes to political or public matters. Harry fails to see what Hannah Arendt says the ancient Greeks understood: that political friendship—the engagement in "sober and cool" discourse about common things—is distinct from the "sentimental" or "intimate" friendship of the private sphere.[66] You do not have to like your political allies, and you do not have to hate your political enemies.

Still, when it comes to Hermione's quest for house-elf liberation, it is clear that in some ways friendship does matter. Though they do it grudgingly, Harry and Ron are the first Hogwarts students to buy S.P.E.W. badges, and Hermione assumes some level of support from them. Their willingness to endure Hermione's "vociferous" speeches on behalf of the house-elves probably help embolden her—or, at least, prevent her from feeling the full brunt of mockery that most other students send in her direction.[67] Although she is willing to risk her friendships as she fights for the cause of house-elf liberation, Ron and Harry do not abandon her—and their willingness to stay by her side probably matters. To that extent, this storyline fits well within the series' broader themes. Throughout the series, each member of the trio is willing to take tremendous risks on behalf of their friendship, but it is also their friendship that enables them to take tremendous risks. Hermione's bravery in confronting house-elf slavery is both a matter of her internal moral conviction and the loyalty shown to her by friends. Even a little loyalty can make a big difference.

In a somewhat related fashion, the house-elf storyline reinforces another political theme of the series: because every human being is an imperfect creature, a healthy political society depends on the active engagement of many members working in concert with each other. No one person can do everything alone—even if that person is as able as Albus Dumbledore. Besides Hermione, Dumbledore is the only character who seems to understand the true nature of the house-elves' enslavement. Like Hermione, he speaks about their enslavement as a matter of convention and not nature. For instance, he tells Harry that "Kreacher is what he has been made by wizards"—in other words, that house-elves have been conditioned to behave the way they do. He laments Sirius's mistreatment of Kreacher, saying that Sirius never "saw Kreacher as a being with feelings as acute as a human's." Sirius died, Dumbledore informs Harry, because "he regarded him as a servant unworthy of much interest or notice." According to Dumbledore, "We wizards have mistreated and abused our fellows for too long, and now we are reaping our reward."[68] Moreover, after the house-elves Dobby and Winky become free, Dumbledore begins to pay them a fair wage and tells them they are allowed to criticize him if they want.

So the question has to be raised: Why doesn't Dumbledore free the house-elves himself? The simple answer is that he can't. It is not within Dumbledore's immediate power to free *all* house-elves—to effect their political liberation—so all he could do would be to free the Hogwarts house-elves. But then he would be freeing them into a world where, because of legal and social prejudice, they have no chance of procuring gainful employment outside the Hogwarts gates. He would in effect be taking a private action on the model of Helga Hufflepuff and Harry Potter—and Dumbledore is smart enough to see the serious limitations of that approach.

And throughout the series, Dumbledore is engaged in his own moral and political battles, both with Lord Voldemort and the Ministry of Magic, each of which demands immediate and almost total attention. For Dumbledore, all other political concerns take second billing. (It is because he fears a freed Kreacher would give help to Voldemort's Death Eaters that Dumbledore tells Harry not to free him.) Dumbledore, like all human beings, is a creature who is limited: limited in time, limited in energy, and limited in opportunity. Despite his extraordinary capacities, Dumbledore is not superhuman and thus not capable of fighting every noble cause by himself. (He is not even able to complete the fight of his life, against Lord Voldemort, without the dedication of the other members of the Order of the Phoenix, the Hogwarts staff, and the students in Dumbledore's Army—and even then the fight is not completed within Dumbledore's lifetime.) Still, Dumbledore welcomes and encourages Hermione's abolitionist efforts, teaching her and giving her support, which is his own way of contributing to the liberation of the house-elves. Given the many moral and political responsibilities on his own shoulders, Dumbledore *must* entrust the heavy lifting to Hermione's shoulders.

One of the great themes of the *Harry Potter* series is that as individuals, human beings are incomplete—no matter how many magical powers we have. As individuals, Ron and Harry and Hermione each remain incomplete in some way; their faults get in the way of their strengths from time to time. But through their friendship, they are able overcome their individual weaknesses to a certain extent—and it is clear throughout the series that all three have to work together, and rely on many others, to defeat Lord Voldemort. None—not even Harry—could do it alone. Though he is laudable in many ways, Albus Dumbledore is an imperfect and incomplete being, requiring others to help him realize not only a better society, but also his better self. And even Hermione's moral vision is incomplete; she dismisses the legal subordination of goblins as unimportant, even though their position in the wizarding world is almost as tenuous as that of the house-elves.[69] Hermione will require some more education, from someone else, to enlighten her.

Because Rowling teaches that human beings would be incomplete even if we were to have magical powers, her books emphasize that the need for *politics* in human life will never disappear. Even magic could not make human beings complete, and so politics—the public negotiation of the terms of human life—will always be part of human existence. For as Arlene Saxonhouse has written, "The city arises to satisfy our incompletion, our failure to reach our *eidos*, our form, our own."[70] And if politics is a fixed feature of human life, a site of enduring public contestation among incomplete beings who must negotiate many of the terms by which we live, then dedicated citizenship is essential. Throughout the *Harry Potter* series, Rowling returns again and again to the necessity of good citizenship, a citizenship that is both a way of acting and a way of being in the world that is based on love, trust, and courage.

Even if human beings had all the science and technology in the world—even if we had magic!—we could not conquer the eternal problems of meanness, cruelty, and injustice. Even magic would not allow us to transcend these permanent fixtures of human life, and our need to respond to them in kind. Throughout the series, Rowling suggests that humans must respond to those threats with love, loyalty, and sacrifice. No matter what level of technological mastery human beings acquire, Rowling teaches, those non-technological forces are the most powerful in human life. Love, as Dumbledore reminds Harry over and again, transcends more technical magic.

Dobby's Sacrifice

The story of the house-elves is key to that grander narrative. That fact is realized on the biggest scale when the Hogwarts house-elves, of their own volition, take an important role in the final Battle of Hogwarts. But it is most poignantly realized in Dobby's final act—an act of great courage taken on behalf of a good cause. Dobby dies while performing one of the most heroic deeds in any of the books: He sneaks into the Malfoy Manor, where Harry and Ron and Hermione among others are trapped and being tortured, and he rescues all of them. Critically, to do so, Dobby uses some of the powerful house-elf magic—the power of apparation—that he would not have been permitted to use had he not been emancipated. He yells to the dark wizards, who are astounded to see a house-elf use such sophisticated magic, "Dobby has no master! Dobby is a free elf, and Dobby has come to save Harry Potter and his friends!"[71] But just as he has set them all free, Dobby is struck by a knife thrown by the evil Bellatrix Lestrange—a knife that she had aimed at

Harry. Dobby dies while saving Harry, and Dobby dies from a weapon that was meant for Harry. Dobby bleeds in Harry's place.

Dobby's sacrifice of himself, on behalf of the common cause, makes him an exemplar of virtue, as these books have us understand what virtue is. When Dumbledore says that the one thing Voldemort fails to understand is "the precise and terrible power of that sacrifice," he is speaking of Lily Potter's willingness to give up her life for Harry, but he might as well be talking about Dobby.[72] Again and again, in these books Rowling heralds the willingness to sacrifice oneself for others or the common good as the supreme human capacity—and it is precisely that capacity that Dobby, the house-elf, illustrates. Dobby shows exactly the same courage, the same considered willingness to lay down his life on behalf of a friend, that the human heroes in this series show. And without Dobby's willingness to take that ultimate risk, Voldemort never would have been defeated.

Critically, Dobby never would have been able to make that sacrifice—to be that virtuous creature—if he hadn't been free. Harry recognizes this, and though the stakes of the moment are high, and Harry has the weight of the wizarding world bearing down upon him, he insists on holding a real funeral for Dobby. Harry digs Dobby's grave with a shovel—"I want to do it properly," he says, "not by magic." He digs "with a kind of fury, relishing the manual work, glorying in the non-magic of it, for every drop of his sweat and every blister felt like a gift to the elf who had saved their lives." Harry closes Dobby's eyes, puts him in the grave, and writes: "Here Lies Dobby, a Free Elf."[73]

In these books, freedom is inseparable from virtue, since—as Rowling indicates again and again—the ultimate expression of virtue is the willingness to sacrifice oneself for others, and the willingness to sacrifice oneself for others only has meaning when it is freely chosen. In the *Harry Potter* series, Rowling uses Dobby to exemplify the relationship she sees between virtue, freedom, and citizenship. True virtue *requires* freedom, since virtuous behavior needs to be chosen freely. And that freedom, in turn, turns on citizenship and public recognition. "Freedom is exclusively located in the political realm," in the realm of choice beyond necessity, as Arendt puts it.[74]

As Rowling tells it, Dobby dies a free elf not merely because Harry Potter freed him in the second book of the series but because Dobby used that freedom to fight—and die—for the freedom of others. As the house-elves' story suggests, when we allow our actions to be dictated by the fear of death, or the fear of a bad reputation, or fear of the unknown, we are letting ourselves be mastered, letting ourselves be enslaved. But when we love others enough to be brave for them—when we love enough to secure and use *our own* freedom to then try to secure that freedom for others, to try to see to it that, as Dumbledore puts it, "fewer souls are maimed, fewer families are torn apart"—only then are we truly free.[75] That is how, in the *Harry Potter* series at least, creatures demonstrate their virtue and their good citizenship and their love of freedom. We only become free, we learn in these books, when we decide that life on certain terms is *not* worth living—that sometimes it is worth risking our lives for a good greater than ourselves. That is what Hermione does when she seeks the liberation of the house-elves. That is what the many members of the Order of the Phoenix and Dumbledore's Army do when they fight Voldemort. And that is what Dobby does when he commits that final, daring rescue.

In the end, it turns out that—just as the defenders of house-elf slavery argued all along—the desire to serve others *is* in Dobby the house-elf's nature. But it also turns out that Dobby is most fully able to realize his desire to serve others not in a condition of enforced servitude, but rather in a condition of freedom. Dobby serves others—serves the common good—more as a free house-elf than he possibly could have done while enslaved. Likewise, the other house-elves do their most significant service to others when they choose, at the end of the series, to join in the battle against Voldemort. They do more for others in the last few pages of the final book—*after* they have been freed—than they did in the preceding six and a half volumes. So it turns out that the strongest argument voiced on behalf of house-elf slavery—that house-elves enjoy serving others—in fact justifies their liberation. House-elves, who enjoy the choice to serve others, turn out to be an example that human beings would do well to follow.

The human wizards in the *Harry Potter* series are enviable for their magical abilities, although their ability to perpetuate and ignore significant injustice is a reminder that, morally speaking, they are not superior to muggles. They have enslaved house-elves and subordinated all sorts of other magical creatures—goblins and werewolves, most notably, but perhaps even owls—who may well be capable of self-governance. And although at the end of the *Harry Potter* series the house-elves have been liberated, those other creatures remain oppressed (and unhappily so).[76] Although Rowling proclaims at the end of the series' final book that "all was well," it may be only a relative statement.[77] Things are better, surely, than they have been—but as the *Harry Potter* books make clear, human society is never entirely well. Injustice is present in all human societies, so that the willingness to engage with and serve the cause of justice is a permanent necessity in human life. As Dumbledore tells Harry, "It is important to fight, and fight again, and keep fighting, for only then can evil be kept at bay, though never quite eradicated."[78]

Notes

For their help and comments on the ideas that became this chapter, I would like to thank Jeffrey Becker, Oona Eisenstadt, Kathleen Fitzpatrick, Margaret Hrezo, Nancy Riley McWilliams, Wilson Carey McWilliams, James Morone, Alison Noll, John M. Parrish, John Seery, George Thomas, and Mariah Zeisberg. I would also like to thank Nina Vertlib and the Pomona Student Union for arranging the event at which I first presented a version of this paper.

1. J.K. Rowling, *Harry Potter and the Sorcerer's Stone* (New York: Scholastic, Inc., 1997), 111.
2. Perry L. Glanzer, "Harry Potter's Provocative Moral World," *Phi Delta Kappan* 89, no. 7 (March 2008): 525-528.
3. When I have presented this argument before, to people singly or in groups, I have been astonished by how readily readers are inclined to take the position that the house-elves are not really slaves, despite the incontrovertible evidence that they are.
4. Elaine Ostry, "Accepting Mudbloods: The Ambivalent Social Vision of J.K. Rowling's Fairy Tales," in *Reading Harry Potter*, ed. Giselle Liza Anatol (Greenwood Publishing Group, 2003), 89-102.
5. I do find it plausible—as I have heard argued—that Rowling herself did not take the plight of the house-elves seriously until she wrote the fourth book in the series (the first book she wrote *after* the series became a popular hit), and that she felt compelled later, perhaps as a result of reader response, to approach the situation of the house-elves with a greater degree of moral seriousness. Still, I am not sure that alternate interpretation of authorial intent would much change the content of this argument.
6. J.K Rowling, *Harry Potter and the Goblet of Fire* (New York: Scholastic, Inc., 2000), 238.
7. Ibid., 182.
8. Ibid., 213.
9. In many of her interviews, Rowling has said this point-blank. "The house-elves are slaves," she told a BBC interviewer. See "The Full JK Rowling Interview," conducted by Gillian MacKay, <http://news.bbc.co.uk/cbbcnews/hi/newsid_4690000/newsid_4690800/4690885.stm> (18 July 2005).
10. Rowling, *Harry Potter and the Goblet of Fire*, 538-539.
11. Ibid.
12. J.K. Rowling, *Harry Potter and the Order of the Phoenix* (New York: Scholastic, Inc., 2003), 76.
13. Ibid., 109-110.
14. Hokey, the only house-elf I do not discuss further in this chapter, is framed and convicted for a murder she did not commit. Dumbledore emphasizes to Harry, when discussing Hokey's case, that the Ministry was "predisposed to suspect Hokey"

because she was a house-elf. It is Hokey's story that makes Harry begin to feel "sympathy with the society Hermione had set up, S.P.E.W." See Rowling, *Harry Potter and the Half-Blood Prince* (New York: Scholastic, Inc., 2005), 439.

15. J.K. Rowling, *Harry Potter and the Chamber of Secrets* (New York: Scholastic, Inc., 1999), 14ff.

16. Ibid., 13.

17. Brycchan Carey, "Hermione and the House-Elves: The Literary and Historical Contexts of J.K. Rowling's Anti-Slavery Campaign," in *Reading Harry Potter*, ed. Giselle Liza Anatol (Greenwood Publishing Group, 2003), 103-116.

18. Rowling, *Harry Potter and the Chamber of Secrets*, 28.

19. For Aristotle, in fact, it would be enough that Dobby demonstrates the ability to reason independently; the natural slave is one who "participates in reason enough to apprehend, but not to have." See Aristotle, *The Politics and the Constitution of Athens*, ed. Stephen Everson (Cambridge: Cambridge University Press), 17 [1254].

20. Jacob Saulwick, "We Muggles Yearn To Escape Economic Reality," in the *Sydney Morning Herald* (July 6, 2007), 16.

21. Teresa Malcom, "Of House-Elves and Children's Tales," *National Catholic Reporter*, 3 August 2007, 14-15.

22. Rowling, *Harry Potter and the Goblet of Fire*, 224.

23. Farah Mendlesohn, "Crowning the King," in *The Ivory Tower and Harry Potter*, ed. Lana Whited (Columbia, MO: University of Missouri Press, 2002), 159-181.

24. Rowling, *Harry Potter and the Goblet of Fire*, 239.

25. Ibid., 265.

26. Rowling, *Harry Potter and the Chamber of Secrets*, 29.

27. Herodotus, *The History*, trans. David Grene (Chicago: University of Chicago Press, 1987), 228 [3.38].

28. Rowling introduces Mr. Weasley's support for house-elf liberation in passing. During a frantic scene at the beginning of the fourth book, Hermione is yelling about the treatment of house-elves, calling it "disgusting." Mr. Weasley hushes her, saying that he agrees with her position but that "now is not the time to discuss elf rights." See Rowling, *Harry Potter and the Goblet of Fire*, 139.

29. Bonnie Honig, *Democracy and the Foreigner* (Princeton: Princeton University Press, 2003), 16.

30. See Roxanne Euben, "The Comparative Politics of Travel," *parallax* 9 (2003), 18-28.

31. Rowling, *Harry Potter and the Half-Blood Prince*, 52-53.

32. I would like to thank Alison Noll for pointing this out to me.

33. According to one psychological reading of the series, this avoidance falls in line with everything else Harry does: Harry has an "avoidant" attachment style, compared with Ron's "anxious" attachment style, and Hermione's "secure" attachment style. See Wind Goodfriend, "Attachment Styles at Hogwarts: From Infancy to Adulthood," in *The Psychology of Harry Potter*, ed. Neil Mulholland (Dallas: BenBella Books, 2006), 75-90.

34. Rebecca Skulnick and Jesse Goodman, "The Civic Leadership of *Harry Potter*: Agency, Ritual, and Schooling," in *Harry Potter's World*, ed. Elizabeth E. Hellman (New York: RoutledgeFalmer, 2003), 261-278.

35. John Granger, *Unlocking Harry Potter: Five Keys for the Serious Reader* (Wayne, PA: Zossima Press, 2007), 187.

36. Melissa Anelli, et al., "PotterCast 130: The One With J.K. Rowling" <http://pottercast.the-leaky-cauldron.org/transcript/show/166?ordernum=1> (December 17, 2007).

37. To be clear, I am thinking of the way that Professor Slughorn forces Hogwarts house-elves to "test" drinks that he fears are poisoned.

38. Rowling, *Harry Potter and the Goblet of Fire*, 125.

39. Ibid., 225.

40. Ibid., 239.

41. Ibid., 378.

42. Ibid., 239.

43. Ibid., 132.

44. Karen A. Brown, *Prejudice in "Harry Potter"* (College Station, TX: Virtual-BookWorm Publishing, 2008), 90.

45. Ibid., 88.

46. Although we don't see in the books what becomes of Winky, Rowling has been adamant in interviews that she comes to enjoy freedom—proving Hermione's point. According to Rowling, Winky eventually gets over her addiction to butterbeer and accepts gainful employment. See "J.K. Rowling and the Live Chat, Bloomsbury. com" <http://www.accio-quote.org/articles/2007/0730-bloomsbury-chat.html> (July 30, 2007).

47. My understanding of Socratic *parrhesia* owes much to Cornel West's elucidation of it. "The Socratic commitment to questioning requires a relentless self-examination and critique of institutions of authority," he writes. "It is manifest in a fearless speech—*parrhesia*—that unsettles, unnerves, and unhouses people from their uncritical sleepwalking." See his *Democracy Matters: Winning the Fight Against Imperialism* (New York: Penguin Press, 2004), 16.

48. See Gordon W. Allport, *The Nature of Prejudice* (New York: Basic Books, 1979).

49. Rowling, *Harry Potter and the Goblet of Fire*, 239.

50. Sarah Zettel, "Hermione Granger and the Charge of Sexism," in *Mapping the World of the Sorcerer's Apprentice*, ed. Mercedes Lackey (Dallas: BenBella Books, 2005), 83-100.

51. Rowling, *Harry Potter and the Deathly Hallows* (New York: Scholastic, Inc., 2007), 198.

52. Ibid.

53. Harry does this simply by being more friendly and giving Kreacher a locket that once belonged to Regulus Black. Even though Ron deems the gift "overkill," it changes Kreacher's whole approach to the young wizards. He even starts to work with renewed vigor (Rowling, *Harry Potter and the Deathly Hallows*, 200).

54. For instance, one of the evil Lord Voldemort's greatest mistakes—a mistake that will turn out to contribute mightily to his undoing—is that he neglects to consider that house-elves might be equal creatures. "Of course, Voldemort would have considered the ways of house-elves far beneath his notice, just like all the purebloods who treat them like animals," Hermione observes. "It would never have occurred to him that they might have magic that he didn't" (Rowling, *Harry Potter and the Deathly Hallows*, 195).

55. Albert O. Hirschmann, *Exit, Voice, and Loyalty: Responses to Decline in Firms, Organizations, and States* (Cambridge: Harvard University Press, 1970).

56. Rowling, *Harry Potter and the Half-Blood Prince*, 439.

57. Marc Bousquet, "Harry Potter, the War against Evil, and the Melodramatization of Public Culture," in *Critical Perspectives on Harry Potter*, ed. Elizabeth Hellman (New York: Routledge, 2009), 177-196.

58. Rowling, *Harry Potter and the Deathly Hallows*, 625.

59. Rowling, *Harry Potter and the Chamber of Secrets*, 333.

60. Andy Lea, "Harry's Elf Warning," *Sunday Star* (July 1, 2007), 28.

61. Rowling, *Harry Potter and the Goblet of Fire*, 709.

62. Ibid., 320.

63. Rowling, *Harry Potter and the Sorcerer's Stone*, 306.

64. Harry's inability to trust Dumbledore when it comes to Severus Snape signifies a broader character weakness. As I go on to describe, Rowling considers trust in others—particularly friends—to be a definitive quality of good citizenship.

65. The question of "Snape: Good or Bad?" was a matter of frequent debate during the years in between the release of the first and last books in the series. Rebecca Traister describes one such public debate in "Potterpalooza," in *Salon*, <http://www.salon.com> (June 1, 2007).

66. Hannah Arendt, *Men in Dark Times* (San Diego: Harcourt Brace and Company, 1970), 24-25.

67. Rowling, *Harry Potter and the Goblet of Fire*, 239.

68. Rowling, *Harry Potter and the Order of the Phoenix*, 832-834.

69. See *Harry Potter and the Goblet of Fire*, 375.

70. Arlene W. Saxonhouse, "Eros and the Female in Greek Political Thought: An Interpretation of Plato's *Symposium*," in *Political Theory* 12.1 (February, 1984), 19.

71. Rowling, *Harry Potter and the Deathly Hallows*, 474.

72. Ibid., 710.

73. Ibid., 478-481.

74. Hannah Arendt, "The Public and the Private Realm," in *The Portable Hannah Arendt*, ed. Peter Baehr (New York: Penguin, 2000), 187.

75. Rowling, *Harry Potter and the Deathly Hallows*, 722.

76. Griphook the goblin makes the case on behalf of his kind—and complains bitterly about the oppressions of human wizards—in *Harry Potter and the Deathly Hallows*, 488-489.

77. Ibid., 759

78. Rowling, *Harry Potter and the Half-Blood Prince*, 644-645.

PART IV

DILEMMAS OF
COMMUNITY AND CHOICE

~

CHAPTER EIGHT

Responsible Life in Paradise

Margaret S. Hrezo

It would seem an odd book on moral and ethical dilemmas that did not attempt to come to grips with the religious moral view and its implications for political life. I will explore two complementary visions of the religious moral view in this chapter, both of which replace virtue defined as the following of dogmas and moral strictures in order to attain salvation with virtue defined as the challenge to live a responsible life—that is, a life grounded in the power of faith, hope, and love.[1] Our windows into this ethical vision are Toni Morrison's novel *Paradise* and the works of Dietrich Bonhoeffer. Although both Morrison and Bonhoeffer have deeply Christian roots, they eschew any moral certainty and any thought that either conscience or rules are infallible moral guides. Instead, they immerse us in contingency, the tangles of the unknowable, and an understanding of life as an "adventure of choice on the edge of freedom and necessity."[2] For both, the responsible life recognizes both freedom and obligation. Freedom manifests itself in self-examination and "the venture of a concrete decision"; obligation takes the form of deputyship in the world.[3] Neither deontologists nor consequentialists, they are pilgrims of the *metaxy* engaged in a search for the spiritual substance of order.

Plato used the term *metaxy* (middle) in discussions of human existence in the cosmos.[4] In his descriptions, human life (and consequently human decision making) takes place in a reality experienced both as constructed by human beings through will, choice, and intention, and as participation in a mysterious and more comprehensive reality not subject to human choice. For Plato, the story of human life was one of joint participation of gods and human beings in the middle.[5] Existence *ta metaxy* (in the middle) incorporates both the reality of being an individual who experiences herself as a subject in the world *and* as a creature living within a reality that both transcends and inter-penetrates every individual. As a subject, a self makes and carries out decisions in an attempt to control and order her life (and those of the people she meets along the way). However, human beings also experience the world as participation in a mystery, a drama that exists outside the individual and exerts power over her irrespective of her wishes. This is the experience of life in the middle, of life as a subject of something or someone else. "I heard the music from *Sleeping Beauty* and was moved by a power beyond myself to dance." This reality transcends time, space, the individual human life, and the world of existent objects. Human beings experience the *metaxy* as a tension in existence between mortality and immortality, between the call of the passions or ego and the call of some larger story to move beyond self.

What is important in understanding Plato's vision is the experience of tension and mediation between the poles of existence—body and soul, beginning and beyond, mortality and immortality. To live in the Platonic *metaxy* is to continually re-orient oneself in order to respond to the tension between these poles in a way that fosters participation in both levels of experienced reality. Thus, *metaxy* is every place, for "presence," "spirit," and "mystery" are the backdrop of and permeate all human life.

Morrison's novels and Bonhoeffer's theology offer different, but equivalent, spiritual experiences of these tensional poles that can assist an inquiry into moral decision making. Reading them together amplifies understanding of each separately. Both Morrison and Bonhoeffer experienced the deformations that had arisen in modern social and religious systems. Politically, Bonhoeffer's experience of modernity led him to envision a religion-less Christianity and prepared him to take part in an assassination plot against Hitler.[6] Morrison's work is filled with allusions to the deformation of America's spiritual substance resulting from racism, sexism, hyper-individualism, and empire.[7]

In addition, both Bonhoeffer's and Morrison's work exhibit dislike of an understanding of religion that turned the hard work of Christian discipleship into what Bonhoeffer called "cheap grace" (the belief that grace meant salvation without any further effort on our part). Genuine acceptance of grace requires conformation with Christ. It is not enough to live a pious life. Instead, the Christian must live in the world without judging it, love it, and serve it. One must "excuse the sin of another, but never his own."[8] Bonhoeffer considered much of bourgeois religion a deformation of Christianity that failed to realize the individual's responsibility to make Christ present in the world. He also saw how quickly and easily both churches and congregants capitulated to Nazism. He argued that the roots of both these deformations of Christianity lay in modernity's increasing loss of spiritual substance and in the failure to recognize that Christianity is a social, not an individual concept. An ethical life is one focused on "whether my action is at this moment helping my neighbor to become a man before God."[9] Modern Christianity, he argued, views salvation as totally up to the individual, forgetting that economic need or injustice hold up "the gifts of salvation to ridicule" and turn Christians into "liars"[10] by increasing the barriers between man and God. Further, the Christian notion of conscience, because it makes the individual the origin of right and wrong, often is the enemy of responsibility.

Thus, the only genuine innocence lies in giving oneself up to the fellowship of guilt. For Bonhoeffer, all human beings are sinners and trying to rely on conscience or virtue just widens the individual's separation from God. Action in the world, even action based on a desire for conformation with Christ, entails sin and guilt. Still, a Christian should "become a sinner again and again every day, and be bold about it" by acting in the world in an attempt to make Christ present.[11] Thus, for Bonhoeffer, the individual who "stands fast" and makes good moral decisions is not the person of conscience, virtue, duty, freedom, or reason.[12] Nor is the person who "stands fast" the one who goes to church every Sunday and follows the rules of conventional morality. All these, even scripture, may stand in the way of responding to the "call of the Word of God."[13] Rather she stands fast who engages in "responsible action" in the world. The world is full of grace. Conformation with Christ, not religion, demonstrates acceptance of that grace. Thus, conformation empowers the individual to act in the world. Bonhoeffer called action in the world deputyship, or discipleship. For Bonhoeffer, as in 2 Timothy 2.7, "God did not give us a spirit of cowardice but rather of power and love and self-control." Human beings must act as God's deputies in this world, taking full responsibility for their actions.

Morrison's complex moral and ethical sensibility also suggests the need for reinterpreting traditional religious ideas. Toni Morrison converted to Catholicism when she was 12, and *Paradise* exhibits Catholic roots. Consolata (Connie), the book's dominant character, was raised in a convent, expresses love for the nun's spirituality, and would like to have that same spirituality. At the end of the novel, as Jill Matus's excellent study of Morrison's work makes clear, Consolata (consolation) is in the arms of Piedade (Portuguese for mercy or compassion). Thus, "mercy and compassion attend consolation."[14] This is a long-standing aspect of Catholic doctrine, but Morrison goes further. In this novel Morrison explores and implicitly criticizes the deformation of Christianity into a fundamentalism focused on an ethic of purity, separation, and exclusion. Connie's spirituality, which incorporates elements of Roman Catholicism, second-century Christian Gnosticism's call to the individual to develop her own experience of Christ (to meet the Christ within),[15] and the Afro-Brazilian religion of Candomblé (a syncretism of Catholic and African spiritual beliefs), demonstrates not only Morrison's vision of *metaxy*, but also a belief that much of traditional Christianity has become stagnant, selfish, and loveless.

Third, both Morrison and Bonhoeffer experience the tension of the *metaxy*. For each in their own way, the world is full of grace, of spiritual presence and power, and the essence of responsible action in the world is the harnessing of that spiritual power in the service of humanity. Bonhoeffer symbolizes *metaxy* in Christ, who mediates the tension between human passions and the love of a God who must be "recognized at the centre of life."[16] God is neither a tutor nor a stopgap. In *Paradise* Toni Morrison portrays the porosity of the veil separating physical from spiritual reality. Presence, grace, often is visible and powerful. The complications, questions, and moral dilemmas that drive her stories always arise out of some characters' felt need to respond to the tension of living in-between two realities. The characters that find peace in her novels are those that accept their own story as part of an ongoing drama of being—a drama only part of which they can understand and control. Responsible action occurs when characters live in acknowledgment of the push and pull of both realities.

Finally, important political implications arise from each of their ethical viewpoints. The individual and political moral issues that arise in *Paradise* echo Bonhoeffer's exploration of moral decision making and its sociopolitical implications in *Ethics*. Both Morrison and Bonhoeffer begin with the law. Neither ends with it. Neither adopts the view that law and order are the same things. The richness and complexity of their portrayals render their view worthy of consideration in the contemporary political world. *Paradise* is Toni Morrison's only overtly religious book.[17] It also is her most overtly political book in which she examines the nature of community, civic duty, and community security.

I will argue that in *Paradise* an inability to understand the in-between nature of human life leads to the reification of ideas about virtue, justice, and the importance of community. For Morrison, the town's concentration on an ethic of purity paralyzes the townspeople's moral sense. They fall into moral blindness, lose the power of grace, and are unable to confront moral dilemmas or make moral choices. The results of this paralysis are tragic. Haunting the story's background is America's own failures in moral choice in its handling of racial, gender, and international relations. However, *Paradise* stands, in the end, as a warning to the deformative dangers of overreliance on *homonoia* (like-mindedness), with its accompanying ossification of moral values into whatever reinforces the dominance of a particular regime within social and political communities. Underlying everything that happens is the importance of ethical clear-sightedness in political as well as individual life.

Paradise as a Human Construction

The in-between character of life means that human beings are not the sole creators of either their personal or their communal lives. In one of the Joseph stories by Thomas Mann, Joseph exclaims, "What a story we are in!" A little later, Joseph will say, "I don't know . . . what sort of man I am. One does not know beforehand how one will behave in one's story; but when the time comes it is clear enough and then a man gets acquainted with himself."[18] For Mann, we are our stories and those stories take place in the theatre of God. Toni Morrison may not believe her stories take place in the theatre of God; however, it is evident that for Morrison human beings are their stories and those stories take place within some larger reality. We cannot get outside those stories without deforming ourselves and those around us. It is only within those stories that moral decisions have any meaning; we are not allowed to "watch" those stories from some exterior vantage point; and those individual stories take place within some larger story from which we cannot remove ourselves, even through death. If you want to think about it the way Shakespeare did, remember that "All the world's a stage, And all the men and women merely players."[19] Beginning, present, beyond—all are linked. Reality is bigger than the physical world and that larger reality will invade our nice, neat, rational spaces when and where it (not we) sees fit.

In order to give her readers the experience of living in such a story, Morrison appears to many readers to write her stories backwards and inside out. She drags us into her stories and makes us live them along with the characters and in the same way the characters must live them—with partial knowledge of the "facts," with incomplete understanding of the big picture, and with whatever strengths or weaknesses we bring to what happens to us in this world that often appears to us to be random or weird or unexplainable. *Paradise* embodies all these aspects of Morrison's writing style, and the reader does not understand the plot fully until the end. Though difficult to summarize, *Paradise* is a spiritual, political, and psychological exploration of a town that tries to stand outside its story, eliminate uncertainty, and render itself immortal.

Paradise asks the reader to live six years (1970-1976) in the life of Ruby, Oklahoma, a town that fits all of Daniel Elazar's requirements for a covenantal community.[20] The story revolves around the town's interaction with and reaction to five women who live at what used to be a convent school for Arapaho Indian girls located 17 miles outside of town. Four of the women are newcomers running from their pasts: Mavis Albright (the only one who seems to have a last name) is an abused wife haunted by the death of her twin infants, who suffocated in the back seat of the car as she bought hot dogs for her husband's dinner; Seneca is a "cutter," abandoned at 5 by her "sister" (who really was her mother), shuffled from foster home to foster home and sexually abused early and often; Pallas (Divine) is pregnant and in denial after running away from high school with her boyfriend who wound up sleeping with her mother; and the tough flamboyant Grace (Gigi) with no mother and a father on death row, who openly flaunts her sexuality and sexual availability. The fifth woman, Consolata (Connie) is leftover from the convent days—an orphan "stolen" by the nuns from the streets of a Brazilian city on their return to the United States. All five are wanderers floating through the present, branded with past scars, and without constructive thoughts as to their futures. In the view of the men of the town, these women are "detritus"(4)—unwanted, immoral, and vulgar throwaways— totally unacceptable in a town that prides itself on isolation and self-sufficiency, a town whose citizens cannot "tolerate anybody but themselves" (13).[21] They seem to have arrived from nowhere and, in the eyes of the town fathers, to have no morality and no sense. Unlike the town's women, they dance, drink, and wear makeup and up-to-date clothes. More importantly, they are racially impure. As time goes by, the townspeople, especially the men, will make these women the scapegoats for sick babies, unhappy wives, and seemingly disrespectful children. In the end, these eminently rational and commonsense men become incapable of reaching rational decisions or taking responsible action in the world. On a July dawn in 1976, after discussing the problems they see as facing their town, they attack the convent women, "God at their side" (18), to preserve "the only black town worth the effort" (279).

As the men bent on destroying the convent dwellers search the convent cellar, the men encounter the outlines of their bodies drawn by the women and the depiction on those outlines of the harms that had been done to them in the past. To the women the drawings were part of a psychic and spiritual cleansing that could lead to healing. From the men's perspective they were "filth." In Ruby external signs of virtue become the equivalent of genuine virtue. Moral decisions are those that reinforce the town's unique covenant.

Ruby is an all-black town, but one with a twist. That twist has its origins in the covenant. The original nine founding families all were very dark (8-rock, or 8-R, like deeply mined coal). Though never slaves, these families experienced all the terrors and degradations of the post-Reconstruction South. To escape, they migrated from Louisiana to Oklahoma; however, every black town refused them admission. The ultimate "disallowing," one that "rocked them, and changed them for all time" (95), occurred in 1890 when the families asked for help in Fairly, Oklahoma, and were refused entrance because they were too black and too poor.

The group first founded a town called Haven, and even before they constructed permanent homes, they built a community oven inscribed "Beware the furrow of his brow." That oven symbolized the unity of the community and its dedication to righteousness. Meals were cooked on it. Deliberations were conducted and important community decisions were made there. No one was quite sure exactly what the phrase meant or why their leader, Zechariah Morgan, had chosen it. Some interpreted the phrase to mean they must make no choice that would furrow God's brow; others thought maybe the brow they were told to keep smooth was that of Zechariah Morgan. Whatever the phrase meant, the oven evoked the community's spiritual substance—the essence of what Haven was about. God would protect the people of Haven as long as they remained true to Him and maintained the purity of the community.

When after World War II it was no longer possible to keep Haven prosperous *and* untouched by the rest of the world, fifteen families dismantled the oven and moved deeper into Oklahoma. They called the new town Ruby and its guiding principle was "May God bless the pure and holy and may nothing keep us apart from each other nor from the One who does the blessing" (205). Ruby would be a new start, but it still would honor the covenant of purity and exclusion.

In Ruby the founders constructed their vision of paradise—one seemingly free from sin and safe from racism. It was clean, close-knit, safe, religious, and prosperous. If they could not sleep, women could wander the streets alone in the middle of the night without fear. Citizens were at ease with their neighbors and assisted them in times of trouble. If anyone was tempted to forget the covenant, Zechariah's grandsons, the twins Deacon and Steward, would remind them. The most important part of educating the town's children was the stories told in the evenings at home about the exodus, the "disallowing," and the redemption of the community in Ruby (110).

The citizens of Ruby believed that they alone had created paradise and could preserve it through faithful adherence to a founding covenant. In the words of a newcomer to Ruby, the town believed "it had created the pasture it grazed" (212), one in which their wives and children were safe and they could control their own lives, their own stories. It "neither had nor needed a jail" (8). In the eyes of its citizens, Ruby was a place of great harmony and order.

Yet *Paradise* opens with the ultimate disorder, murder, and close examination of life in Ruby reveals that murder is not the only disorder in the most orderly town in Oklahoma—the town without a "slack or sloven" woman (8). What Toni Morrison portrays in *Paradise* is a community that is very orderly at the level of intentional reality. Its citizens have constructed a code and follow it. They are pious, God-fearing people who regularly attend church. They display all the virtues accounted important by the liberal tradition: "discretion, caution, enterprise, industry, assiduity, constancy, perseverance, considerateness, secrecy, order."[22] The town appears to reap the rewards of its virtue. The twin brothers Steward and Deacon Morgan (Zechariah's grandsons) make money almost effortlessly because of their hard work, rectitude, and attention to the covenant. So do others.

Single-minded commitment to the life of intention, however, harms those who adopt it. Steward's wife, Dovey, believes Steward's financial success has come at a cost. A man who loves wide-open spaces, he has sold much of his ranch for development. Over the years he also has lost his ability to enjoy people, food, and conversation (82). As the story unfolds, Morrison shows the reader that Ruby's emphasis on its self-constructed reality produces an outward order and prosperity that masks an interior impoverishment and disorder. The disorder it masks is very similar to that which Dietrich Bonhoeffer protested against in Germany before and during World War II when he wrote in a letter to Helmuth Rossler that the church was unable to proclaim "God's commandments in any concrete form." Just as Bonhoeffer condemned German Lutheranism for losing sight of the substance of Christian spirituality, Morrison seems to suggest that the citizens of Ruby have built walls that keep out important pieces of reality, rather than windows or doors that will allow a larger reality to illuminate the world of action and intention. For Bonhoeffer, the religion he saw in Germany precluded responsible citizenship and responsible Christianity. I would argue that Morrison implies the same thing about Ruby.

Despite its overt religiosity, the citizens of Ruby maintain their hard-won sense of order only by reducing all existence to their own will. They become God. Their view of virtue and vice is the only one possible. Organized religion operates in Ruby to reinforce the founding myth and the town's narrow moral ethic. Reverend Senior Pulliam, the Methodist minister, comes from the community. His God is the jealous and vengeful God of the Old Testament. His religion demands fear of God, weekly church attendance, and absolute adherence to the Ten Commandments in their most literal form. Although Deacon and Steward Morgan attend the Baptist church because it is the most powerful, the Baptist minister, Reverend Richard Misner, is an outsider. Thus, they carefully evaluate Reverend Misner's opinions "to judge which were recommendations easily ignored and which were orders they ought to obey" (56-57). Men of rectitude and conscience, they would decide what God wanted based on their own judgment.

According to Reverend Pulliam, no one deserves love. Love is not natural and "God is not interested in you" (143). Because no one deserves love, no one deserves God. One has to "earn God" and only earning Him gives one the right to love. Love is a hard-won prize, not an empowering gift, earned only through virtue of the sort displayed by the Morgan men and by following the words on the oven in the narrowest form. "Beware the furrow of his brow" and "God bless the pure and the holy" (142) are the golden calves of Ruby.

Pat's Dilemma and Moral Decision Making

These golden calves frame the moral choice at the heart of this chapter. Pat Best's decision to burn her genealogical research epitomizes the constrained ethical thinking that Morrison ascribes to Ruby. Because that decision is rooted solely in her own will and desire to be reasonable, Pat will fail to see its profound ethical consequences.

Pat is the town's schoolteacher and historian. She has compiled a genealogy of Ruby as a gift to its citizens. By 1975, however, she has decided the genealogy is fit only for her own eyes (187). What that genealogy reveals—that "unadulterated and unadulteried 8-rock blood held its magic as long as it resided in Ruby" (217)—will require her to choose whether to harm her community's sense of itself or to harm her daughter. Should she protect the community's good name and sense of its own virtue, or should she reveal Ruby's "secret" to her daughter so that Billie Delia will understand why she is considered a "loose woman" whose conduct is continually under scrutiny and comment?

The secret Pat had discovered was how Ruby managed to remain 8-rock pure and the lengths to which it would go to exclude those who violated the covenant. Anyone who does not marry "8-rock" (and their spouses) is marginalized by the town as no longer "pure and holy." When old men needed care and women were spinsters in a town closed to outsiders and intent on its racial and sexual purity "takeovers" among close relatives became common. Was the "takeover" arrangement merely a cover for incest? Were some of these individuals ever legally married? Her genealogy reveals that "the small m. was a joke, a dream, a violation of law" (187). Ruby has reduced all of moral decision making to the maintenance of the purity of 8-rock blood. In this town women and their conduct remain "always the key" (61) to the town's success or failure. Their actions must be watched and controlled because keeping the covenant means there must be no adultery and all marriages must be between 8-rocks. No change can challenge the covenant. Change, whether social, political, or spiritual, threatens Ruby's immortality.

Her insight is confirmed at the Christmas play, which now depicts only seven holy families. Her own family is one of those eliminated because her father was the first member of the community to marry a woman that was not 8-R. He was the one Steward Morgan said brought "along the dung we leaving behind" (201). Delia and Roger Best were subtly but surely excluded from the main life of the town. Pat has not been accepted fully either, and the evening of the Christmas pageant she recognizes that she always had seen her daughter, Billie Delia, as a "liability" because of her skin color. Pat also will ask herself whether in her attempts to fit into the community she had "defended Billie Delia or sacrificed her" (203). Her father had spent his entire life in Ruby trying to atone for a wife, a child, and a grandchild who were the wrong color. And, Pat realized, so had she, for when in October 1973 she and Billie Delia had a fight that drove Billie Delia away from the town for good, the iron she held "was there to smash the young girl that lived in the minds of the 8-rocks, not the girl her daughter was" (204). Still, Pat refuses to act. Instead, she burns her research. She will regret that decision too late. Pat is a good-hearted and intelligent woman and she understands the problem she is facing. However, her desire for acceptance renders her incapable of standing fast against an ethic she knows to be destructive.

Pat is unable to decide whether to act when confronted by a conflict between the town's sense of itself and her daughter. This is not the sort of grand moral dilemma one finds in political dramas. There is no ticking bomb. This is the sort of dilemma that can happen in any society, particularly one which believes that its continued strength and goodness must be firmly grounded in the civic virtue of its citizens. How much like-mindedness and citizen identification with community values is required to keep a political community secure? When should a society engage in examination of its values? It is morally wrong to willfully and knowingly harm either one's community or one's child. Should not the citizens of Ruby, all worried about the "four damaged infants" in the Fleetwood family (11), think about the effects on increasingly in-bred families of its single-minded commitment to racial and sexual purity? Should she not protest the town's exclusivity and contempt for anything that is different from itself for its own good? For Morrison, any society that declares itself the sole arbiter of conduct and will not accept difference turns itself into God and harms both individuals and the society as a whole. Like Bonhoeffer, *Paradise* suggests that it is wrong to show contempt for or judge another human being. Rather the disciple (for Bonhoeffer) or the moral person (for Morrison) works to create human conditions that will allow others to see all of reality.

Pat faces a moral and ethical crossroads and chooses blindness. She elects to be reasonable and becomes a confirmation of Bonhoeffer's warning that reasonable people "think that with a little reason they can bend back into position the framework that has got out of joint. In their lack of vision they want to do justice to all sides, and so the conflicting forces wear them down with nothing achieved."[23] It can be argued that Pat's decision allows the book's tragic conclusion to occur, as men who worry about the polluting effects of women determine that anything that is uncertain, that could not be controlled, and that might dilute the town's racial purity must be destroyed. When unreason masks itself as reason, the reasonable approach is no help.

Pat, at one level, sees more than most of Ruby's citizens. Yet she refuses what she sees and supports an ethic she understands is harmful. Like most of the townspeople, she wants to be able to define life, to tame it and make it safe. In Reverend Misner's words: "How exquisitely human was the wish for permanent happiness, and how thin human imagination became trying to achieve it" (306). Pat demonstrates the tragedy of human moral choice. There will be times when we will not know the correct moral choice. Sometimes we will not know (as Pat did not) that it is a moral choice we are making. Yet choice remains, and according to Bonhoeffer must be exercised—thoughtfully, by immersing ourselves in the mystery and clutter of life without recourse to virtue or personal consequence and in full understanding of the guilt we may incur by making that choice. The wise individual is the one with *opsis* (clear-sightedness), who "sees reality as it is, and who sees into the depths of things."[24] Pat refuses to look deeply enough.

Responsible Action in Paradise

Throughout *Paradise* Morrison contrasts the narrow, exclusive sense of reality, spirituality, and virtue found in the town with a wider perspective, one grounded in *opsis* (clear-sightedness). In presenting this perspective, Morrison suggests that genuinely moral decisions arise only out of a consciousness that, instead of building walls, keeps open its doors and windows to a larger and more comprehensive reality—one open to learning, with St. Paul, that "my grace is sufficient for you, for power is made perfect in weakness" (2 Cor. 12:9). An important message of Morrison's story, whether intended or not, is that moral decision making can only take place in a consciousness attuned to all of reality. Thus, the ethical framework Toni Morrison appears to support in *Paradise* finds echoes in Dietrich Bonhoeffer's discussions of responsible action in a world full of grace where religion is not the sole precondition for faith.

In *Paradise* the barriers are thin and permeable between a reality composed of physical objects and a mysterious, unseen reality within which the physical world exists. This unseen reality is present, in fact pervades, the physical world. In other words, grace is omnipresent in this world, if human beings only had the eyes to see it. This is a crucial link between Morrison's novel and Bonhoeffer's theology, a link inherent in the experience of *metaxy* and in their views of spirituality.

We see this pervasive presence of grace in the stranger that periodically walks through Dovey Morgan's backyard and stops to talk. She has no idea who he is or where he comes from and when he appears she feels that she talks "nonsense." However the stranger always displays interest in her sorrows, her joys, and her ideas about the world. What she says matters to him. And she knows that if she asks who he is, as soon as she attempts to tie him to the physical world of objects and intentions, he would disappear forever (92-93). This same stranger also visits Connie at the convent.

The convent sits at the crossroads of both parts of reality. It too becomes a place full of grace. At its inception, the convent represented the experience of living a story told within the theatre of transcendence. It was not the physical building that made this so; it was the presence of the sisters. As long as Mother Mary Magna lived, some order prevailed at the convent. Once Mother Superior dies, disorder reigns there as well, but disorder of a different sort than that which occupies Ruby. The women who one-by-one find shelter at the convent reek of "disorder, deception, and drift" (221). Each views the convent as a refuge from both their personal demons and the disorder of the outside world. Yet they are incapable of overcoming their own internal disorder. Even Connie, who grew up at the convent, has succumbed in her despair over the death of the Mother Superior and now drinks most of the time. The harms they have suffered and their lack of maturity have driven them from the world of intentionality to self-indulgent apathy. Ultimately, Connie recovers and leads the women in a process of healing whose foundation is experience of both poles of life in the *metaxy*. Connie's message is simple: Body and soul are one, "Never break them in two. Never put one over the other. Eve is Mary's mother. Mary is the daughter of Eve" (263). Responsibility toward oneself and others can only be achieved by openness to both. The world of the spirit is just as true and real as the world of the body. Responsible life requires understanding and participating in both. In Bonhoeffer's words, "God, our brother, and the earth belong together."[25] Yet, even at the time of their worst disorder these women are capable of helping those who seek them out. And the women of Ruby do seek them out, walking the 17-mile dirt road between the town and the convent in loneliness, despair, or desperation. All found refuge. A few found peace.

The mystery surrounding what happens to the women's bodies after the raid on the convent is a third symbol of the permeability of the boundaries between the two realities discussed in this chapter. When Lone DuPres, Dovey and Soane Morgan, and Lone's male relatives arrive at the convent in a failed attempt to stop the men, they find two dead women. The rest escaped the building and were shot down running across the fields. However, when Roger Best arrives with his hearse to remove the bodies, they are gone. A thorough search is conducted, but no bodies are found. In the book's brief final chapter the reader sees each woman engage in an act of reconciliation with someone from her past from whom she had been estranged, either physically or emotionally, in life. The manner in which the women mysteriously appear and disappear suggests that they are apparitions. However, the people they meet experience them as flesh and blood.

The most telling of the vignettes is Connie's. Connie is lying with her head in the lap of a mysterious figure she remembers from her childhood called Piedade, listening to her sing. She is totally at peace. They are sitting by the ocean. "Around them on the beach, sea trash gleams. Discarded bottle caps sparkle near a broken sandal. A small dead radio plays the quiet surf" (318). They watch a ship come into port, "crew and passengers, lost and saved, atremble, for they have been disconsolate for some time. Now they will rest before shouldering the endless work they were created to do down here in paradise" (318). Morrison's paradise is not someplace "out there" and it is not achieved by being virtuous and following the rules. Paradise is the recognition of a world full of grace where humans share in the hard work Bonhoeffer called "forgiving men their sins." Here Morrison sounds much like Bonhoeffer did in a letter written concerning what he viewed as the mistake Christians often made in their understanding of redemption:

> The Christian, unlike the devotees of the redemption myths, has no last line of escape available from earthly tasks and difficulties into the eternal, but, like

Christ himself . . . , he must drink the earthly cup to the dregs. . . . Redemption myths arise from human boundary-experiences, but Christ takes hold of a man at the centre of his life.[26]

For both Morrison and Bonhoeffer, "now is the Kingdom and now is the day"[27] for human beings to recognize and act in paradise.

Two characters in the book, Lone DuPres and Richard Misner, particularly embody Bonhoeffer's understanding of responsible action, one that goes beyond the local ethic of Ruby's community. Both feel the call of grace to action in the world. However, theirs is not the conventional morality of rite, ritual, and commandment.

Lone DuPres is a very old woman who has acted as the town's midwife all her grown life. An orphan, she "knew" as a toddler that the migrating group would be coming past her house and positioned herself in a way that she would be seen and "adopted." Lone, it seems, was born with *opsis*, but she also nourished the gift. The town no longer wants her services as midwife; a few consider her a witch because of the herbs she gathers to concoct natural remedies and because she has an uncanny ability to know what others are thinking. She also is a person of deep spiritual faith. Overhearing the conversation at the oven during which the men plan the attack on the convent, Lone immediately knows that she must act. In Lone's mind God is a guide and teacher who taught one "how to see for yourself . . . if you stopped steeping in vanity's sour juice and paid attention to his world" (273). Connie, too, possesses a natural *opsis*, but her Catholic training tells her it is wrong. For her "stepping in" (a belief, present in many cultures and given a variety of names, in which one person enters into another and pulls them back from death) is witchcraft or magic; for Lone it is the ability to experience all of reality and, as such, an act of pure faith. Ultimately, Connie will call it "seeing in" and accept the gift as "in sight" (247)—an ability to see into the essence of people. As her physical eyesight weakens, Connie finds that her insight grows.

Reverend Richard Misner is the new young Baptist minister who has been inspired by Martin Luther King Jr. and the civil rights movement. His clear-sightedness arises from his faith. To Reverend Misner, as opposed to Reverend Pulliam, the cross is the symbol of the coming together of God and the world in love. The crucified Christ is the point at which these truths become physically evident. Spiritual reality is very alive for him. At the end of *Paradise*, Reverend Misner and Anna Flood (who were out of town at the time of the murders) return to the convent to try to make sense of the several different stories they have been told. They find little physical evidence that can help. As they leave, they stop in the garden to gather the last of the hot peppers for which the convent is famous. And there, for only a second, they see in the midst of the overgrown plants a door or a window. What can it be? Neither Anna nor Misner question the reality of what they experience. They discuss whether they saw a door or a window, not whether they actually saw anything at all (305-306).

Misner's Christianity is much like Bonhoeffer's and very different from Reverend Pulliam's. Both Misner and Bonhoeffer agree that God (as Misner puts it) is "a permanent interior engine that, once ignited, roared, purred and moved you to do your own work as well as His—but if idle, rusted, immobilizing the soul like a frozen clutch" (142). In other words, the power of God is the power of love that energizes people to live and act in His place. The full force of that power only can be felt by openness to all of reality; that is, by firmly grounding oneself in the experience of *metaxy*. Misner believes the unity of God and man in Christ changed the human relationship with God radically "from CEO and supplicant to one on one" (146). The cross is both the symbol of that transformation and the embodiment of love; it made human beings responsible for the world and for each other. Love is not a "silly word" as Pulliam maintains (141); through Christ love has become the ground of human life, for love is, in Bonhoeffer's words, the "revelation of God and the revelation of God is Jesus Christ."[28] God makes no distinctions and loves all peoples. He does not permit human beings to classify and judge others based on their own standards,[29] which is exactly what the men of Ruby did. Instead, He shows us that "death was life, don't you know, and every life, don't you know, was gold, don't you know, in His eyesight" (160).

For Bonhoeffer and for Morrison, the good is decided in the middle of human relationships and experiences.[30] Some vision of abstract good is not the same thing as the good lived in the *metaxy*—in the midst of reality as a whole. There is only one reality, "the reality of God."[31] Transcendence is not "infinite and unattainable"; rather, it is the "neighbor who is within reach in any given situation."[32] That reality expresses itself in concern for both the ultimate and the penultimate; that is, in concern for both poles of existence—for the last things and for those things that come before the last. Life is "held in tension" between the beginning and the beyond—the "two poles of eternity."[33] Pat and most of Ruby's residents have built walls of isolation and righteousness designed to keep out challenges to the complex, the uncontrollable, and the mysterious.

Commitment to this vision of God and of reality will lead Bonhoeffer to embrace what he called "religionless" Christianity. Grounded in his readings of the epistles of St. Paul (in particular Ephesians and 1 and 2 Corinthinians), elements of religionless Christianity may be found in Bonhoeffer's discussions of the Body of Christ in *The Cost of Discipleship*. Further groundwork for his understanding of this idea is evident in Bonhoeffer's *Ethics*. Taken together these works emphasize his experience of Christ as *metaxy* and the implications of that experience for human life on earth. For Bonhoeffer, "the Body of Christ is the place of atonement and peace between God and man."[34] As in Ephesians 2:11-22,

> He has abolished the law with its commandments and ordinances, that he might create in himself one new humanity in place of the two, thus making peace, and might reconcile both groups to God in one body through the cross, thus putting to death that hostility through it.

Christ, he wrote, is the only "place where one can experience God and the world at the same time."[35] The church is not an institution but a person—the new man, and Christ is that new man.[36] We must, he wrote, "put on the new man," but we must also understand that salvation is a collective endeavor and not an individual work. The only way to experience God is by living totally in the world. *Ethics* makes clear that the only way in which we can consider ourselves part of the Body of Christ is by selfless action in the world on behalf of the other, that is, by love. To "allow the hungry man to remain hungry would be blasphemy against God and one's neighbor, for what is nearest to God is precisely the need of one's neighbor."[37] For Bonhoeffer, love is a power and without that power there is no *opsis*—no ability to see transformations or the fact that every moment, even every ending, is a new beginning. He is not seeking to enlist an army of social reformers. He is seeking to include all people in the Body of Christ. We find the transcendent in our neighbor.

Building on these ideas from his earlier works, Bonhoeffer arrives at his call for religionless Christianity in *Letters and Papers from Prison*. There, he again maintains that religion is not a requirement for salvation. Through his death and resurrection, Christ cleansed the world and its people; thus, we may not consider any people unacceptable. He also writes about how much more comfortable he is speaking with non-religious people about God than with the religious. Religious people, he says, only resort to talking about God when "human knowledge has come to an end."[38] Such talk pushes God farther and farther out of the world and renders Him superfluous. Instead, we must interpret miracle and God in the world in terms of the Body of Christ: "It is not with the beyond that we are concerned, but with this world as created and preserved, subjected to laws, reconciled, and restored."[39] We are called, he wrote, to find ways of translating "repentance, faith, justification, rebirth, and sanctification" into everyday terms and of incorporating them into daily life.[40] We must get beyond the law in order to follow Christ.

Thus, the "sum of the commandments" is "to live in fellowship with Christ."[41] Living in fellowship with Christ means living in fellowship with our fellow man. Living that fellowship requires thought and discussion. Ethics, for the Du Pres family of which Lone is a part, revolves around talk about the problems each member faces. "And always the turn was on the ethics of a deed, the clarity of motives, whether a behavior advanced His glory and kept His trust" (284). Decisions are neither automatic nor necessarily easy. The individual who understands, accepts, and lives that truth, Bonhoeffer would suggest, is clear-sighted. In Ruby, economic prosperity, maintenance of the 8-rock line, and the ethic of purity seem to the townspeople to heal any "wounds of guilt" the town possibly should feel about how it treats the Best family, Menus Jury, Reverend Misner, the convent women, or any outsider.[42] They also lead to moral blindness.

It is interesting to note that the characters that appear to be the most clear-sighted and the most capable of Bonhoeffer's responsible action in the world stand somewhat "outside" mainstream religious space. Lone and Connie combine Christian orthodoxy with other experiences of spirituality. Richard Misner is different from the other ministers in Ruby. Certainly he calls the people of Ruby away from a narrow piety to participation in the world. In this he is similar to Bonhoeffer.

Bonhoeffer was strongly critical of traditional twentieth-century Christianity, almost as critical as Freud, though from a very different perspective. He accused it of refusal to meet reality and refusal to accept God's responsibility. Therefore Bonhoeffer refused to equate God with religion. For too long, he wrote, human beings relegated God to the "other world." For too long man has dealt with his life in bits and pieces. There was a secular part, and a religious part, and a family part, and a political part, and so on until mankind's wholeness was shattered into a thousand pieces. Man could and should take interest and joy in each of his fragments, but unless they are bound into a whole and given some form and pattern, they can only be illusory and insecure. The pieces are not reality, only the whole can be that. For Bonhoeffer, what binds the pieces together is Christ, understood as the point at which God through the Incarnation encounters man, the point where the transcendent breaks through into the physical world. The genuine Christian knows that life "is not pushed back into a single dimension, but is kept multidimensional and polyphonous."[43] It is through Christ that man is redeemed and reconciled with God, and therefore, with herself. Christ only can do this, however, if He is freed from the box of religion and set loose to pervade all aspects of human life. God will not be pushed out of this world—even by religion. For Bonhoeffer, *opsis* results when one can "recognize the significant in the factual," and that cannot happen as long as "God and the world are torn asunder."[44]

It is for this reason that Bonhoeffer could embrace the godless or religionless character of the contemporary world. The "godless" world understands that the religious act is something partial, whereas life is a whole. The contemporary world has come of age and it is God's will that man should now think and act as if he could get along without God, while at the same time recognizing God "in the middle of the village."[45] There are not two realities, one sacred and another profane. There is only one reality—God manifest through Christ. Thus, Christ's place is not at the boundaries of existence, where man's religious nature is inclined to push God, but at its center. Humankind must live in the secular, "godless" world without explaining it religiously, or embossing it, or judging it, or despising it, because it is God's world.

The key to spiritual faith for Bonhoeffer and (I argue) for Morrison is not holiness or strict adherence to formulas or rites. Originally Bonhoeffer thought he could acquire faith by living a holy life.[46] Over time, he wrote, he came to realize that religion is not the condition of faith and salvation. By the time of his imprisonment he believed that faith meant humankind must live unreservedly in life's problems, successes, and failures. This is what it means to be a Christian in Bonhoeffer's theology, not to be pious or virtuous. Reason, conscience, pious observation of such rites and mandates as circumcision—sometimes even scripture—could be a barrier to discipleship.[47] Bonhoeffer argues that only by living unreservedly and genuinely in life does an individual demonstrate the utmost faith and the ultimate acceptance of reality. She knowingly throws herself "into the arms of God" taking seriously not her own sufferings but those "of God in the world."[48] Only by living in the world and serving it does man come to terms with his guilt and alienation and overcome the split between body and spirit. For Bonhoeffer, and I think for Morrison, in the end paradise "turns on man"[49]—not in the sense of constructing heavens on earth to escape reality, but in the sense of embracing life in between and doing the work that must done on earth to help all people remember how to return to what Morrison called "love begun" (318). There is no guarantee of order, but there is a path humanity can follow.

Politics and the Possibility of Paradise

The search for control of rather than participation in the drama of being, and the murders that result from that desire, bring trouble and change to Ruby.

The convent women are gone but still have an impact on the town; one of the Fleetwood children dies; rifts occur in lifelong friendships that will not heal easily (if at all). Many have learned nothing. However, Deacon Morgan has realized that he has become the very thing he hated, and the individual Bonhoeffer called the "antitype" to one who attempts to conform with Christ[50]—judge, jury, and executioner of the needy and different.

For both Bonhoeffer and Morrison, participation in the full drama of being must be part of both individual and communal life. Without that participation, what is left is a rationalized and mechanized world in which technology "has become an end in itself" and "has a soul of its own"[51]—in other words, the contemporary political world. In such a world it is inconceivable to think about politics as anything but economic and physical power. That is true for those like Bonhoeffer who accept transcendence as well as for spiritual realists such as Camus.[52] For those who see life as occurring within the *metaxy*, whether atheist, agnostic, or believer, the essence of politics is the tension between power and spirit (Necessity and Freedom). Morrison and Bonhoeffer offer an important critique of contemporary politics' emphasis on rights, personalism, faction, instrumental reason, and materialism. They also suggest that there is a need both to enlarge our view of reality and politics and to distrust political power (no matter who holds it) that has recourse to formulas and platitudes to solve the tension between Necessity and Freedom. The Christian life is not the life of "bourgeois respectability,"[53] not in the thought of Dietrich Bonhoeffer and not in the novels of Toni Morrison. It is hard for human beings to live without succumbing to the temptation to build the sorts of illusory realities one sees in Ruby. Bonhoeffer called it a very narrow road, because discipleship requires loving, with "the infinite love of Jesus Christ," one's personal enemies and the enemies of everything one believes.[54] Morrison's *Paradise* portrays graphically just how challenging that requirement can be.

This, they say, is life in the *metaxy*, where human beings and political communities understand morality and ethics as a "narrative unity of human life,"[55] and conform themselves to that life by concern for real people. Moral lives are more important than moral choices, and moral lives come from responsible action in the world. There are no saints, supermen, or heroes. There are only people like Connie, Richard Misner, and Lone DuPres, who possess the insight to know that there is only one reality and it is a mysterious, cluttered, slippery in-between in which we not only choose and act but also to which we must conform ourselves. As Bonhoeffer wrote: "We can only live life; we cannot define it"—the very mistake that Ruby repeatedly makes.[56] In this mysterious in-between, such people strive for the wholeness of life, the knitting together of body and soul that Lone and Bonhoeffer advocate and that Connie tries to teach the other women at the convent.

In *Paradise*, as in Bonhoeffer's thought, human beings as they presently act in this world deal not with reality but with self-spun illusion because they do not understand or cannot accept the two-in-one nature of reality. Conscience and law remain important to this life, but they are a starting point. Conscience and principle lead to tragedy in Ruby. Thinking about this novel increases our understanding of the obstacles to genuine vision in politics as well as in individual human life. Neither individuals nor political communities can escape life in the middle. Neither the individual nor the political community will ever corner the market on Truth or moral reasoning. Insight and a corresponding ability to engage in genuine moral thinking and action arise in the eyes of Morrison only from participation in the *metaxy*. Lack of clear-sightedness was Ruby's failure. Ruby's selective memory, tunnel vision, and obsession with its own purity, isolation, and exclusion warn us of the dangers posed by a contemporary politics dominated by a desire for ideological purity. Like individuals, societies need to remember who they are and what story they are living. Ruby forgot who and what it was and so wrote itself into the wrong story. There is a warning there for any political community. Wall yourself off too much from life in the *metaxy* and you are likely to see yourself as the only author of your story. Individuals and societies whose major goals are total security and control often wind up in the wrong story and miss those important windows and doors that await us beyond our security and outside our control.

Notes

1. The Greek word for power in action, usually *dünamis*, appears frequently in the gospels and epistles and usually is associated with actions of faith, hope, and love grounded in the call and power of the Holy Spirit (grace). See, for example, Hebrews 2.4 and 3.15-16; 2 Corinthians 3.1-6 and 4.7; Ephesians 1.18; and Philippians 3.10. All biblical quotations are taken from Donald Senior, Mary Ann Getty, Carroll Stuhlmueller, and John J. Collins, ed., *New American Bible* (Oxford University Press, 1990).

2. Eric Voegelin, *Order and History Volume I: Israel and Revelation* (Baton Rouge, LA: Louisiana State University Press, 1956), 1.

3. Dietrich Bonhoeffer, *Ethics* (New York: MacMillan, 1971), 220.

4. Plato, "Symposium," in *Great Dialogues of Plato*, trans. W.H.D. Rouse (New York: Penguin Mentor Book, 1984), 202a-203a.

5. Diotima tells Socrates that Love is a great spirit whose work is to "interpret and ferry across to the gods things given by men and to men things from the gods . . .

and being in the middle it completes them and binds all together into a whole" (*Symposium*, 202).

6. In contrast with Trotsky and Arendt (as discussed by Charles Turner in chapter 3 in this book), Bonhoeffer, although agreeing about the importance of context, would not attempt to justify assassination. He would see it as part of a balancing of freedom and the obligation of deputyship, but would accept the guilt inherent in murder.

7. See for example, Peter Widdowson, "The American Dream Refashioned: History, Politics and Gender in Toni Morrison's *Paradise*," *Journal of American Studies* 35 (Summer 2001): 313-35; Marni Gauthier, "The Other Side of Paradise: Toni Morrison's (Un)Making of Mythic History," *African-American Review* 39 (2005): 395-414; Ana Maria Fraile-Marcos, "Hybridizing the 'City upon a Hill' in Toni Morrison's *Paradise*," *MELUS* 28.4 (2003): 3-33; Candice M. Jenkins, "Class, Color, and Intraracial Politics in Toni Morrison's *Paradise*," *MFS Modern Fiction Studies* 52.2 (Summer 2006): 270-96; Carola Hilfrich, "Anti-Exodus: Countermemory, Gender, Race, and Everyday life in Toni Morrison's *Paradise*," 52.2 *MFS Modern Fiction Studies* (Summer 2006): 320-49; Larry M. Preston, "Theorizing Differences: Voices from the Margin," *American Political Science Review* 89.4 (December 1995): 941-533; Cyrus R.K. Patell, *Negative Liberties* (Durham: Duke University Press, 2001); and George Shulman, "Political Culture, Prophetic Narration and Toni Morrison's *Beloved*," *Political Theory* 24.2 (May 1996): 295-314.

8. Bonhoeffer, *Ethics*, 83.

9. Ibid., 86.

10. Dietrich Bonhoeffer, *The Cost of Discipleship* (New York: MacMillan, 1949), 287.

11. Ibid., 57.

12. Dietrich Bonhoeffer, *Letters and Papers from Prison* (New York: MacMillan, 1953), 5.

13. Bonhoeffer, *The Cost of Discipleship*, 87.

14. Jill Matus, *Toni Morrison* (Manchester: University of Manchester Press, 1998), 167.

15. See Elaine Pagels, *The Gnostic Gospels* (New York: Random House, 1979). As several Morrison scholars have noted, Morrison and Pagels are friends and the epigraph in *Paradise* is from one of the Gnostic gospels found at Nag Hammadi, *Thunder, Perfect Mind*.

16. Dietrich Bonhoeffer, *Letters and Papers from Prison*, 311-12.

17. Deirdre Donahus, "Morrison's Slice of 'Paradise,'" *USA Today* 22 (January 1999).

18. Thomas Mann, *Joseph the Provider* (New York: Alfred Knopf, 1944), 352.

19. William Shakespeare, *As You Like It*, Act II, Scene 7.

20. See Daniel J. Elazar, *Covenant and Polity in Biblical Israel: Vol. 1, Of the Covenant Tradition in Politics* (New Brunswick, NJ: Transaction Publishers, 1995), 22-23. Elazar defines a covenant as "a mutually informed agreement or pact based upon

voluntary consent, established by mutual oaths or promises, involving or witnessed by some transcendent or higher authority, between peoples or parties having independent status, equal in connection with the purposes of the pact, that provides for joint action or obligation to achieve defined ends."

21. Parenthetical citations are from Toni Morrison, *Paradise* (New York: Penguin Plume, 1999).

22. David Hume, *An Enquiry Concerning the Principles of Morals* (Lasalle, IL: Open Court Books, 1966), 78.

23. Bonhoeffer, *Letters and Papers from Prison*, 4.

24. Bonhoeffer, *Ethics*, 70-71.

25. Dietrich Bonhoeffer, *Creation and Fall* (New York: MacMillan, 1959), 40.

26. Bonhoeffer, *Letters and Papers from Prison*, 336.

27. Marty Haugen, "Gather Us In" ©1982 G.I.A. Publications.

28. Bonhoeffer, *Ethics*, 53.

29. Ibid., 73.

30. Ibid., 211.

31. Ibid., 195.

32. Bonheoffer, *Letters and Papers from Prison*, 381.

33. Bonhoeffer, *Ethics*, 121.

34. Bonhoeffer, *Cost of Discipleship*, 276.

35. Bonhoeffer, *Ethics*, 71.

36. Bonhoeffer, *Cost of Discipleship*, 269-70.

37. Bonhoeffer, *Ethics*, 136.

38. Bonhoeffer, *Letters and Papers from Prison*, 281.

39. Ibid., 283.

40. Bonhoeffer, *Ethics*, 283.

41. Bonhoeffer, *Cost of Discipleship*, 82.

42. Bonhoeffer, *Ethics*, 77.

43. Bonhoeffer, *Letters and Papers from Prison*, 311.

44. Bonhoeffer, *Ethics*, 70-71.

45. Bonhoeffer, *Letters and Papers from Prison*, 326-29.

46. Ibid., 369.

47. Bonhoeffer, *Cost of Discipleship*, 87.

48. Bonhoeffer, *Letters and Papers from* Prison, 370.

49. Ibid., 380.

50. Bonhoeffer, *Ethics*, 111.

51. Ibid., 99.

52. For the spiritual realist, modernity results in increased secularization and loss of spiritual substance in political and social life and, therefore, makes it difficult to construct orderly societies. Voegelin argues that, although each took a different direction in the attempt to provide such a substance as an alternative to blind material power, Machiavelli, Hobbes, Dante, and Bodin were spiritual realists. Albert Camus was a contemporary spiritual realist. See, in particular, *The First Man*, trans. David

Hapgood (New York: Alfred A. Knopf, Inc., 1995), 192-97. For Camus, every human being is forced by the mystery and immensity of life to construct without aid some sense of morality and truth. Each human being must "one by one, try to learn to live without roots and without faith . . . they had to learn to live in relation to others" and recognize that all shared common hopes, fears, and destiny (195-96). See *The Collected Works of Eric Voegelin, Vol. 19: History of Political Ideas, Vol. I, Hellenism. Rome, and Early Christianity*, ed. Athanasios Moulakis (Columbia: University of Missouri Press, 1997), 24-25; *The Collected Works of Eric Voegelin, Vol. 21: History of Political Ideas, Vol. III, The Later Middle Ages*, ed. David Walsh (Columbia: University of Missouri Press, 1998), 69-72; and *The Collected Works of Eric Voegelin, Vol. 25: History of Political Ideas, Vol. VII, The New Order and the Last Orientation*, ed. Jürgen Gebhardt and Thomas A. Hollweck (Columbia: University of Missouri Press, 1999), 33-34.

53. Bonhoeffer, *The Cost of Discipleship*, 54.

54. Ibid., 211.

55. Alasdair MacIntyre, *After Virtue* (Notre Dame, IN: University of Notre Dame Press, 1984).

56. Bonhoeffer, *Ethics*, 214.

CHAPTER NINE

~

Amoral Dilemmas
and the Temptation
to Tyranny in *A Simple Plan*

Travis D. Smith

In *A Simple Plan*, three ordinary small-town fellows uncover a plane buried under the snow out in the woods. Accompanying its pilot's frozen remains they discover a duffel bag containing 4.4 million dollars. After some dispute and deliberation, they opt to keep the money and keep it quiet. Once winter passes, if it looks safe, they will split up their newfound fortune and skip town, each to live the good life as it pleases him. The consequences of this injudicious decision are grim, as people who know not how to be altogether bad conspire altogether badly.

Amoral Dilemmas

I see in *A Simple Plan* an opportunity to examine the premises and effects of modern ethics, the philosophical origins of which lie in the explicitly amoral political theory of Hobbes, itself derivative of the merrily immoral teachings of Machiavelli.[1] Hobbes's political science is an adaptation of the Machiavellian proposal that men should seek to conquer fortune and become masters of their own lives. Its mission is openly hostile to classical ethical concerns regarding good character. It reduces virtue to the skills and the will for achieving worldly success. Machiavelli knew that his teaching was suited to extraordinary individuals. Hobbes, however, insinuates Machiavellian modes of thought and behavior, now liberalized and democratized, into the souls of all men and women, disordering them for the sake of constructing a new order upon them.[2] *A Simple Plan* is saturated with the language, imagery,

189

and ideas of early modern political philosophy. Following a brief overview of modernity's premises and purposes and an outline of their implications for morality, I will synthesize from the film a critical examination of modern man's chances for happiness within a secularized, commercial social order ruled in conformity with a technological mind-set.

Hobbes labors to convince men that they shall secure relatively good lives for themselves within a system premised on the supposition that a man's happiness is nothing other than his getting what he thinks he wants and doing what he happens to like, without end, until he dies (Lev VI:58, XI:1-2). Death, the ultimate buzzkill, is one thing we can all agree is bad. Political society should be conceived of as a voluntary association for mutual self-preservation, as every man must keep on living in order to keep the good feelings coming—at least sometimes, or eventually, or so he hopes. This system needs men who are inoffensive and complacent, seeking comfort and contentment. Neither hating nor loving each other, they should leave each other alone except to engage in consensual exchanges of perceived benefits.[3] Men ought to be left free to pursue the satisfaction of their appetites so long as they do not disrupt the civil peace in so doing. They must heed the laws that everyone is said to consent to because they are declared needful for maintaining the system that helps everyone to stimulate their pleasure centers. A fear of getting caught and being punished is needed to keep men in line, but the power that punishes should not seem oppressive or else men might discover causes for courage. Instead, men should pride themselves on their enlightened timidity, equating law-abidingness with righteousness.

So as to dispel the quarrels that arise from disagreements regarding right and wrong, Hobbes teaches that good and evil are merely points of view and that justice is strictly conventional, an expedient social construct that we can all justify and uphold for our own self-interested purposes. Hobbes acknowledges a catalogue of virtues, but they are only labels for the rules of behavior that conduce to self-preservation and appetite-satisfaction, not enduring states of soul that embody human excellences, constitutive of a happiness that transcends mundane pleasures and possessions.[4] Although men should worry that unlawful behavior will be detected and punished by the civil state in this life, they should not be terrified of suffering "torments everlasting" for their sins after death (Lev XXXVIII:14). Hobbes discourages the belief that anything should be held sinful apart from the intention to break the law (Lev XXVII:1-2, XXIX:7), for fear that some might try to impose peculiar private preferences and prejudices on others rather than submitting uniformly to those practices and opinions that presently enjoy public approval.

How much less dependable is conventional justice when it is explicitly constructed upon sheer self-interest, relying only on the fear of getting caught by secular powers? What if a man who is educated to prize control over his circumstances so as to satisfy his appetites feels confident that he could get away with breaking the laws, discovering that they represent only inconvenient obstacles to his getting what he thinks he might want (cf. Rep 358e-361b)? Why should someone obey the laws when they appear to do the opposite of what they are supposed to do? Here is the kind of situation that will feel like a compelling dilemma to such a man: shall I (a) continue obeying laws theoretically authored by me, if indirectly through my representatives (Lev XVI:5, 14, XVII:13, XVIII:6), because they hypothetically serve my self-interest in roundabout fashion, or (b) disobey, even if I agree that the laws usually do their job well enough, when breaking the law in some particular present instance seems to serve my future interests much better (cf. Lev XV:4)? Admittedly, to call this kind of scenario a moral dilemma would be malapropos. Since taking care of oneself and one's own is not inherently immoral (NE 1169a10, Pol 1263b1), let us just label it an *amoral dilemma*, the type men face when they have agreed that right and wrong refer only to what works and what does not for the sake of self-preservation, pleasure, and personal success.

Many factors facilitate the rationalization of lawbreaking. If laws are justified as mechanisms for the prevention of harms and no manifest harm to anyone is foreseeable, disobedience ceases to seem like such a tough call. If a man's life circumstances have deprived him of the experience necessary to measure and take risks, he is more prone to proceed recklessly. A man is more apt to try anything if he believes that happiness is comprised of appetite satisfactions, independent of the actions and habits that shape his character. Imagining that obedience is an indication of weakness may spur a man on, especially when he is made aware that others disobey with impunity and without misgivings. Unconcern for supernatural entities or cosmic principles that hold men accountable for their deeds and desires when earthly powers do not also helps. Needless to say, the magnitude of the payoff intensifies the temptation, as does the slightness of the anticipated effort. *A Simple Plan* puts circumstances such as these on full display. For example, the principal protagonist of the film, Hank Mitchell (Bill Paxton), specifically makes the plea that actions are wrong only if somebody gets hurt. As the story unravels, the fragility of conventional justice premised on material self-interest, the inadequacy of treating the power to satisfy appetites as the measure of happiness, and the vanity of man's attempt to conquer fortune are exposed, shaking the foundations of the modern moral-political complex.

Hank's brother Jacob (Billy Bob Thornton) compares the money found in the plane to "lost treasure." His words recall Book XI of Plato's *Laws,* in which the Athenian Stranger, discussing laws regarding property, asks, what if someone "deposited in the earth" for safekeeping "a very great mass of treasure"? He argues, "I should never pray to the gods that I may find it; nor, if I do find it, should I move it." By not taking or even desiring riches that do not belong to him, he says that the justice and virtue of his soul would increase more than his material wealth (something of lesser value) would grow by keeping them.[5] Of course, ethical arguments like this only reach those who remain open to the possibility that happiness has something to do with good character. Among them are many who have difficulty resisting the temptation to do wrong when opportunities arise. As a general rule, those who are unsure whether or not they should indulge in wrongdoing (let alone whether or not they could get away with it) should refrain from trying, but they need to be dissuaded. People who know how to succeed at behaving badly are not so troubled by self-doubt. Moral arguments only interest them as instruments for swindling others.

In order to profit from their sudden discovery, one of the men who found the money would have had to make immediate use of the loaded hunting rifle that Jacob happens to have on hand and be prepared to start an altogether new life. Machiavelli teaches that a new power that arises suddenly will not last unless "those who have suddenly become princes have so much virtue that they know immediately how to prepare to keep what fortune has placed in their laps" (Pr VII 26). For Machiavelli, virtue and goodness are practically antonyms. Like most of us, none of the men in this story possess the qualities of character, not to mention the experience or contacts, needed to improvise and resolutely execute such a deceptively simple plan. They are insufficiently bad to commit great wrongs well.

Character Matters

The film's setting is a small, worn town in snowy, rural Wright County—which *sounds* like Right County, i.e., a place that is just (and hence, not a big city). The law there is represented by Carl Jenkins (Chelcie Ross), an affable and credulous sheriff's deputy well suited to a beat where criminality is slight.

The three men who find the plane are the aforementioned Mitchell brothers and Jacob's best bud Lou Chambers (Brent Briscoe). Hank, "a nice, sweet, normal guy," works as the accountant at the local feed mill. Whereas Hank's father was a crop farmer, Hank manages the money that somebody else's business makes by selling processed crops back to farms. His job brings to mind the commercialization of agrarian life and the division of labor. His quotidian tasks focus his attention on small-scale money-making. Thanks to this "good job," as his wife refers to it before the prospect of prodigious riches alters her assessment, Hank lives more comfortably than his father, who went broke and lost the farm. In the film's opening monologue, forebodingly delivered in the past tense, Hank reminisces, "for a while there, without hardly even realizing it," he possessed the humble happiness that his struggling father dreamed of, comprised of "simple things, really: a wife he loves, a decent job, friends and neighbors who like and respect him." Incidentally, he omits mention of his wife loving him. Also, nothing in the film confirms that he actually has any friends. It is furthermore telling that he did not know that this was supposed to be happiness while he enjoyed it, calling into question its sufficiency as a definition of happiness, seeing as it lacks reference to qualities of mind and character (NE 1098a15, 1100b10-20). Maybe Hank hoped for something more, if subconsciously, making him predisposed to risking it all when the opportunity unexpectedly arises. Hank is self-involved without being self-aware, and he is relatively oblivious to the problems facing those who are less well off. He is proficient at self-deception but inexperienced at deceiving others or detecting the deceptions of others. It never occurred to him that his brother has never kissed a girl, that his wife is unfulfilled by a job for which she is overqualified, that his college tuition contributed to his father's financial ruin, or that the automobile accident in which his parents perished was no accident. He is reflexively law-abiding until he decides to keep the money, after which time he suffers from a "terrifying anticipation of punishment" (Pr XIX 73). His better judgment is easily overturned, his resolution readily wavers, and he relies on his wife for strength and direction. Hank's unmanliness is a running theme (cf. Rep 359b), as Jacob calls his shoes "pussyloafers" and Lou remarks, "he runs like my wife."

Jacob is unattractive, overweight, and disheveled. He is incapable of taking good care of himself, although in this individualistic society he is left on his own to try. Perennially unemployed and on welfare, Jacob lands only "the occasional odd job," performing wage labor suited to "those who lack any art but are useful only for their bodies" (Pol 1258b25; cf. 1254b20).[6] He is also preoccupied with his childhood memories. Apart from Lou, his only friend is his (male) dog, Mary Beth, named after the only girl who ever dated him. Despite knowing that she only did it to win a bet, Jacob forgives and speaks fondly of her (ASP 4, 172f).

"A forty-year-old, unemployed high school dropout who's proud when people call him the town drunk" is how Hank describes Lou. Masking his insecurity and resentment with buffoonery, Lou nevertheless possesses the most self-knowledge of them all. Mooning the others out the window of Jacob's truck in his first appearance, Lou later admits, "maybe sometimes I can come off a little bit like an asshole." He is irresponsible, irreverent, impatient, inconstant, and dishonest. None of his many bad qualities make him a good co-conspirator. His wife, Nancy (Becky Ann Baker), works to support them both. They abuse each other verbally but remain devoted to each other, and Lou confides in her.

Hank cannot help himself from blabbing to his own wife, either. Sarah (Bridget Fonda) grew up elsewhere and met Hank in college. Now she works at the local public library. As the story commences, she is very pregnant. More booksmart than streetsmart, Sarah believes what the FBI is quoted as saying in the newspapers and she overestimates her own talent for intrigue. She deserves credit for realizing well before Hank that Jacob and Lou are liabilities, not partners, and for figuring out that the FBI agent who interrogates Hank is really the villain in disguise—a wanted murderer who played a part in a kidnapping from which the plunder in the plane was the ransom. Sarah displays a feminine concern for appearances, maintaining a nice-looking home and affecting domestic contentment. When we first meet her she dispassionately voices affirmations of conventional morality in response to hypothetical questions. Needless to say, knowing how to solve made-up moral dilemmas (let alone amoral dilemmas) is not itself moral virtue (NE 1105b10-15). Regrettably, Sarah harbors within herself the girlish fantasy of living like a princess. Spellbound by the bundles of hundreds tumbling across her dining room table, she laughs like her biblical namesake does upon discovering that her greatest desire, which she had given up on, is to be miraculously fulfilled. In Lady Macbethesque fashion, Sarah must embolden her husband to act on their behalf. She freaks out about bloodstains, too. Sarah proves willing to consider or excuse almost anything, although I doubt that she would consider dashing out her daughter's brains. Amanda is born midway through the film, and nobody seems to realize how much her existence complicates any bid to keep the booty. It is no coincidence that Sarah conceives of her most devious plot the moment her baby suckles her for the first time (Rep 460b-d). Although she fancies herself the most competent of the bunch, Sarah is mainly just more determined. The messes made by her maneuverings reveal her to be an amateur manipulator.

Elements of Hobbes

That *A Simple Plan* takes place within a world shaped by Hobbesian premises may be demonstrated by showing how shot through it is with images and situations reminiscent of Hobbes's account of the natural condition of man. Hobbes's state of nature teaching is the conjectural beginning of his political philosophy. Because man's natural condition is so miserable, he argues, we must agree to obey the laws of our society. Hobbes not only frets about entire societies slipping into a condition of out-and-out civil war. The state of nature remains ever-present, if in the background, even in the midst of relatively well-ordered and prosperous regimes (Lev XIII:10). It can only be suppressed, not eliminated once and for all. Indeed, the eruption of the state of nature depicted in *A Simple Plan* illustrates how men may become forgetful of their vulnerability to the dangers of the state of nature by the very success of the Hobbesian project. People who enjoy peace and prosperity for a long time take their good fortune for granted and become arrogant and complacent, leading them to overrate themselves and underestimate others.

A fox raids a chicken coop as the film opens, making a startling statement about the natural order of things. A hen in its jaws, this fox darts in front of Jacob's truck, causing it to crash. This accident leads to the discovery of the plane when Jacob chases after the fox into a "nature preserve." Taking his rifle, Jacob plans on "collecting a debt." Every man decides for himself the reaction merited by any perceived transgression in the state of nature, and death is the most predicable sentence (Lev XIII:5, XXVIII:2).[7] "You can't hunt here," protests Hank. But hunting is not only permissible wherever nature is preserved; it is to be expected. The conspirators do not, however, foresee all that will be required of them once they decide to situate themselves outside of the law. Henceforth, they must abide the foremost law of nature at all times and defend themselves and their fortune *"by all means"* (Lev XIV:4). In nature, "force and fraud are," Hobbes says, "the two Cardinal virtues" (Lev XIII:13). Deputy Jenkins arrives on the scene, but in failing to notice the payload of Jacob's pickup, the state of nature and all of its drawbacks get hauled back into the city.

In Hobbes's state of nature, no promises may be reckoned on, there are no property rights, and nothing may be called unjust. All of these features are made manifest in the story. Promises are only reliable when they can be enforced (Lev XIV:15, 18, XV:5), and criminal conspirators cannot rely on the law to assist them in their illegal activities or defend them against each other. At one point, in order to keep Jacob on board, Hank has to promise to help him buy back their father's farm by agreeing to provide him with a cover story. Hank knows that he cannot risk keeping this promise. (The only way he can help Jacob buy the farm is figuratively—which eventually, of course, he does.) Other empty promises include the agreement between Hank and Lou not to let their wives in on things, Hank's guaranteeing Jacob immunity from being caught after they kill a local farmer named Stephanson (Tom

Carey) who nearly discovers them revisiting the plane,[8] Hank's acceding to split up the loot sooner than previously agreed so that Lou may resolve some incautiously incurred personal liabilities, and Hank's promise of happiness to Jacob in the future.

In trusting Hank's promise to divide the take later on (so long as he holds on to it all in the meantime), Lou and Jacob "betray" themselves as do all who "performeth first" in some unenforceable agreement (Lev XIV:18). There is "no *mine* and *thine* distinct," in the state of nature, "but only that to be every man's that he can get, and for so long as he can keep it" (Lev XIII:13). "Just because you have it doesn't mean it's yours. Part of that is my money," Lou reminds him, hoping for an advance. "Part of it might be your money," replies Hank, "if we decide to keep it"—that is, if he condescends to give him any. Until then, the whole stash is Hank's to keep or else destroy if he suspects danger or treachery (Lev XIV:18). Jacob eventually comprehends their predicament. "We should've never let him keep the money," he tells Lou. "Look how he's looking at us, like he's better," he complains, then elaborates, to Hank, "like you own us, or something." Technically, Hobbes would point out, human life has no inherent, objective value that must be respected by others in every circumstance (Lev X:16), and no man possesses an exclusive right to his own person in the state of nature (Lev XIV:4). Thus, Hank does own Lou and Jacob, although no more so than they own him. What Hobbes calls the Right of Nature therefore fully sanctions Lou's reaction, when, having discerned that Hank and Jacob have ganged up on him, he fetches his shotgun (Lev XIV:1).

The question of whose money it is arises repeatedly. Hank's initial reaction is that the money is "a police matter," since keeping it will land them in prison. Obedience to the law out of a fear of punishment is his ingrained instinct. Lou jokes that the dead pilot "won't mind" their relieving him of it, and they quickly convince themselves that it is "dirty money" in order to justify treating it as up for grabs. Even though no external power compels him, Hank apparently intends to keep his promise to divvy it up, evidencing a kind of "generosity" (Lev XIV:31).[9] He even offers Lou's share to Nancy while her face and dressing gown are freshly sprinkled with her husband's lifeblood. In her rage she assumes, quite naturally, that Hank intends to "take all the money." So, she goes and gets her pistol.[10] After shooting Carl toward the story's conclusion, the kidnapper, Vernon Bokovsky (Gary Cole), presses Hank, "Where's my money?" This no-nonsense question epitomizes his theory of natural justice. To a man like him, nothing may be denied and no gain is ill-gotten, irrespective of the means by which it is attained, the current set of circumstances, or the claims of others. Not all that differently, Sarah proceeds as if the treasure-trove is all hers, or rather, her most immediate family's, even though she knows that keeping it has "always been stealing."

There are no crimes in the state of nature, Hobbes observes (Lev XXVII:3). He contends further that there are no standards of right or wrong there, except the unlimited right to preserve oneself (Lev XIII:13; cf. VI:7). When Jacob strikes Stephanson, he initially defends himself in Hobbesian fashion, protesting, "What else was I gonna do?" Jacob did what his private judgment deemed "the aptest means" to preserve himself, as natural liberty recommends (Lev XIV:1). When Hank pronounces Stephanson dead, however, Jacob replies, "That's not right," revealing that he does not fully grasp his state of affairs. Stephanson regains consciousness and murmurs, "Get the police." To his misfortune, it is the absence of law enforcement that practically defines the situation wherever nature is preserved or emerges (Lev XIII:13). Lou and Nancy are killed in their home, located outside the city limits and beyond the nature preserve. It is no coincidence that Carl gets shot in the nature preserve where, symbolically speaking, he has no authority. The kidnapper meets his end in the nature preserve, too, where even the weakest can kill the strongest (Lev XIII:1). The solitary and poor Jacob, burdened by nasty memories of brutish acts, finds his life cut short there as well (Lev XIII:9).

Hobbes says that "the passion to be reckoned upon is fear" (Lev XIV:31). To keep nature at bay, fear of the law is needful, but it only works to keep men in line when men are convinced of the competence of its agents and their commitment to follow through on its threats. Fear of "the power of spirits invisible" (Lev XIV:31) affects Hank not at all. His unreligious personality is put in relief by the signs of Christmastime present throughout the film.[11] Instead, he exemplifies Hobbes's insistence that the fear of the law is "the greater fear" (Lev XIV:31).[12] In anticipation of his initial interrogation by the FBI, Hank dolefully predicts that "they're gonna know" about everything he has done. Hobbes, who recommends conceiving of the government as a God on earth (Lev XVII:13), would be gratified to hear the state reckoned omniscient, its justice inexorable. After his final debriefing, Hank is so alarmed that he rushes home to burn the bills straightaway, even though he remains unsuspected. Still, it must not be forgotten that a heated conversation with the likes of Lou and Jacob was enough to cause his fear to abate a bit at the outset. The possibility of securing "commodious living" (Lev XIII:14) without having to obtain it through "his own industry" (Lev XI:4; cf. XVII:13, XXVII:10) was too hard to resist. Lou proclaimed their discovery "the American Dream in a goddamned gym bag." (Take note, it is stuffed with the denomination depicting Benjamin Franklin.) Even though Hank momentarily showed appreciation for the Dream as something "you work for," he caved once Lou appealed to his role as provider for his family.

In a well run Hobbesian commonwealth, fear of breaking the law would be like background radiation. Because modernity proves so successful at producing and distributing the benefits of civil society, the law-abiding life proves pretty good—meaning that people need not be kept in a constant state of terror. Too much palpable fear would yield unnecessary inefficiencies and discontentment. Modern society works hard to convince men that they have it within themselves to be whatever they want to be and that they deserve to be free to do and get whatever pleases them. Hobbesian man learns that rules of right and wrong are human artifacts designed to advance self-interest. He obeys the laws, keeps his word, respects the property of others, and refrains from meddling so that he, too, may live unmolested, acquiring goods and feeling good. Men, however, are naturally proud (Lev XV:21, XVII:2). The ongoing prevalence of criminality demonstrates that to better secure their self-interest, even within the fairest regime hitherto constructed, men remain sorely tempted to privilege themselves, rationalize anything, and overestimate their chances.

Machiavellian Legacy

Having identified the law as a social construct creating an obstruction to their future happiness, the conspirators in A Simple Plan exempt themselves from its rule. They proceed as if they are better than their neighbors, to the point of committing murder. Residing in the state of nature in principle, they position themselves outside of society, which is to say, above it. Re-assuming their natural sovereignty, they become like unto wild lions. They also parasitically proceed in practice as if the benefits and protections of civil society were still theirs to fully enjoy. In chasing a fox, the three men enter into a situation requiring the emulation of foxes. These particular characters, however, have known only a life of domesticated captivity. None of them "know well how to use the beast" (Pr XVIII 69).[13] They are sheep in foxes' clothing.

As Machiavelli is the great advocate of behaving like a beast in order to master fortune, I will now examine some of the Machiavellian elements of this story. Machiavelli's counsel is directed at those who deserve to be greater than other men (Disc DL), those who are ready and able to attempt anything. Anyone can be tempted to follow his advice, but those who are not suited to it will not be well served by trying to live in accordance with it. Hobbesian politics, in its attempt to bring society as a whole under control, universalizes and democratizes Machiavelli's decidedly immoral outlook and approach, educating everyone to a diluted, milder version of it, providing them with paltry protection against its siren call.[14] Hobbesian society teaches men that self-interest is the real foundation of all human behavior, and that this is fine. It grants individuals a tremendous degree of liberty to live as they please so long as they bring no injury to others (cf. Lev XIV:7, XXI:6-7). It fails, however, to make people happier because its conception of happiness, defined in terms of endless appetite satisfactions, is deficient. It breeds instead perpetual anxiety, dissatisfaction, and isolation even in the midst of large communities enjoying relative safety and plenty. Even if behaving decently proves generally advantageous, modern men are liable to succumb to delusions of grandeur when duly tempted, daring to disregard the restrictions to which everyone is supposed to have consented in order to chase their dreams.

Although anybody can try one, Machiavelli notes that few conspiracies worthy of notice meet with success (Disc III.6.1, Pr XIX 73). Success generally depends on opportune circumstances exploited by conspirators of rare qualities sharing strong bonds of allegiance. An ordinary man's "stained conscience" and his "false imagination" of being caught will commonly undo him (Disc III.6.16). When Hank learns that the FBI wants to question him, he nearly breaks down and only recovers upon Sarah's chastisement.

If "divided cities are immediately lost," as Machiavelli warns, "when the enemy approaches" (Pr XX 84; cf. Disc III.6.3), then conspiracies, being less stable, are especially endangered by faction. Hank, Jacob, and Lou are accidental allies, and the divisions between them that predate their uniting strongly manifest themselves soon afterward. Without consulting Hank, Lou decides that it is a bright idea for Jacob to tell the deputy that they "might have heard [a plane] with engine trouble," as if this unusual remark will put them beyond suspicion later. They need to be cautious and unified in their endeavor, but they almost botch everything up right from the get-go.

Having learned that Hank was forced to smother Stephanson after Jacob failed to finish off the old man with one stroke of his truck's jack, Lou tries to blackmail him. A distraught Hank whines and wonders how Jacob could divulge that secret. Struck by Hank's distress, Jacob explains that the three of them are "all in this together." Initially insisting, "there's no sides," he unwittingly but tellingly revises his position for the worse, claiming, "I'm on both your sides." He does not appreciate the impracticality of being an ally of both his brother and his brother's enemy. Claiming to be on opposing sides only places one on an especially vulnerable third side, Machiavelli maintains, but "he who is friendly to you will ask that you declare yourself with arms" (Pr XXI 90; cf. 89). Hank confronts Jacob, forces him to choose, and enlists him in a plot to tape Lou pretending to be Hank confessing to Stephanson's murder. Then Hank could credibly threaten to bear false witness against him. Sarah concocts this convoluted plan, and in the novel it is playfully referred to as "her simple plan" (ASP 167).[15] What Sarah and Hank fail to anticipate is that a whiskey-filled Lou will react to this stratagem by assessing his situation as kill-or-be-killed (cf. Disc III.6.11). With Lou and Nancy consequently eliminated (cf. Lev XV:34), the plan inadvertently succeeds at doing what a better plan would have intended.

Modern life aims at taking the future out of fortune's hands. Wise men, to gain and maintain control, "not only have to have regard for present troubles but also for future ones," for by "seeing inconveniences from afar," Machiavelli maintains, the capable can "always [find] remedies for them" (Pr III 12; cf. Disc III.31.1). Having decided to keep the money, Sarah is aware that "from now on" she and Hank need to be "careful" and "thinking ahead all the time." She is unaware that the likelihood of their succeeding is dependent on their having learned to live in this manner long ago. Ironically, the best counsel in the film is offered by Lou moments before the plane is discovered. When Jacob grumbles that he is thirsty, Lou produces a can of beer and proclaims, "Always be prepared" (cf. Pr XIV 59f, XXV 98ff).[16] Having "always kept to a life of crime" (Pr VIII 34; cf. ASP 286, 339), the villainous kidnappers are the most prepared. They might have gotten away with their murderous enterprise if some unanticipated misfortune had not crashed the plane. Vernon's impersonation of an FBI agent as he hunts for his missing brother is both sly and bold. Callously killing an officer of the law is all in a day's work for him. Still, the kidnappers apparently underestimated the FBI's ability to track unmarked ransom. Plus, Vernon never expected that anyone would see through his disguise, as Sarah does, or that Hank had recently become "the cold-blooded type."

When he recounts their original plan to Sarah, Hank comically overestimates his abilities, not to mention his confederates', declaring, "there's no risk, we'll always be in control." Throughout the story, multiple machinations misfire. Sarah's masterminding leads not only to the aforementioned unintended demise of Nancy and Lou but also that of Stephanson. As if returning to the scene of the crime is a good idea, she convinces Hank to return five hundred thousand to the plane (leaving 3.9 million total, or thirteen hundred thousand for each of the three parties),[17] arguing that the authorities would then never suspect that it had ever been disturbed. Given the outcomes of Sarah's schemes, Hank later threatens to return the rest of the riches, shouting, "everything's gonna be just like it used to be," as if that were a possibility after everything they have been through. After Deputy Jenkins requests his presence at the station for questioning, Hank panics and suggests to Sarah that they should "take the money, the baby—and just leave the country." Later, as Hank prepares to feed the fireplace,[18] Sarah implores him, "we could go to South America or to Australia, someplace far away!" Take the money and run sounds like the simplest plan of all, but these people never develop contingency plans for speedy implementation in case of emergency, nor would they know how. Such a plan is complex in its execution, and it needed the right kind of man to put it into motion unhesitatingly when the plane was first discovered.[19] The longer these small-town residents with their so far ordinary lives try to retain control over the fortune that they found, the further they lose control over their lives. The only plan that achieves its end is at the film's end, when Jacob realizes that he cannot go on living feeling so much evil in his soul. Also figuring out that the only way that his niece might benefit from the money is with him removed from the picture, he persuades Hank to shoot him and "make it look like the bad guy did it" (cf. Disc I.9.2).

Having little talent for anticipating and mastering the future, the conspirators rely heavily on trying to change the past. Hank frequently finds himself trying to cover things up, make things disappear, and put things back. He disguises Stephanson's murder as a snowmobile accident. He reports that Lou and Nancy slew each other in a domestic squabble. Burning the money is his handy fallback option. Attempts to erase old evidence tend, however, to leave new forms of evidence. To his credit, Hank knows that his powers of concealment are poor, observing, "it wouldn't be that hard for somebody to just put it all together."

Hank is generally unaware of the extent to which he relies on an astonishing run of good luck, something that is typically a recipe for ruin (Pr VI 22, XXV 99, Disc II.29.2).[20] Mary Beth just about uncovers the cash while Deputy Jenkins looks on. A snowfall covers Hank's tracks following Stephanson's murder, and no autopsy is performed on the farmer's body. No forensics team investigates the Chambers' deaths. The feds do not closely inspect the confusing cluster of footprints bunched about the bodies of Carl, Jacob, and Vernon, nor do they detect any bloodstains or shreds of fabric that would evidence Hank's having rummaged around the plane on two previous occasions. Nothing leads the authorities to obtain a warrant to search the Mitchells' home. Nobody seems to notice just how terrible Hank is at lying.[21] He even emerges unscathed from five short-range gunshots from Nancy and two more from the kidnapper.

Conspirators must dispense with commonplace and abstract notions of justice (Pr XV 61). Sarah proves superior to the men at this.[22] Her rote affirmation of the illegality and, hence, wrongness of theft evaporates the moment she sees the money. Subsequently, she cares only about securing a life of affluence for her and Amanda. Whether their actions will prevent or lead to their getting caught is what concerns her,[23] although she has confidence that nobody will suspect them. She cares nothing about the immorality of actions such as Stephanson's murder. It does not occur to her to consider what effect becoming a killer might have on the state of mind of her husband until he prompts her to act sympathetically. Her indifference furthermore implies a presumption that a murderer and his accomplice can make perfectly good parents, given sufficient wealth.

Excelling at dissimulation and being "altogether wicked" when necessary, conspirators must be extraordinary actors capable of extraordinary action (Disc I.26.1, I.27 T; cf. I.42.1, Pr XVIII 70). The film's four protagonists—an apprehensive bookkeeper, his disappointed wife, a defective Prince Myshkin, and a drunken lout—are not at all prepared to succeed. Unfortunately for them, they have been raised to believe that self-interest rules, and what is more, that anyone can accomplish anything on which they set their minds. Sarah recognizes that a reputation for good character has its advantages, but only Jacob senses that it is the actual orientation of one's soul that is crucial.

A Classical Take

A Simple Plan depicts modern life in an unflattering way, with its effort to conquer fortune by any means, engendering insatiable acquisitiveness and entailing the unceasing manipulation of things, rendering society as but an instrumental artifact in the service of individualistic motives, rejecting objective morality, discounting good character, and disavowing divine scrutiny. In this section I will briefly point out how classical concerns regarding the relationship between character and happiness contribute further to the criticism of modernity in this story.

In comparison with the outright vicious Vernon, an example of wholehearted, unflinching villainy, the conspirators are relatively ordinary, less than virtuous individuals behaving badly for reasons they regard as not so bad, getting in over their heads as a result. Their giving in to temptation is understandable, given that modernity positively encourages it.[24] They are lukewarm in their goodness as well as their badness. What goodness they exhibit is the product of social convention and fear. The most goodness is found in Jacob, but it was left uncultivated and became compromised.

Consistent with his unsophisticated innocence, he translates the bonanza that befalls them in terms of redistributive justice misapplied, inferring that "if this guy's a dope dealer," meaning the pilot, "then that means we're like Robin Hood." Lou does not correct his friend—especially under the circumstances (NE 1167a15)—their relationship being premised on accepting each other just the way they are (cf. NE 1159b5, 1165b15, 1172a5-10). All the conspirators lack settled, genuinely good qualities of character, making it difficult for them to enjoy what contentment the circumstances of their lives may permit. As mentioned, Hank admits that he did not know that he was "happy" before all of this started. They also lack the less admirable qualities needed to really succeed in the modern world on its own terms.

The discovery of the treasure mirrors the story of the Ring of Gyges retold by Glaucon in Book II of Plato's *Republic* in remarkable detail. The plane buried under snow corresponds to the hollow bronze horse found underground there; the kidnapper's frozen remains to the inhuman corpse; the greenbacks to the golden ring (Rep 359d-e). That ring bestows the power of invisibility; the money prompts the conspirators to simulate invisibility. The money and the ring alike signify "license to do whatever [one] wants" (Rep 359c). The conspirators' choices corroborate Glaucon's proto-Hobbesian conjecture that "no one is willingly just but only when compelled to be so," and "all men suppose injustice is far more to their private profit than justice" (Rep 360c; cf. 367d-e). It is this account of human behavior that Socrates challenges in the *Republic*. It turns men into tyrannical types who fail to become happy even should they enjoy substantial success at getting what they think they want, evermore enslaved to a lust for greater power (Rep 571a-580a).

The characters imagine that the money is sufficient to make anything possible, not yet realizing they have started down a path along which anything and everything will always prove insufficient. Only Jacob's desires are not so immoderate. He yearns to live an idealized version of his father's life.[25] A baffled Hank tries to explain, "you've got the whole world," adding, "you can go anywhere you want,"[26] but all Jacob wants is to reclaim the family farm.[27] Radically autonomous individuality holds no appeal for him. Sarah, in contrast, represents what happens when a natural love of one's own is unbound. The frightening scope and intensity of her desires as well as her sense of entitlement are laid bare when a hysterical Hank threatens to replace all of the money. She delivers an unruly tirade exposing her loathing for a life of moderation and responsibility. "What about me?" she wails,

> Spending the rest of my life, eight hours a day with a fake smile plastered on my face, checking out books. And then coming home to cook dinner for you,

the same meals over and over again, whatever the week's coupons will allow, only going out to restaurants for "special occasions"—birthdays or anniversaries—and even then having to watch what we order, skipping the appetizer, coming home for dessert? You think that's gonna make me happy?

Her harangue pertains to more than foie gras and crème brûlée. Disdaining her ordinary yet respectable life and livelihood, she claims to deserve more than that which she has helped to build on the basis of her own choices and efforts under relatively enviable life circumstances. Feeling that she must have wrongly settled for or fallen into the life she has, resenting the decent man who loves her dearly for not sacrificing enough of himself for her, Sarah cares not how many people must suffer so that she can indulge her taste for luxuries and her daughter can have new toys and fancy clothes. In the *Republic*, Plato shows that the love of one's own is the root of injustice and that quarrel is the inevitable consequence of giving in to the human desire for "relishes and desserts" (Rep 372d). Because that desire is ineradicable,[28] it needs to be well tempered. Constantly tempting and teasing people is therefore counterproductive. It is almost a little too fitting that Sarah foretells that "everybody's going to get what they deserve" (ASP 193). She lacks sufficient self-knowledge to know what she deserves for meddling in business that is not hers (cf. Rep 433b).[29]

During the concluding monologue, Hank reflects that his best days henceforth are those rare days in which he "manage[s] not to think of anything at all." He used to live an unconscious life unwittingly. Now he must work to suppress his conscious mind. In an effort to rise above other men he needed to emulate foxes and lions, creatures of lower rank than man, only to find himself preferring to resemble vegetables, life forms of lower rank still (cf. NE 1097b30-98a5, 1102a30-b10, Pol 1256b15). He used to dread the punishments of the law. He learns that being left to live with himself can be a worse fate.[30] Worse than that, as an unbeliever, the solace offered by the gift of forgiveness escapes him.[31]

The Bitter End

Democracies are prone to deteriorating into tyrannies, Plato argues, and democratic souls, attached to subjectivistic liberty, unimpressed by virtue, preoccupied with pleasures and property, and resentful of anyone who enjoys more than they do, are but one step removed from tyrannical souls. Thankfully, most people do not make that transition as swiftly as Sarah. Deposited there by the premises and purposes of modern society, however, modern man dwells on that decline, tempted by the prospect of becoming a law unto himself. *A Simple Plan* transposes onto a spectacular scale the kinds of decisions that ordinary people confront and sometimes make on a smaller scale in everyday situations. They may not have the same dramatic effect as the prospects confronting the characters in this story, but they have a cumulative effect, bringing about not inconsiderable dissatisfaction through the pursuit of happiness wrongly construed—as if much more of the same will achieve what so much obtained to date has not.

I am not saying that Hank and the others are the worst sort of people. They are ordinary people in an imperfect society that has raised them, by design, to be weak in the face of temptation and proficient at making excuses for themselves. When seeking to live just as one pleases is officially recognized as the legitimate, universal foundation of human motivation, the toughest decisions a man must tackle involve calculating which courses of action will allow him to better execute his personal life-plan. Spread the opinion that people ought to succeed and dissatisfaction will soon turn to aggravation and desperation. Hope mixed with a sense of entitlement and emboldened by inexperience will make men audacious when given the opportunity. Overestimating their potential for translating hard choices into change that works, they risk supposing, as Sarah does, "we can't lose anything by trying."

Notes

Throughout this chapter quotations are drawn from the film version of *A Simple Plan* (Paramount Pictures, 1998), directed by Sam Raimi, unless otherwise indicated. All quotations from the original novel are from A SIMPLE PLAN by Scott Smith, copyright © 1993 by Scott B. Smith, Inc. Used by permission of Alfred A. Knopf, a division of Random House, Inc. Earlier versions of this chapter were presented at the 2002 American Political Science Association annual meeting and the 2009 New York State Political Science Association annual meeting. The author thanks Scott Smith for a copy of his screenplay and Leah Bradshaw, Michaele L. Ferguson, Margaret Hrezo, Mary P. Nichols, John Michael Parrish, and Avery Plaw for their incisive comments on previous drafts.

The primary source texts on which I predominantly depend are cited in parentheses using the following abbreviations:

ASP   Scott Smith, *A Simple Plan* (New York: St. Martin's Press, 1993)

Disc   Niccolò Machiavelli, *Discourses on Livy*, trans. Harvey C. Mansfield and Nathan Tarcov (Chicago: University of Chicago Press, 1996)

Lev   Thomas Hobbes, *Leviathan*, ed. Edwin Curley (Indianapolis: Hackett, 1994)

NE   Aristotle, *Nicomachean Ethics*, trans. Terence Irwin (Indianapolis: Hackett, 1985)

Pol   Aristotle, *The Politics*, trans. Carnes Lord (Chicago: University of Chicago Press, 1984)

Pr   Niccolò Machiavelli, *The Prince*, trans. Harvey C. Mansfield Jr. (Chicago: University of Chicago Press, 1985)

Rep   Plato, *The Republic*, 2nd ed., trans. Allan Bloom (New York: Basic Books, 1991)

1. Whether or not Kantianisms, Marxisms, or postmodernisms constitute real alternatives to Machiavelli and Hobbes is a longer and further question.

2. See John M. Parrish, *Paradoxes of Political Ethics* (Cambridge: Cambridge University Press, 2007), 115ff, 173f, 180f. Aside: throughout this chapter I normally employ the unfashionable convention of using gendered nouns and pronouns. That's my bad. It is worth mentioning that the bending and blending of traditional gender roles and attributes is one of the intended consequences of the modern project.

3. See Travis D. Smith, "Hobbes on Getting By with Little Help from Friends," in *Friendship & Politics: Essays in Political Thought*, ed. John von Heyking and Richard Avramenko (Notre Dame: University of Notre Dame Press, 2008), 214-47.

4. Contrast the fourteenth and fifteenth chapters of Hobbes's *Leviathan* with the second book of Aristotle's *Nicomachean Ethics*.

5. Plato, *The Laws*, trans. Thomas L. Pangle (Chicago: University of Chicago Press, 1988), 913a-d. People who do not care about virtue should be kept fearful of punishments both civil and divine, the Stranger adds (Ibid., 913d-914a). Not only do modern states disregard otherworldly affairs, they operate lotteries to tantalize their citizens with extravagant prizes.

6. Crows have "a weird job," remarks Jacob, "always waiting on something to die so they can eat it." The beastly things would surely crow that they at least have a job, and maybe make some crack about expectations regarding inheritance.

7. See also John Locke, *Second Treatise of Government*, ed. C. B. Macpherson (Indianapolis: Hackett, 1980), §§7-8, 12-13.

8. Coincidentally, the fox that they chased preyed on Stephanson's chickens.

9. On Hobbes on giving and receiving, see Travis D. Smith, "On the Fourth Law of Nature," *Hobbes Studies* 16 (2003): 84-94.

10. Gloating and goofing around while holding Hank at gunpoint, Lou allowed Jacob time to retrieve his rifle and keep his brother safe. Living out on the county road with a rowdy husband who "owe[s] people money," Nancy probably thought that owning a gun was a good idea—although learning how to use it would have been an even better idea. Of the principal characters, only the college-educated Hank and Sarah own no firearms. Hank imagines himself capable of leading a conspiracy without any experience in wielding arms, costing Carl his life and him nearly his. He is sharp enough to borrow a handgun from the sheriff's office without asking, but he is clueless as to which caliber of bullets to load (cf. Pr XIII 55ff).

11. Hank crosses himself at the Chambers' funeral, praying aloud to the Trinity along with everyone else, but he is only going through the motions ceremonially. Not

adhering reflexively to established social customs in a public setting would be out of character for him. He shows no signs of any kind of piety otherwise. Jacob is incensed when Hank presumes to channel their father's approval of their venture. When he first espies the pile of money, Hank exclaims, "God Almighty!" He explains to Jacob that in order to secure their happiness, "goddamn it, this is what it costs," referring to all of their misdeeds. "If it looks like there's even the slightest chance of us getting caught," he vows in another revealing moment, "I swear to God, it's all gonna vanish." If God were there to swear by, burning the money would make everything all right only if He does not care when people worship Mammon, take His name in vain, murder, steal, bear false witness, or covet.

12. Lou, a professional public nuisance, is not so afraid. He tries to instigate a bar brawl as if he were no stranger to such altercations. He urinates on the grounds of the cemetery in broad daylight. Who knows how many minor transgressions he routinely commits without ever being held to account. Such neglect amounts to an invitation to escalating misconduct, Hobbes points out (Lev XXVII:32). No wonder Lou tells Hank that his fear of going to prison is "bullshit." The film, however, also provides evidence on top of insinuations that Lou is a bad gambler.

13. Another beast mentioned in the film is the snake, which Jacob suggests Hank will imitate by going to the sheriff's office and confessing. Lou agrees that Hank would "rat on us just to get off the hook," promiscuously adding vermin and fish to the bestiary thereby. Although snakes often represent treachery, they may also represent wisdom. See Matthew 10:16. Hank, however, makes no confession.

14. Before Hobbes democratized Machiavelli's teaching, Francis Bacon exploited it to propel modern technological science forward for the ostensible benefit of all mankind, animating truth seekers to undertake "the stopping and turning back of the powerful course of nature" by "means hitherto unattempted." Francis Bacon, "History of Life and Death," in *The Works of Francis Bacon*, vol. 5, ed. James Spedding, Robert Leslie Ellis, and Douglas Denon Heath (London: Longman, 1858), 267.

15. It is possible, however unlikely, that the story as a whole conforms to a simple plan akin to that which organizes Maimonides, *The Guide of the Perplexed* (Chicago: University of Chicago Press, 1963), vol. 1, xiii, or "the design of the work" to be discovered in Montesquieu, *The Spirit of the Laws* (Cambridge: Cambridge University Press, 1989), xliii. Whereas a film written, directed, and produced by the selfsame people could be so well crafted (see Steven J. Lenzner, "A Cinematic Call for Self-Knowledge: An Interpretation of *Miller's Crossing*," *Perspectives on Political Science* 30, no. 2 (Spring 2001): 85-92), the author of *A Simple Plan* is at the mercy of Thornton's improvisations and a talented director who could accidentally spoil any such plan. That said, Raimi, a friend of the Coens, was crafty enough to place the most significant moment in *Spider-Man 2* precisely at the exact center of that film.

16. If Machiavelli and Jesus agree on anything, it is the need to be prepared. See Matthew 24:44, Luke 12:40.

17. For the sake of argument, in this chapter I follow the reading of Machiavelli that discovers a single, coherent teaching in his *Discourses on Livy* and *The Prince*,

recognizing that this interpretation is decidedly controversial. See Leo Strauss, *Thoughts on Machiavelli* (Chicago: University of Chicago Press, 1958), 29, 52.

18. The FBI informs Hank that the serial numbers of one-tenth of the bills had been recorded. His fear of the law's long arm is not entirely unfounded. Discoursing upon the art of catching criminals, Agent Renkins (Bob Davis) explains, "to someone who's been properly trained, there are many ways to detect a liar." For instance, "sometimes the suspect will cover his mouth with his hand as he speaks." Interestingly, as he tells Hank about the serial numbers, he covers his mouth with his hand. Either way, it is probably for the best that Hank burns the money since he would have made some fatal mistake eventually. To imagine that Hank and Sarah could have lived happily ever after beggars belief. Indeed, Sarah has already left some highly suspicious evidence, including a paper trail in the library system created by her requests for newspaper articles about the kidnapping from another branch, not to mention her undoubtedly recorded phone call to the offices of the FBI asking after a nonexistent Agent Baxter, the assumed name that Vernon took.

19. If you are waiting for specifics, I apologize. I'm not capable of it. (I am not sure that one who is capable of it would supply them. I am certain that he would not be laboring as a professor of political science.)

20. For a reading that gives Hank too much credit, see Rosellen Brown, "Choosing Evil," *New York Times Book Review*, 19 September 1993, 9.

21. Hank's reputation sees him through (cf. Pr XVII 68). In a brief scene at the feed mill, however, a Mr. Schmitt (John Paxton, in an astute casting decision) wrongly accuses Hank of overcharging him on the previous month's invoice. Hank is taken aback. His sense of himself as an honest-dealing businessman has not been affected by his recent misconduct. Though mistaken in this instance, the wizened Schmitt (whose name unmistakably evokes that of the screenwriter) trusts that all bourgeois men are tempted to cheat from time to time.

22. Cf. Carol Gilligan, *In a Different Voice* (Cambridge: Harvard University Press, 1993), 19ff, 164ff, 171ff.

23. Concerns about getting caught do preoccupy the characters, but this does not mean that the story is essentially about whether or not they will get caught. Contrast Bruce Russell, "The Philosophical Limits of Film," *Film and Philosophy* (Special Edition, 2000): 163-67.

24. Locke, *Second Treatise*, §51.

25. Jacob's strong devotion to his father recalls the classical notion of piety, and his dedication to the restoration of his father's house carries religious connotations. Whereas his confederates bear the names of secular kings, his is biblical. Only Jacob expresses feelings of guilt, wants to confess, speaks of "evil" as something real, and utters prayers witnessed by no other man. Worried about being unclean, he feels uncomfortable in close proximity to baby Amanda until Hank reenacts a bedtime ritual that their father taught them. He believes that if he kills himself he will be "fucked." (Apparently, he also believes that there is a loophole permitting assisted suicide; it is what his father committed in volunteering a random truck driver to help do him in.

Cf. Friedrich Nietzsche, *Human, All Too Human*, trans. R.J. Hollingdale [Cambridge University Press, 1986], §II.1.94). According to the novel, his less than perfect father taught him that money is "the root of happiness" (ASP 176), which helps to explain why Jacob mistook a literal "treasure hidden in a field" for the greatest of blessings. Cf. Matthew 13:44, 1 Timothy 6:10.

26. Hank is unaware that the life of a wanderer is a curse. Inside the plane, Hank is pecked on the forehead by a crow, leaving a mark suggestive of Cain's, foreshadowing the fratricide to come. The closing monologue implies that Hank is never punished for murder so long as he lives, again evocative of Cain.

27. Jacob is a low expectation romantic. He probably would have flourished in a small, pre-modern agrarian community, married to "a normal, normal woman" (cf. Pol 1318b5-15).

28. Even though the desire for luxuries may not be universal, those who are not so enthralled commonly find themselves feeling compelled to win the favor of those who are.

29. When she is initially asked how she would react if she stumbled upon a fantastic fortune, Sarah declares, "I wouldn't take it. That's just me. I wouldn't." She has been living a lie with respect to the things most precious to her (Rep 382a-b).

30. Cf. Plato, *Gorgias*, trans. Donald J. Zeyl (Indianapolis: Hackett, 1987), 472e.

31. The less-than-perfect darkness under which the conspirators make their initial getaway alludes to the sort of deals purportedly made in the pale moonlight. In constrast, when Hank tells his lies about the Chambers' deaths, a trick of the light creates a faint image of a cross hovering in the sheriff's office. Raimi's own religious heritage may raise a doubt regarding the intentionality of this peculiarity, to be sure, but he is shooting a story cast against a Christian backdrop for an audience still largely accustomed to Christian imagery. Moreover, taking total control over every image that appears onscreen is his principal responsibility.

Index

~

About the Contributors

Paul A. Cantor is Clifton Waller Barrett Professor of English at the University of Virginia. He has taught in both the English and Government departments at Harvard University, and served on the National Council on the Humanities, 1992–1999. He has published widely on popular culture, on such subjects as *The Simpsons*, *South Park*, *24*, *Star Trek*, Martin Scorsese, Edgar Ulmer, and film *noir*. His book *Gilligan Unbound: Pop Culture in the Age of Globalization* was named one of the best nonfiction books of 2001 by the *Los Angeles Times*. His latest book, coedited with Stephen Cox, is *Literature and the Economics of Liberty: Spontaneous Order in Culture*.

Margaret S. Hrezo is associate professor of political science at Radford University. She has written on W.E.B. DuBois, Simone Weil, Eric Voegelin, and the films of Robert Altman and King Vidor. Along with Nick Pappas, she is working on a book called *Hungry Hearts: Mythopoesis and the Search for Order*.

Joel A. Johnson is associate professor in the Department of Government and International Affairs at Augustana College (SD). A graduate of Gustavus Adolphus College, he received his Ph.D. in Political Science from Harvard University. His research and teaching interests include American political thought, politics and literature, and theories of justice. He is the author of *Beyond Practical Virtue: A Defense of Liberal Democracy through Literature* (2007), in addition to articles in journals such as *Perspectives on Politics*, *The*

Review of Politics, and *Proceedings of the American Antiquarian Society*. He is currently writing a book of political philosophy, tentatively entitled *The Life of Politics*.

Susan McWilliams is assistant professor of politics at Pomona College, where she has won the Wig Distinguished Professor Award for excellence in teaching. Her work has appeared in a number of edited volumes and journals, and she is a contributing editor at *Front Porch Republic*. Currently, she is working on a book about the place of travel literature in political theory.

John M. Parrish is associate professor of political science at Loyola Marymount University. He is the author of *Paradoxes of Political Ethics: From Dirty Hands to the Invisible Hand* (2007), as well as articles in such journals as *International Theory*, *History of Political Thought*, and *The Historical Journal*, and several book chapters. He is also the coeditor (with Wayne Le Cheminant) of *Manipulating Democracy: Democratic Theory, Political Psychology, and Mass Media* (forthcoming). He is engaged in two book-length projects: a study of the development of mercy as a political concept (with Alex Tuckness), and an examination of the metaphor of politics as theater.

Travis D. Smith is assistant professor of political science at Concordia University in Montreal, where he teaches political theory.

Charles C. Turner is associate professor and chair of the Department of Political Science at California State University, Chico. He enjoys reading everything by Stephen King. He also writes about elite decision making behavior, most recently that of the Supreme Court.

A. Craig Waggaman is associate professor of political science at Radford University, where he teaches and writes about political philosophy and international relations. He has used Cormac McCarthy, J.R.R. Tolkien, and Ray Bradbury with some frequency to explore key questions in the study of politics.

Breinigsville, PA USA
20 April 2010
236480BV00002B/15/P

9 780739 138137